Amiga™ Programming Guide

Tim Knight

Que™ Corporation
Indianapolis, Indiana

About the Author

Tim Knight

Tim Knight of Santa Clara, California, is the author of 15 other computer books as well as numerous articles for newspapers and magazines. Among his published titles are *Graphics and Sounds on the IBM PC, Excel on Your Atari 660XL/800XL, Basic BASIC Programs on the Adam, and Probots and People: The Age of the Personal Robot.* Having a special interest in robots, Mr. Knight is a partner in Valley Robotics, a mail-order firm devoted exclusively to educational personal robots.

Product Director
Chris DeVoney

Editorial Director
David F. Noble, Ph.D.

Managing Editor
Gregory Croy

Editors
Kathie-Jo Arnoff
Jeannine Freudenberger, M.A.
Pamela Fullerton

Technical Editor
Richard Shoemaker
Founder, North American Amiga Users Group

Table of Contents

3   Advanced Amiga BASIC 55

4   Creating Graphics with Amiga BASIC .. 79

7   Programming in C

Acknowledgments

The author wishes to thank Hamid R. Moazed and Mike Massing for writing the majority of the C code for Chapter 7.

Que Corporation is grateful to Terry Ward for providing technical expertise for Chapter 7.

Composed by Que Corporation in
Garamond and Que digital

Cover designed by
Listenberger Design Associates

Screen shots courtesy of
DOMUS Software, Ltd.
Ottawa, Ontario, Canada

Trademark
Acknowledgments

Que Corporation has made every effort to supply trademark information about company names, products, and services mentioned in this book. Trademarks indicated below were derived from various sources. Que Corporation cannot attest to the accuracy of this information.

1-2-3 and Symphony are registered trademarks of Lotus Development Corporation.

A Mind Forever Voyaging, Cutthroats, Suspect, and Wishbringer are trademarks and Enchanter, Infidel, Planetfall, Seastalker, Starcross, Suspended, The Witness, Zork I, Zork II, and Zork III are registered trademarks of Infocom, Inc.

Aegis Draw is copyrighted by The Next Frontier Corporation.

Amiga and Amiga C are trademarks and Digitizer, Genlock Interface, Graphicraft, Kickstart, Musicraft, Textcraft, The 1200 RS, Trumpcard, and Workbench are registered trademarks of Commodore-Amiga, Inc.

Archon, Arcticfox, Deluxe Video Construction Set, Marble Madness, One-on-One, Return to Atlantis, Seven Cities of Gold, and Skyfox are trademarks and Pinball Construction Set is a registered trademark of Electronic Arts.

Commodore and Commodore 64 are registered trademarks of Commodore Electronics, Limited.

CompuServe Incorporated is a registered trademark of H&R Block, Inc.

CompuServe Information Service is a registered trademark of CompuServe Incorporated and H&R Block, Inc.

CP/M is a registered trademark of Digital Research Inc.

Enable is a trademark of The Software Group.

Hitchhiker's Guide to the Galaxy is a trademark of Douglas Adams.

IBM is a registered trademark of International Business Machines Corporation.

Lotus and 1-2-3 are registered trademarks of Lotus Development Corporation.

Macintosh is a trademark of McIntosh Laboratory, Inc., licensed to Apple Computer, Inc., and is used with its express permission.

MacPaint is a trademark and Apple II and ProDOS are registered trademarks of Apple Computer, Inc.

Microsoft BASIC and MS-DOS are registered trademarks of Microsoft Corporation.

Rags to Riches is a trademark of Chang Laboratories, Inc.

T-card, T-disk, T-modem, and T-tape are trademarks of Tecmar, Inc.

The Source is a service mark of Source Telecomputing Corporation, a subsidiary of The Reader's Digest Association, Inc.

ThinkTank is a trademark of Living Videotext, Inc.

Introduction

You finally make the decision to buy a personal computer, you bring home your new machine, and the first question your friends ask is "What can it do?" Soon this question begins to annoy you, and you too begin to wonder: "Have I just been taken in by a trend or do I truly have a machine that can do something useful?"

In my early years working with personal computers, I never really questioned their usefulness. I simply loved using and programming computers. I recall my first computer fondly, in spite of its pitiful graphics, inadequate sound, and its mere 16,000 bytes of memory. And yet, when I discovered how to use machine language to make the computer beep out a few notes of "The Yellow Rose of Texas," I was ecstatic. But after writing my first few computer books, I began to realize that the home computers being sold at that time weren't very useful for most people. The irony of that discovery was that I had been preaching through my books how wonderful computers were for ordinary people.

The computer industry has come a long way since then, and today I no longer have to question the usefulness or value of personal computers. The technology has progressed very quickly, bringing to the public such machines as the Apple II®, the IBM® PC, and the Macintosh™. These computers were major milestones in the industry, and each machine that was introduced had capabilities that were improvements over its predecessor. In particular, significant improvements were made in the areas of graphics, sound, speed, memory capacity, and mass storage capability.

Among these new computers, the Amiga™ from Commodore-Amiga, Inc., stands out as one of the most powerful and exciting personal computers in existence today. The more you know about computers, the more astounded you are at all the Amiga is capable of doing.

What Are the Amiga's Capabilities?

Marking another major milestone in the personal computer industry, the Amiga features many powerful capabilities at a low cost. Among the Amiga's capabilities are

- High-resolution graphics with 4,096 available colors

- Sound and music generation in stereo with as many as four "voices" (channels)

- Easy operation with the mouse

- A full 512K of user memory

- A complete keyboard with cursor-control keys and a numeric keypad

- The sophisticated and powerful 68000 Motorola microprocessor

Two of the Amiga's strengths are particularly outstanding: graphics and sound capabilities. Graphics are the pictures the computer can produce on the screen. By using the Amiga's graphics commands, you can draw a variety of shapes and colors on the screen with surprising ease. The sounds you can produce with the Amiga can be sound effects in a game or musical pieces. You can create music using as many as four separate instruments playing simultaneously. To program the computer to make graphics and sounds and to serve other useful functions, you need to learn the fundamentals of three computer languages: Amiga BASIC, TLC™ Logo, and C. The *Amiga Programming Guide* concentrates on the Amiga's graphics and sound capabilities, as well as on the computer languages you need to learn to use the Amiga.

What Does This Book Contain?

This book is organized so that you gradually learn about programming as you work your way through each chapter. You need not be an expert in computer programming in order to learn from this book because it is a tutorial, not a reference guide. Through programming examples and descriptions of keywords (specific words in a computer language that cause the computer to perform tasks), you can learn, step-by-step, the fundamentals of programming. This knowledge will give you the basic foundation, from which you can use your own imagination to build and create more powerful programs. A brief overview of the material presented in this book follows.

In Chapter 1, "Introducing the Amiga," you will learn how to set up the Amiga, use the mouse and keyboard, and use the Workbench program.

Chapter 2 provides an introduction to the fundamental concepts of programming in Amiga BASIC, the language that comes with your computer. You will learn about line numbers, variables, and some simple commands.

Chapter 3, "Advanced Amiga BASIC," provides explanations of variable arrays, program development, and other more advanced topics. The material in this chapter will help you begin writing more sophisticated programs.

Because much of the Amiga's power is in its graphics capability, all of Chapter 4 is devoted to Amiga BASIC's graphics commands and ways to use them.

You easily can produce sounds, music, and speech through Amiga BASIC commands. In Chapter 5, "Sounds, Music, and Speech," you will learn how to use these commands in your own programs.

Chapter 6 teaches you the basics of Logo. This language is popular both for children and adults who are interested in artificial intelligence. Even if you don't own a Logo software package, you still can profit from a look at how another programming language works.

C is a fast, powerful language that is popular among professional programmers. Chapter 7, "Programming in C," gives you a brief introduction to the language and explains what you will need to use it.

Chapter 8, "Using AmigaDOS," explains the disk operating system that is included with your Amiga's software. AmigaDOS can help you manage your computer's information efficiently.

To learn even more advanced commands for the disk operating system, you can explore the commands and DOS program descriptions presented in Chapter 9, "Advanced AmigaDOS."

Finally, Chapter 10, "Amiga at Work and Play," contains information that can help you make the Amiga a useful tool for your home or office. This chapter also offers ideas for using your Amiga for entertainment. Once you understand all that the Amiga is capable of doing, you will be able to answer confidently the question "What can it do?" The power of the Amiga is immense, and after you have finished reading this book, you will have the knowledge to begin tapping that power.

Introducing the Amiga

The Amiga is one of today's most sophisticated personal computers for the home and for the small business (see fig. 1.1). This computer features unparalleled graphics, versatile sounds and music, easy-to-use input and output devices, a fast microprocessor, and a library of powerful software. The combination of these features, made possible by recent advances in high technology, make this computer an excellent value.

Fig. 1.1. The Amiga.

Although the manual that comes with the Amiga system provides general instructions for setting up the system, using the Work-bench®, and programming in Amiga BASIC, these items—as well as other topics—are covered in much more detail in this book. In this chapter, you will learn how to set up the Amiga; how to use the keyboard, the disks, and the mouse; and how to start running the computer.

Setting Up the Amiga

Before setting up the computer, you must find a place to put it. Although this may seem to be a minor topic, giving the location some advance thought can prevent costly accidents and aching backs. Some important requirements for the location of the computer are the following:

1. The surface should be smooth and flat with plenty of room for laying down such items as books, diskettes, and program listings.

2. The location should be near an electrical outlet so that the computer can be plugged in without the risk of someone's tripping over the cord and pulling out the plug.

3. Your computer workstation should be equipped with a comfortable chair, preferably an adjustable office chair like you would use at a typewriter table. If you spend a few hours at your computer sitting on the old dining room chair, the ache in your back will tell you why an appropriate chair is important for your workstation. A comfortable office chair, which has adjustable height and back support, puts minimum stress on your back. Adjustable office chairs are available in most office supply centers for less than $100.

4. If possible, your electrical outlet should be equipped with a surge protector, which you can purchase at most computer outlets. This device eliminates the changes in electrical power that can cause loss of information in the computer's memory.

Components

Once you have designated an appropriate workstation, you can begin to arrange the computer's components and to make the necessary hookups. The Amiga computer comes with the following components:

The main computer unit and power cord: The main unit contains all the hardware of the computer. The microprocessor, memory, input/output electronics, and the rest of the actual computer are housed in this case.

The keyboard and cable: The Amiga keyboard resembles a typewriter keyboard but has extra keys, such as the numeric keypad, function keys, and other special keys.

The mouse: To move the computer's pointer around the screen, you use the mouse. By moving the pointer to selections on the screen and pressing the left button on the mouse, you can select options and open programs easily.

Three disks: Included with your Amiga system are three disks: Kickstart®, which gets the computer running when you first turn it on; Workbench, the "home base" for getting other programs up and running; and Amiga Extras, which has the Amiga Tutor and the Amiga BASIC programming language.

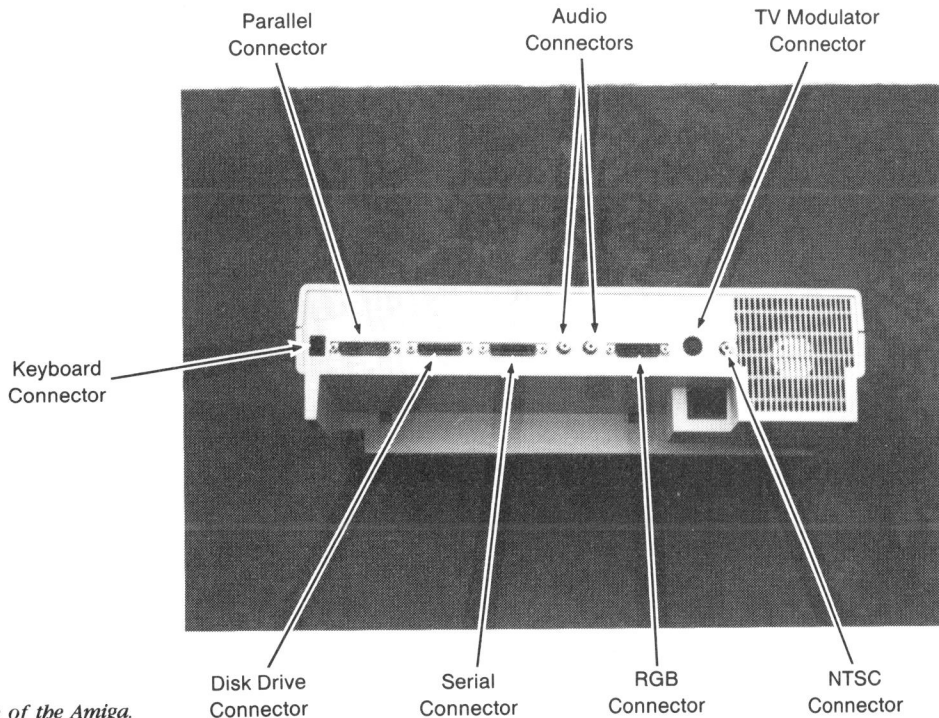

Fig. 1.2. The back of the Amiga.

Parallel Connector · Audio Connectors · TV Modulator Connector · Keyboard Connector · Disk Drive Connector · Serial Connector · RGB Connector · NTSC Connector

Hookups

When you have all your components out of their cartons, you can begin setting up the Amiga and making the necessary hookups. Follow these instructions in the order given, and in a few minutes your Amiga will be up and running. (Refer to fig. 1.2 for the locations of the connectors.)

1. Place the main computer unit on the desk that you will be using. Make sure that the slot for the disk drive is facing you. Now take the cable for the keyboard (the one that resembles a telephone cord) and plug the straight end into the leftmost connector on the back of the main computer unit.

2. Set the keyboard (so that it faces you) in front of the Amiga and plug the free end of the keyboard cable into the connector located on the extreme left side of the back of the keyboard. The keyboard is now hooked up to the Amiga, and you can tuck the keyboard cord underneath the main computer unit, which has an opening for the cable to pass through.

   If you want to tilt the keyboard, put down the legs on the right and left sides underneath the keyboard. When you put these legs back up (so that the keyboard lies flat), you can slip the keyboard completely underneath the main computer unit for storage. This feature is convenient if you need the extra space when the computer is turned off.

3. Now take the mouse and set it on the desk to the right of the keyboard. (If you are left-handed, you can place the mouse on the left side if you prefer.) Plug the end of the mouse's cord into the connector labeled "1" on the right side of the main computer unit. Your mouse is now attached and ready to use.

   When you start using the computer, you may discover that the computer is sluggish and is not as responsive to the mouse as you would like. If the problem stems from the computer not being sensitive to the mouse's movements, you can solve this problem easily; see the section titled "The Preferences Tool" later in this chapter.

If the surface that the mouse is on is smooth and is not providing good traction for the rubber ball within the mouse, you may want to place the mouse on something that gives better traction. A piece of linoleum tile or the back of a clipboard often does the job well. If you want something fancier, you can purchase a pad for the mouse, such as Mousepad from Moustrak, Inc., of St. Helena, California (707/963-8179). You can find these pads at just about any well-stocked computer or software store.

4. Next, you hook up your video monitor. Because different Amiga users have different monitors, each type of monitor will be examined separately here.

The *Amiga monitor from Commodore-Amiga, Inc.,* is a high-resolution color monitor that produces crisply and clearly all the graphics and sounds of the Amiga. The monitor is called an RGB monitor because it produces the red, green, and blue (R, G, and B) color levels separately before they are displayed collectively on the monitor. This method results in a sharp picture with a wide range of colors.

To hook up the Amiga monitor, plug the smaller end of the video cable supplied with the monitor into the connector on the back of the monitor. Plug the larger end of the cable into the connector labeled "RGB connector" on the back of the main computer unit.

If you are using a *composite (NTSC) video monitor* or a *television with an NTSC connector,* take a high-quality phono cable (a shielded cable used with stereo equipment and video games) and plug one end into the round connector in the back of the main computer unit and the other end into the connector on the monitor or television. Be sure that the cable is not coiled around or near the power cords and that the cable is firmly inserted on both ends; otherwise, you might get a poor picture.

Using a *television* for the Amiga is wasteful because a TV can't take advantage of the Amiga's full potential. However, if you do use a TV, use a phono cable the same way you would with an NTSC monitor with an RF modulator and a TV switch box. The methods of

connecting a television to a computer vary from TV to
TV, so check the instructions that come with the
modulator to find the proper procedure.

5. Now you are ready to bring the Amiga to life. Plug the
six-sided plug on the power cable into the
corresponding connector on the back of the main
computer unit; then plug the other end into a three-
prong electrical outlet. To turn on your computer, flip
the switch on the left side of the main computer unit.

Connecting a stereo to the Amiga is optional. If you do
so, however, you can enjoy the results of the programs
in Chapter 5 in stereo sound. To hook up your stereo,
get two phono cables and, on the back of the main
computer unit, plug one of them into the circular
connector for the left stereo channel and plug the
other into the circular connector for the right stereo
channel (see fig. 1.2). Then take the other ends of
each cable and plug them into the corresponding input
connectors of your stereo system.

Important Dos and Don'ts

Before you go any farther, stop and memorize the following three
rules for using your Amiga. Learn and live by these rules, or else
you will find yourself with a trashed disk or computer.

*If you have just turned off your computer, wait five seconds before
turning it on again.*

*Never do a software reset when a disk—especially the Workbench
disk—is running.*

A software reset, which you do by pressing the CTRL key and two
Amiga keys simultaneously, is a sort of "panic button." You use this
procedure to get out of any mess you may get into with the Amiga
(such as when the Amiga gets stuck in a routine). Pressing CTRL
and the two Amiga keys is fine as long as the disk drive isn't running.
If the disk drive is running, you could accidentally wipe out your
information and programs.

Never remove a disk when the disk drive is running.

If your files are not closed and you remove the diskette, it will be
rendered useless. Therefore, whenever the disk drive is running—the

disk drive's light is on—never remove your diskette. (Another valuable caution is not to insert a disk in any drive before a picture is displayed.)

I mention these three rules because they may not be obvious to the new Amiga user, and perhaps not even to a computer veteran. I wiped out my Workbench disk within half an hour after getting my Amiga, which greatly humbled this long-time computer user.

In addition to the three absolute rules for using your Amiga, you should keep a few common sense rules in mind for the care of your computer. In general, you should treat your Amiga system like any other high-quality home appliance, such as a fine stereo. Keep drinks and food away from the computer; don't subject it to harsh blows and direct sunlight; and keep it clean and properly maintained. If you have any problem with your Amiga, don't try any repairs yourself; go back to your Amiga dealer or Amiga Service Center and let someone there open up the main computer unit to investigate the problem. If you open up the Amiga yourself, you will void the warranty.

Using Input and Output Devices

You can get information to and from the Amiga in many ways. These include the keyboard, the disk drive, modems, printers, the mouse, and other peripherals. For now, examine the input and output devices that come with the base Amiga system.

The Keyboard

Begin with the keyboard (see fig. 1.3). Most of the Amiga's keyboard is like an ordinary typewriter's, complete with alphanumerics (letters and numbers), punctuation symbols, and SHIFT keys. In addition, the Amiga has some extras that you should know about in order to make the most use of your computer:

Numeric keypad: When you are entering many numbers, the numeric keypad is the fastest way to get data into the computer. Once you have worked with the keypad for a while, you will surprise yourself with just how fast you can enter numbers.

Function keys: The function keys do different things in different programs. In a word-processing program, these keys may be used for deleting words, moving pieces of a

Function Keys

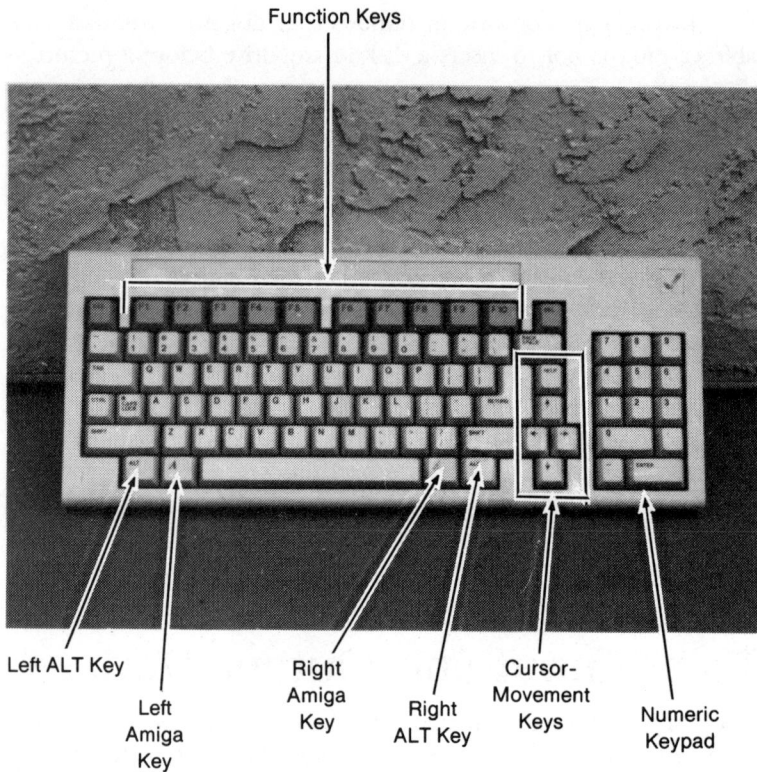

Left ALT Key

Left
Amiga
Key

Right
Amiga
Key

Right
ALT Key

Cursor-
Movement
Keys

Numeric
Keypad

Fig. 1.3. The keyboard.

document around, or saving and loading files. In a business program, however, the function keys may be used for adding columns of figures and doing mathematical operations. The documentation provided with the specific software tells you what functions, if any, the function keys serve.

Cursor-movement keys: To move the blinking cursor (the blinking box showing where you are working on the screen), use these up-, down-, left-, and right-arrow keys. As mentioned earlier, these keys also are used with the Amiga keys and the SHIFT key to move the pointer around the screen without using the mouse.

CAPS LOCK: If you want to type all capital letters, press this key. The red LED built inside the key will light up. When you want to go back to regular uppercase and lowercase letters, press this key again, and the light will turn off.

Other special keys: Like the function keys, a number of other keys perform different tasks, depending on the software running on the computer. These keys include the CTRL (Control), ALT (Alternate), Amiga, and ENTER keys. Others special keys are ESC (Escape), which usually gets you out of whatever function or program you are in, and BACKSPACE, which moves the cursor back one space, removing the character the cursor lands on.

The Disk Drive and Diskettes

One of the most important input/output devices for your Amiga is the disk drive. The small 3 1/2-inch diskette that your Amiga uses holds more than 800,000 pieces of information.

To help you avoid accidentally erasing an important file or copying over data, the diskette comes with a protect tab. By shifting this tab, you can *protect* or *unprotect* the diskette. If you don't want the disk drive to write anything on a diskette, move the protect tab toward the top of the diskette (so that you can see through the small hole in its upper right corner). If you don't want the diskette to be write-protected, close the hole by pushing the protect tab back down.

The diskette is delicate and should be handled carefully. Although the diskette itself is sealed and protected from the outside environment by its metal slide, you still should not subject the diskette to heat, any kind of magnets (which include telephones, speakers, and motors), or smoke. Also, be sure that you never touch the actual diskette after moving the metal slide and exposing the plastic diskette itself. Touching the diskette almost definitely will ruin it.

The Mouse

Another important input device is the mouse—a pointing device that translates your movements into movements for the pointer on the screen. The mouse works by detecting the movement of a rubber ball inside the mouse; as the ball rolls in a certain direction, the mouse translates the direction into a change in the x- and y-coordinates of the pointer on the screen.

To keep the mouse in good working order so that your computer does not respond sluggishly, you need to give the mouse special care. Every couple of weeks, you should go through the following procedure:

1. Turn the mouse upside down and slide the piece of plastic holding the ball inside the mouse.

2. Lift the piece of plastic off the mouse.

3. Turn the mouse over and catch the ball.

4. Moisten a cotton swab with alcohol or a window-cleaning solution and clean the rollers inside the mouse where the ball used to be.

5. Wipe off the rubber ball and replace it inside the mouse; put the plastic cover back on.

Running the Amiga

When your Amiga is first turned on, you should see a graphics picture of a hand holding a disk called Kickstart. This picture is your signal to put the Kickstart disk in the drive. Insert the Kickstart disk with the metal slide facing forward and the label facing up. (This is the way you insert all disks.)

After you insert the disk, the Amiga reads from the Kickstart disk. The disk drive light stays on as long as the program is reading. In a few seconds, another hand appears on the screen; this hand is holding a Workbench disk (see fig. 1.4). Make sure that the drive light is off and then eject the Kickstart disk by pressing the button on the front of the disk drive. Insert the Workbench disk. In a few moments, the screen displays a title bar and a Workbench disk icon. (An *icon* is a picture representing a program or some other disk or file.)

Now work with the mouse for a few moments to get familiar with its operation. The mouse is your key to easy control of the Workbench features. Try moving the mouse around on a flat surface, and watch how the arrow on the screen moves relative to your movements. When you move the mouse away from you, the pointer arrow moves up the screen; when you move the mouse around in a circular motion, the arrow moves in the same way. The arrow will not go beyond the boundaries of the screen. If you need to move the arrow farther than the space on your desk allows, simply lift the mouse up and move it over. For instance, if you want to move the arrow to the extreme left, but your keyboard prevents you from moving the mouse any farther to the left, you simply lift the mouse up and set it down as far to the right as you can. You then have room to go to the left again. After you have worked with the mouse for a

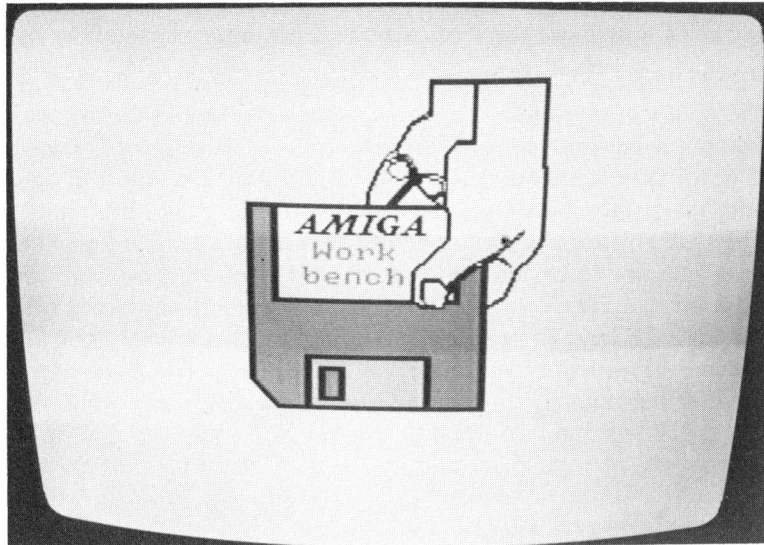

Fig. 1.4. Icon telling you to insert the Workbench disk.

while, the movements will become natural, and you will wonder how computer owners ever managed without a mouse.

You use the buttons on the mouse to select items. You almost always will be using the left button. Assume that you want to select an icon from the Workbench disk. Using the mouse, you move the arrow to the Workbench icon and click the left mouse button. This action *inverts* the icon and tells the computer you have selected that icon. However, nothing happens until you *open* the icon. To open the icon, you press the left mouse button twice without pausing between clicks (*double-click*). The Workbench disk icon then *explodes* into a window where you can see a directory of all the files on that disk.

Go ahead and use the mouse to point to the Workbench disk icon. The pointer must be pointing to some specific part of the disk icon, not just in its general direction. Once you have positioned the pointer on the icon, double-click the left mouse button and watch as the window forms out of the exploding icon.

Another use of the left mouse button is to *drag* an icon. As the term suggests, dragging an icon means that you pull it around on the screen. For example, if you have a file you want to put in the trash, you move the arrow to the file's icon, hold down the left mouse button, and move the mouse to drag that icon to the Trashcan. The file then is disposed of. Try moving the icons that are in the window. Don't move the icons outside of the window, and don't put any of them on top of the Trashcan (or they might get destroyed accidentally). Just move the icons around a bit until you see how the dragging process works.

Using certain keys on the keyboard, you can accomplish many tasks without using the mouse. (You may want to do this, for instance, if your mouse is broken.) Notice the red *A* Amiga keys to the right and left of the space bar on the keyboard. To move the pointer, press either Amiga key with one of the cursor-movement keys (the keys with up, down, left, and right arrows). To select an icon, you position the pointer on the icon and press the left Amiga key with the left ALT key. To open a file, you hold down the left ALT key and quickly press the left Amiga key twice. To speed up the movement of the pointer, you can hold down the SHIFT key while you use the Amiga and cursor-movement keys.

The Menu Bar

Select the icon for the Workbench disk and press the right mouse button. Now notice the Menu Bar that appears on the top of the screen. On the Menu Bar are the words Workbench, Disk, and Special. These menu titles are positioned over three invisible menus. You can make these menus visible by holding down the right button on the mouse while pointing to a menu title (see fig. 1.5).

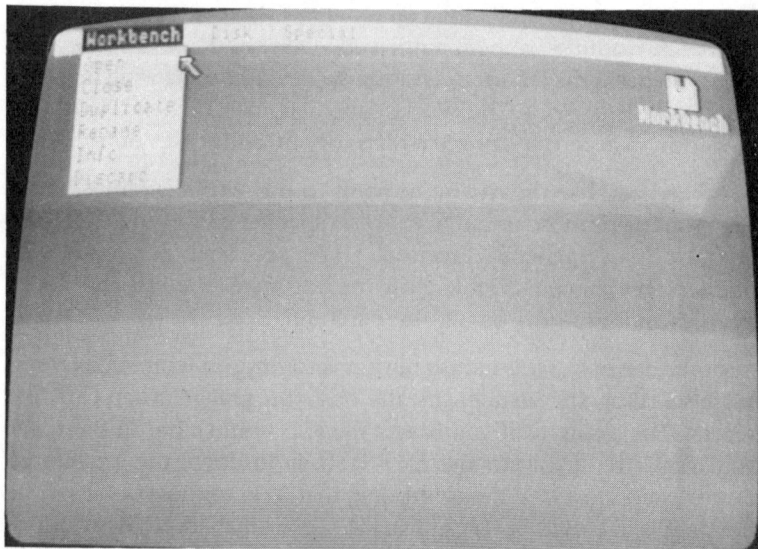

Fig. 1.5. The Workbench window
with a pull-down menu selected.

When you pull down the Workbench menu, you see the following choices:

Open	Opens the icon selected
Close	Closes the file or disk you are working with
Duplicate	Makes a copy of a disk
Rename	Changes the name of the icon or disk
Info	Gives you information regarding the current disk or program
Discard	Throws away the icon you have selected

Because having backup copies of your disks is so important, the Duplicate command deserves special attention. As I mentioned earlier in this chapter, I once accidentally destroyed my Workbench disk. If I had made a backup of Workbench, I would not have had any problem; instead, I had to make a trip to the dealer to get another copy of the disk. In any situation, you should have your own backup copy of a disk.

When you choose Duplicate, the computer tells you when and how often to swap the disks in order to finish the copy. The computer guides you through the entire copying process by instructing you which disk to insert or eject at any one time. (If you are fortunate enough to have a two disk drive system, you do not need to worry about swapping disks in and out of the drive. You simply drag the file's icon to the second disk drive icon and follow the menus.)

The menu under Disk offers the following options:

Empty Trash	Permanently gets rid of the unwanted files you have put into the Trashcan. The Trashcan icon must be selected with the mouse before this command will work.
Initialize	Formats a new disk or erases an old one completely. Be careful when you choose this option; if you go through with this selection, you will erase all the data on the disk in the drive.

Under Special, you have these menu options:

Clean Up	Neatly arranges the icons in a window

Last Error   Tells the computer to display at the top of the screen the most recent error that occurred

Redraw   Redraws the contents of the screen if your screen gets cluttered by other activities

Other disks, programs, and activities have different Menu Bars. Take time to experiment with the Menu Bar on your screen until you get comfortable with how the Menu Bars work.

The Workbench Window

After you have made the disk icon into a window by double-clicking the disk icon, you can examine the Workbench window and its different components. On the screen is a box, called a *window*. In this window are several small pictures called icons, which represent programs or groups of programs.

Icons of the Workbench Window

The icons of the Workbench window are as follows:

Disk icon: This icon represents an entire disk. When you open a disk icon, you see a directory of all the files on the disk. The files also are represented by icons. (Each disk, not only the Workbench disk, has a disk icon.)

Trashcan icon: Throw away unwanted files here. When you deposit an icon in the Trashcan, the computer prompts for verification that you want to throw away something.

Program file icon: This icon represents an actual working program. Often the icon suggests the program's purpose; for instance, a game program's icon might be a tiny action scene from the game.

Drawer icon: This icon looks like a drawer. A drawer icon is a "sub-disk" of sorts because it usually contains a number of files. Therefore, a disk icon with just a few drawers actually may have dozens of files with several programs tucked inside each drawer.

Tool icon: A special icon, such as the Clock, Notepad, or Preferences icon, represents a program that has only one purpose (in the Clock's case, telling the time). When you open a tool icon, the tool is available for your immediate use or reference.

You can drag any icon around the screen, although some, such as the Disk and Trashcan icons don't need to be dragged. If you would like to arrange your screen differently, however, you certainly can.

Parts of the Window

Windows are useful because they provide a quick, easy way to survey the contents of disks. You can have a number of windows on the screen at one time, and each window can be modified to accommodate your needs. Carefully examine the window in figure 1.6 and note the purpose of each part of the window.

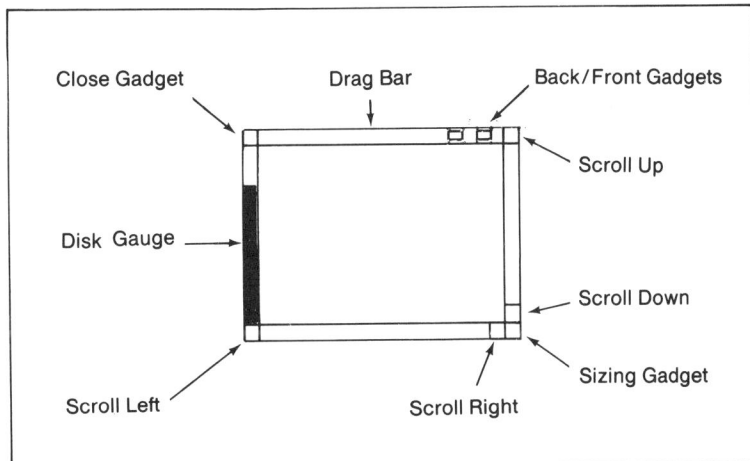

Fig. 1.6. The Workbench window.

Close Gadget: Just as you can open files and icons, you can also close them. If you don't need a window that is on the screen, you point to the Close Gadget in the extreme upper left corner of the window and press the left mouse button. The window goes back into the disk icon. Try closing the window on your screen right now. After the window is closed, open it up again by double-clicking the Workbench disk icon.

Drag Bar: At the top of the window is an area known as the Drag Bar. By moving the pointer to this section and holding down the left mouse button, you can move the window around to different parts of the screen. In the middle of the Drag Bar is the *Disk Identifier*, which tells you the name of the diskette.

Sizing Gadget: At the lower right corner of the window is the Sizing Gadget, which lets you shrink or expand the window. Point to the Sizing Gadget, hold down the left mouse button, and move the mouse. The size of the window changes on your screen. You can make the window wide and short, tall and thin, or very big.

Disk Gauge: On the left side of the window is a "fuel meter" for each diskette. The Disk Gauge indicates how full the diskette is. When the Disk Gauge shows that your diskette is nearly full, you should begin using another diskette in order to ensure that you have plenty of room to work with.

Scroll Arrows: In the corners of the window are arrows pointing left, right, up, and down. You can move the contents of the window around by pointing to an arrow and holding down the left mouse button. If, for example, you can't see all the files in a window because they stretch beyond its boundaries, you can point to the appropriate arrow (corresponding to the direction you want the contents of the window to move) and hold down the left mouse button.

Back and Front Gadgets: Windows often overlap one another. If you want the current window to be in front of another window, move the pointer to the Front Gadget, located in the upper right corner of the current window, and click the left mouse button. If you want the current window to hide behind another window, select the Back Gadget box just to the left of the Front Gadget box.

You will sometimes see on the window a puffy icon filled with Zs. This icon indicates that your Amiga is busy with an operation and can't be interrupted. When the computer is ready to respond to your commands again, the snoring icon changes back to a regular pointer.

Manipulating Windows

To make sure that you have a good understanding of windows, use the mouse to open the drawer called Demos. Then open all three program icons in the Demos window: Dotty Window, Boxer Window, and Lines Window. The Dotty Window draws randomly colored dots inside the window; the Boxer Window draws randomly colored boxes inside the window; and the Lines Window draws random lines bouncing around the window. The functions of all three windows go on simultaneously (see fig. 1.7), which demonstrates the important concept of *multitasking*, the computer's capability to carry on more than one function at a time. Multitasking is possible on the Amiga because of an advanced coprocessor chip, which is important to you in only one respect: you can get several things done at once. For instance, you can receive a program over the telephone line, work on a spreadsheet, and print a letter all at once.

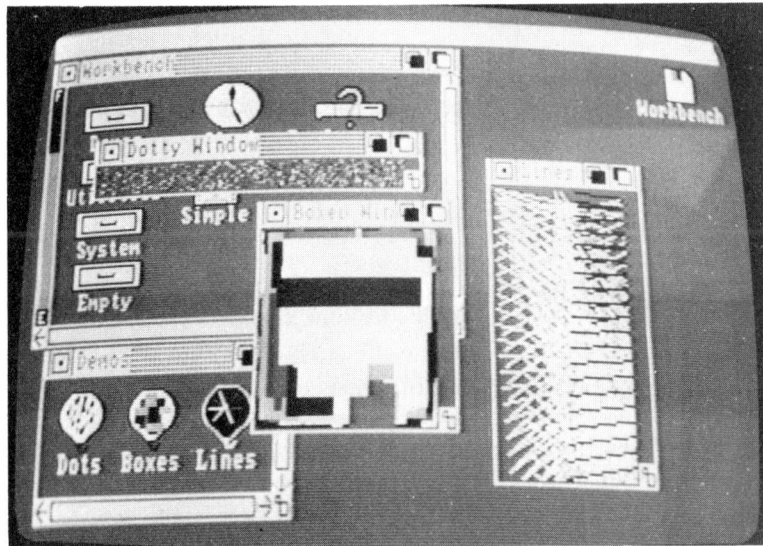

Fig. 1.7. Workbench's multitasking capability in action.

Go ahead and experiment with these three windows. Move them around, expand them, overlap them, and do whatever else you think would be fun and would help you learn more about the functions of windows. Once you have finished experimenting, close the three program windows one at a time.

Transferring Files

When you have more than one window on the screen, you can transfer files from one window (which might represent a disk or drawer) to another. For instance, if you are working with a single disk drive system, and you want to copy the program POLYSCOPE from one disk to another, you simply drag the POLYSCOPE icon from one disk window to the other disk window. The computer then gives you instructions that tell you what disk to insert at what time in order to copy the POLYSCOPE file to another disk. Keep in mind that when you copy the program, POLYSCOPE still will be on the first disk as well as on the second.

You can manipulate more than one icon at a time also. For example, to open three drawers, you simply hold down the SHIFT key and double-click the mouse button on each drawer. All three icons are selected and act as one when you perform the next function.

The Workbench Tools

In the Workbench window are three icon tools that you can use right now. These are the Clock tool, the Notepad tool, and the Preferences tool.

The Clock Tool

After you have closed the Demos window so that no more windows are open on the screen (except the one for the Workbench disk itself), use the mouse to point to the Clock tool and then double-click the left mouse button. A large analog clock will appear on the screen. You can display this clock in digital or analog and 12- or 24-hour mode, and you can even set the alarm. Choose the options you want from the Menu Bar by clicking the right mouse button. Just as windows can be displayed or moved, you can display or move this clock at any time.

The Notepad Tool

In the Utilities drawer is the Notepad tool, which you can use to store short notes and documents. Open the Utilities drawer; then open the Notepad tool by double-clicking it. You can begin typing right away, and your words will appear on the Notepad. You can go forward a page by clicking the small triangle at the lower left corner of the paper, and you can move back to the preceding page by clicking the triangle at the upper right corner of the paper. By using the right mouse button, you will discover a wide variety of Notepad menu options.

The first of the Notepad menu options is Project. Here is a list of the Project Menu Bar options and their functions:

New	Starts a new document
Open	Loads a document from the disk into memory
Save	Saves the current document under its present file name
Save As	Saves the current document under a file name that you supply
Print	Prints the document with the current setting—either high quality or rough draft
Print As	Prints the document as you specify—either high-quality or rough-draft
Quit	Gets out of the Notepad tool

Another option of the Notepad is Edit. Under the Edit Menu Bar are these options:

Undo	Undoes your last operation
Cut	Cuts out a block of text from the document
Copy	Copies a block of text from the document
Paste	Puts the block of text at the current cursor location
Erase	Erases the block of text

From the Notepad's Font Menu Bar, you can select a number of fonts and point sizes. The Amiga software designers chose to name the fonts after precious gems, including Topaz, Ruby, Diamond, Opal, Emerald, Garnet, and Sapphire. All these fonts are at your disposal—most of them with different sizes too.

From the Notepad's Style Menu Bar, you can change the style of the text you are typing by choosing Plain, Italic, Bold, or Underline. You can select any combination of these last three options. Instead of using the mouse, you can change the style of the text by pressing the Amiga key along with the P, I, B, or U keys.

The last option on the Notepad tool is Format. You can use selections from the Format Menu Bar to change the color of the pen or "paper" on the screen.

The Preferences Tool

Changing the time on the clock, along with altering a variety of other characteristics of the Amiga, is accomplished with the Preferences tool. Double-click Preferences. The screen will fill up with the Preferences options, which are controlled through the mouse (see fig. 1.8). If you want to change a setting, place the pointer over the number of the function you want to change and click the mouse. Clicking the mouse on the up or down arrow next to the number increases or decreases the setting. Another way to change characteristics established by the Preferences tool is to point toward an arrow and move the arrow.

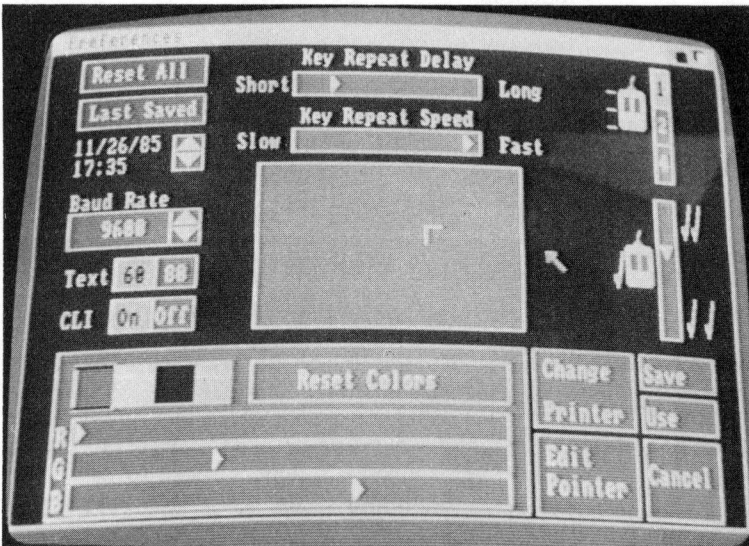

Fig. 1.8. The Preferences window.

Under Preferences, you can control the following functions:

Date and Time: To change the date or time, click the mouse at the number you want to change and use the up and down arrows to adjust the value. The date is set in month/day/year format, and the time is in 24-hour hours:minutes format. Adjusting the time here also changes the time that the Clock tool displays.

Key Repeat Delay: The Amiga has a repeating key function, which means that if you hold down a key, the function of that key will soon begin to repeat. The delay between when you press the key and when the function starts repeating is established by the Key Repeat Delay box. If you want a longer delay, drag the arrow to the right with the mouse; if you want a shorter delay, drag the arrow to the left.

Key Repeat Speed: The speed at which the keys repeat is determined here. Drag the arrow right to make the keys repeat more quickly and drag the arrow left to make the keys repeat more slowly.

Mouse Speed: You can select 1, 2, or 4 here; the larger the number, the less distance the pointer will move across the screen relative to how much you move the mouse.

Double-Click Delay: When you double-click the left mouse button, the computer waits only a certain amount of time between the first and second clicks. If you take too long, the Amiga interprets your actions as two separate clicks and not as a double-click. To increase the time that the Amiga allows between clicks, move the arrow in this rectangle down. To decrease the time, drag the arrow up.

Baud Rate: Baud, which means "bits per second," refers to the speed of the serial port; this term is used (in this case) to describe how fast a computer can send information over a telephone line to another computer. If you have a modem with your Amiga, you can adjust the baud rate up or down by clicking the up and down arrows next to the Baud Rate selection on the screen. If you don't have a modem, you will not need to use this option of Preferences.

Text Size: You can choose to have either 60 or 80 characters per line displayed on the screen. If you are using a high-quality RGB monitor, choose 80 because the screen is capable of displaying 80 characters per line. If you are using a TV, choose 60 to make sure that the characters are displayed as clearly as they can be.

CLI: This option is an acronym for Command Line Interface, which offers you another way to manipulate files on your computer. Select ON if you want the CLI icon to appear in the System drawer so you can use the CLI later. This disk operating system for the Amiga is explored in Chapters 8 and 9; you needn't be concerned with it now.

Workbench Colors: You can change the Workbench's red, green, and blue levels by dragging the appropriate arrows left or right. The Workbench itself uses four colors, and these colors are displayed to the left of the words Reset Colors. Click any one of these colors in order to modify the level of red, green, or blue that the color has, and then use the arrows to adjust the color to your liking. If you prefer different colors, this is the section of Preferences that you use to make the adjustments. If you decide that you would rather go back to the colors you were using, select the Reset Colors box.

Display Centering: In the center of the Preferences window is a box, and near the middle of the box is a symbol that resembles a corner mark. With this symbol, you can change the position of what is being displayed. If your monitor or television is cropping off some of the display, you can use this tool to make the needed adjustment. Move the pointer to the symbol and hold down the left mouse button as you drag the screen to a better position.

Printers: Choosing this part of the Preferences window brings an entirely new window onto the screen (see fig. 1.9). With this window you can tell the computer what kind of printer you are using; what kind of paper you want to use; whether the print should be letter-quality or dot-matrix; what the pitch, space, left and right margins, and paper size are; whether you will be printing graphics; and what kind of printer port you are using.

Edit Pointer: If you want to change the appearance of your pointer, you can select this option and create your own pointer. The Amiga will show you how to create a new pointer by using the mouse and any of the four available colors.

When you are satisfied with the choices you have made in Preferences, you can select Save to put those choices on the disk. If your choices are temporary, choose Use; the computer will use your

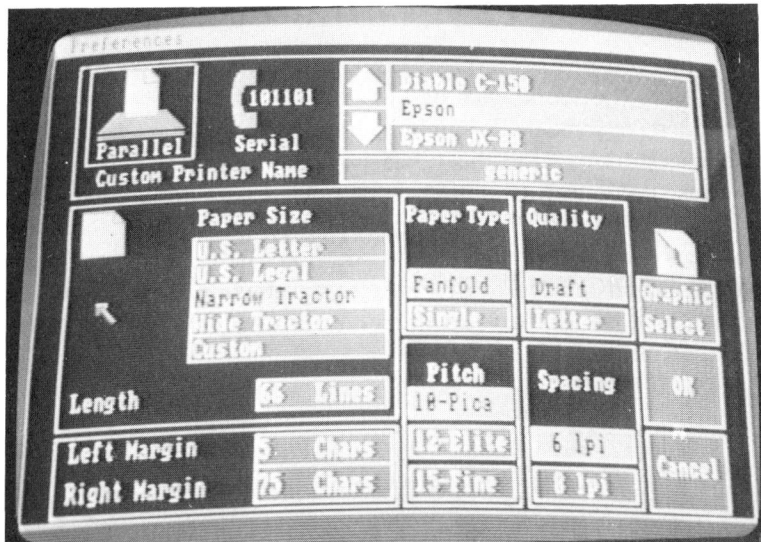

Fig. 1.9. The printer-selection
window.

choices until it is turned off, at which time the Amiga will "remember" only the most recent preferences stored on the disk drive.
If you decide that you want everything set back the way it was when
you bought your Amiga, choose Reset All. If you want to save to the
disk the options you last specified, select Last Saved. (These options
are located in the upper left corner of the Preferences window.)
Finally, if you decide not to save the settings you have chosen, select
Cancel. Any of these selections will return you to the Workbench.
You should spend some time experimenting with the Preferences.
You always can reset them to their original positions.

One interesting feature you should note about working with windows and desktops is that entire screen displays may be moved just
as easily as windows. Right now, move the pointer up to the top of
the screen to the words AmigaWorkbench. Hold down the left mouse
button and drag the screen down as far as you like. You can move
the screen up the same way. When you have several screens in operation, you can shift them up and down in order to work with the
one you want. Moreover, each screen has a Front Gadget and Back
Gadget (in the upper right corner), so you can overlap screens just
as you do windows. Finally, notice that the Amiga will also tell you
(at the top of the screen) how many bytes of memory you have left
to use.

Ready for Programming

Now that you have set up your computer and you have experimented with using the Workbench desktop and its windows, you are ready to undertake some programming. Although you may not have all the languages discussed in this book, you definitely have Amiga BASIC because it comes with your computer. To do the programming discussed in Chapters 6 and 7, you will have to purchase the other languages used. However, even if you don't have all the languages, you will find reading those chapters worthwhile. Throughout the chapters in this book, you will explore many different ways to use the potential of the Amiga.

2
Programming in Amiga BASIC

Amiga BASIC, the Amiga's version of BASIC, is one of the easiest languages to use with the Amiga. BASIC (the acronym for Beginner's All-purpose Symbolic Instruction Code) always has been the most popular microcomputer language for beginning and intermediate users. Although BASIC is not the fastest language available, it is powerful and easy to learn. Amiga BASIC is essentially the BASIC language with some enhancements. Besides being one of the best and most advanced versions of BASIC available, Amiga BASIC is easy to master. Because the words of the language are so much like English, you should be writing simple programs within half an hour. This chapter helps you learn the Amiga BASIC language through the step-by-step creation of short sample programs that demonstrate what different keywords do.

Two methods are available to tell the Amiga what to do when you are using Amiga BASIC. You can type commands from the keyboard or you can create a program.

To use the language in either way, you first double-click the Amiga BASIC icon. You will see two windows: Output and List. The Output window displays the results of your programs. You also use the Output window to enter commands directly (for example, PRINT "HELLO"). The List window, on the other hand, is where you type or edit a program. You can open either window by moving the mouse pointer to that window and clicking the mouse button.

At the top of the Amiga BASIC screen is the Menu Bar, which provides a variety of options. You can do such tasks as suspend a program, stop a program, or alter the contents of the program lines. The items under the Menu Bar are generally self-explanatory, and you can display any menu by moving the pointer to the Menu Bar and pressing the right mouse button.

To edit a program, you open the List window, move the mouse pointer to the part of the program you want to edit, and click the left mouse button. You can use the cursor keys to move around, the BACKSPACE key to delete characters, and the other keys to add characters to a program line (see Chapter 3 for more information about editing programs). As always, input from the keyboard should be followed by pressing the RETURN key. To use a program, type the RUN command from the Output window.

As mentioned, you have two ways to give instructions in Amiga BASIC. The first way is from the Output window. You type a command from the keyboard, which the Amiga executes immediately. For example, if you want the Amiga to tell you what 3 times 5 is, you can type

```
PRINT 3 * 5
```

When you press the RETURN key, the monitor immediately displays

```
15
Ok
```

When you give the computer a direct command, the computer responds immediately to that command.

The second way to get the Amiga to respond to Amiga BASIC is by a program, which you create in the List window. A *program* is an ordered set of instructions for the computer. You tell the Amiga in what order to execute these instructions by means of numbered program lines. When you are typing an Amiga BASIC program, you give a number to each line of instructions. These numbers tell the computer the order in which you want those instructions to be executed. The numbers you use or the order you type them doesn't matter because the Amiga puts the lines in correct numerical order for you.

Creating Programs

To gain an understanding of programming, you should create all the programs given as examples throughout this book. This will make the learning process easier and more fun. Don't be concerned if you don't know what all the statements do yet; you will learn all about them in this chapter and the next.

Enter the short program that follows. Because Amiga BASIC treats uppercase and lowercase letters the same, you do not need to be concerned about them as you type the lines. Every time you get to the end of a line of commands, press the RETURN key to tell the Amiga that you have finished entering that line. Be sure to type the lines exactly as shown here.

```
10 LET A = 5 * 3
5 REM THIS IS A VERY SIMPLE PROGRAM
40 PRINT "THE VALUE OF A IS "; A; "AND THE VALUE OF B
IS "B". SO MUCH FOR ADVANCED MATHEMATICS. "
20 LET B = 2 + 5
50 END
```

When you finish entering this little program, you can display it on the screen. To do so, issue the LIST command and press RETURN. On your screen, you will see the following:

```
LIST
5 REM THIS IS A VERY SIMPLE PROGRAM
10 LET A = 5 * 3
20 LET B = 2 + 5
40 PRINT "THE VALUE OF A IS "; A; "AND THE VALUE OF B IS
"B". SO MUCH FOR ADVANCED MATHEMATICS. "
50 END
Ok
```

Notice that the program lines are now in numerical order but otherwise appear exactly the way you typed them. If you use the RUN command to start this program's execution, you will see the following lines on the computer screen:

```
RUN
THE VALUE OF A IS 15 AND THE VALUE OF B IS 7. SO MUCH FOR
ADVANCED MATHEMATICS.
Ok
```

Line Numbers

The following are the only rules you have to observe about line numbers:

1. Make sure that the numbers are in the order you want the lines to be.

2. Don't use negative numbers or numbers higher than 65529.

3. Don't use decimals in line numbers; for example, you can't have a line number 10.5433.

When you are using line numbers, make sure that the intervals between the numbers are large enough so that you can insert more program lines if you want to. Begin your program with line numbers like 10, 20, 30, and so on, instead of 1, 2, 3. This practice will make it easier to add to the program later.

Line numbers have another purpose besides just getting a program in order. They are used as references for the rest of the program. As the preceding short program stands, the computer will simply do what it is told to do in lines 5, 10, 20, 40, and 50. However, you can make a program "jump" to a different part of itself instead of processing straight through to the end and quitting.

Before you explore how a program "jumps," you need to get rid of the program you were working on. To clear the program from your screen, type *NEW* and press RETURN.

Now type this next short program. Remember to type these lines exactly as they appear and to press the RETURN key after each line you enter.

```
10 REM Here is a program that uses a GOTO command
20 PRINT "Good day. I am the Amiga personal computer. "
30 C = C + 1
40 PRINT "I have said that"C"times already today!"
50 GOTO 20
```

If you make a mistake while typing, just press the BACKSPACE key as often as necessary to erase your mistake. If you press RETURN after typing a program line and the computer tells you that you have made a mistake, examine the line carefully to find your mistake and type the whole line again. You will learn an easier way to correct mistakes later, but for now make the correction by typing the line again.

Infinite Loops

As you may have guessed, the GOTO 20 in line 50 tells the Amiga to go back to line 20. In fact, as the program runs, it will keep coming to line 50, which tells the program to go back to line 20. This is called an *infinite loop* because the program will keep running as long as the Amiga is working properly. The computer has no reason to stop the program. Here's what happens when you execute the program:

```
RUN                     (RETURN)
Good day. I am the Amiga personal computer.
I have said that 1 times already today!
Good day. I am the Amiga personal computer.
I have said that 2 times already today!
Good day. I am the Amiga personal computer.
I have said that 3 times already today!
Good day. I am the Amiga personal computer.
I have said that 4 times already today!
```

The computer will continue being friendly and complaining about how many times it has had to say "Good day" to everyone. This program uses some simple commands, which you now will explore one line at a line. Before you continue, however, press the CTRL and C keys at the same time; this action will stop the program. CTRL-C is used to "break" any Amiga BASIC program's execution.

The first part of the program, line 10, is a REM statement:

```
10 REM Here is a program that uses a GOTO command
```

REM is a short way of saying REMARK. You use REM to make a note or remark to yourself in the program. The computer ignores anything following the word REM in that program line. You even can type

```
10 Remarkable program, isn't it? Thank you very much.
```

The computer will ignore this entire line because it begins with the three letters *Rem*. However, you must follow REM with a blank space so that the computer can recognize REM as a separate keyword. Use REM to make notes to yourself in the program so that you can better understand what certain parts of the program do. This practice also will help you find programming errors easily.

The PRINT Command

Line 20 contains the PRINT command followed by the words that the program prints out:

`20 PRINT "Good day. I am the Amiga personal computer. "`

The PRINT command prints on the screen (displays) whatever comes after the command. Here are some sample PRINT statements and the resulting output:

```
PRINT "HELLO"
HELLO

PRINT "The sum of 2+2 is"; 2+2
The sum of 2+2 is 4

PRINT 10
10

PRINT 5 + 7
12

PRINT 5 * 1000 "is a pretty big number. "
5000 is a pretty big number.
```

You should notice three characteristics of PRINT:

1. PRINT can display both words and numbers.

2. PRINT displays whatever is enclosed in double quotation marks (") exactly as the material is entered.

3. If numbers are outside the quotation marks, PRINT displays the mathematical result.

You have to be careful with quotation marks because the computer doesn't have different symbols for opening and closing quotation marks. The rule is that the first quotation mark means open, the second quotation mark means close, the third quotation mark means open, the fourth quotation mark means close, and so on. What is not enclosed between opening and closing quotation marks is outside the quotation marks and therefore is regarded as a mathematical statement of some sort (which can include variables).

You also should keep in mind that you can use a semicolon (;) at the end of a PRINT statement. Normally, the PRINT statement prints each statement on a separate line. If you don't want the computer to skip to the next line, put a semicolon at the end of the entire PRINT statement.

Using Variables

In the Amiga BASIC language, you can assign values to *variables*, which are symbols made up of letters and numbers. As in algebra, you can let something represent a number, and that "something" can hold the value of the number even if the number changes. For instance, you can let the variable A equal the number 10 by typing the following:

A = 10

Watch the results of the following two PRINT statements after you have assigned the variable A a value of 10:

PRINT "A"
A

PRINT A
10

In the first PRINT statement, the computer did exactly what you told it to do: to print the letter A. Because the letter was enclosed in quotation marks, it was treated as a string and was therefore displayed exactly as entered. (A string is simply a series of one or more characters.) In the second PRINT statement, you told the computer to PRINT A (without quotation marks), and the letter A was interpreted as a variable. The computer therefore displayed the present value of the variable A, which is 10.

As mentioned earlier, the values of variables can change. Look at the third line of this short program:

30 C = C + 1

This line tells the computer to "make the variable C equal to itself plus 1." Every time line 30 is executed, the value of C increases by 1. The statement makes no sense algebraically; in algebra, C always equals C. With computer programming, however, you can bend the rules. By making C equal to itself plus 1, you can change the value of the variable.

The following PRINT statement combines words with a variable:

```
40 PRINT "I have said that"C"times already today!"
```

The PRINT statement is followed by the words *I have said that* in quotation marks. The next part of the statement, the variable C, is not enclosed in quotation marks. C is treated as a variable, and its value is displayed between the first set of words and the second set of words. The second set of words—*times already today!*—is within quotation marks and therefore will be displayed exactly as it appears.

Finally, consider the line

```
50 GOTO 20
```

This command sends the program directly back to line 20. Get rid of this line by typing the line number and pressing RETURN:

```
50      (RETURN)
```

Line 50 is gone now. Type a new line 40. By typing line 40 again, you erase the old line 40 and replace it with the new one. This fact is important to remember when programming because you don't want to wipe out program lines accidentally by using the same line number twice. The new line is

```
40 PRINT "I have said that"C"times already today!" : GOTO 20
```

When you RUN this program, you will discover that it does exactly the same thing as the old one. You attached to the end of line 40 the command that used to be on line 50. Note the colon (:) separating the original line 40 statement and the GOTO 20 statement. You can have many different commands on the same program line, as long as they are separated by colons.

Numbers in Amiga BASIC

At this point, you should take a few minutes to learn the rules for using numbers in Amiga BASIC. Although you can't use decimals (such as 0.653 and 0.1) in program lines, you certainly can use decimals in Amiga BASIC. You also can use negative numbers, signified by the minus sign (-) in front of the number. One important restriction is not to use commas in numbers. In the English language, the number one thousand often is expressed as 1,000. If you typed *A = 1,000* into the Amiga, however, you would get an error message because commas never should be used in numbers. Instead you would type

A = 1000

When you are assigning numbers to variables, three different kinds of variables are available. These are the integer variable, the single-precision variable, and the double-precision variable.

An *integer variable*, denoted by the percentage sign (%), holds any number from -2,147,483,647 to 2,147,483,648. This type of variable will not retain a decimal value; instead, an integer variable rounds off a decimal to the next higher number. Therefore, an integer variable that is assigned the value 16.93 would equal 17. Examples of integer variables are A%, Y1%, RR%, IV%, YCH%, and BC%.

A *single-precision variable*, denoted by an exclamation point (!), is the kind of variable used if you specify otherwise. In other words, the default variable is single precision. Because the computer treats a variable as single precision anyway, you do not need to put the exclamation point at the end of the variable unless you want to. The variables A, Y, T1, U!, WOW!, GWHIZ!, HI, and LOIZ! are all single-precision variables. These variables can support very large numbers (both positive and negative) whether they have fractional parts or not.

If a number is very large, the computer uses scientific notation, which shows a number multiplied by a power of 10. Suppose that the value of a single-precision variable is

A! = 3. 235325e + 10

The exponent is e + 10. The value of this number is 3.235325 times 10 raised to the 10th power (which is a pretty big number). Single-precision variables can support exponents of -38 to +38.

For extremely large numbers, the Amiga has *double-precision variables*, denoted by the pound sign (#). When used with mantissas, double-precision variables—such as RR#, PG#, and TTK#—can support numbers from 10^{-308} to 10^{+307}. One way you can tell when you are dealing with a number so large that the computer denotes the number as double precision is that the exponent has a d in it. Therefore, mantissas such as d + 15 and d + 07 are used instead of e + 10, as in single-precision variables.

Math in Amiga BASIC

You can perform math operations with variables and numbers combined in any way you want. The only requirement is that you have an operator (such as a plus sign or a multiplication symbol) between the variables and numbers. Table 2.1 shows the different types of operators that Amiga BASIC supports.

Table 2.1
Mathematical Operators in Amiga BASIC

Operator	Operation	Results
+	Addition	Adds elements (examples: PRINT 5 + 7 results in 12; A = 5: PRINT A + A results in 10)
–	Subtraction	Subtracts the latter expression from the former (examples: B = 7 - 20 results in the variable B being equal to -13; NN = 20: PRINT 10 + 20 - NN results in a value of 10)
*	Multiplication	Multiplies the first number by the second (examples: PRINT 50 * 10 results in 500; H1 = 23 * 2: PRINT H1 * 3 results in 138)
/	Division	Divides the latter number into the former (examples: PRINT 50/5 results in 10; GJ% = 35: PRINT 105/GJ% results in 3)
^	Exponentiation	Raises the first number to the power of the second (examples: PRINT 2^8 results in 256; E = 7: PRINT 10^E results in 10,000,000)

A simple example of how these operators are used in a program follows. Remember to type *NEW* before you start entering a new program and to press RETURN after each program line.

```
10 CLS
20 PRINT "Math Machine, brought to you by the Amiga personal
computer"
30 PRINT: INPUT "Enter the first value: "; FV
40 INPUT "Enter the second value: "; SV
50 PRINT FV; " plus "; SV; " equals "; FV + SV
60 PRINT FV; " minus "; SV; " equals "; FV - SV
70 PRINT FV; " times "; SV; " equals "; FV * SV
80 PRINT FV; " divided by "; SV; " equals "; FV / SV
90 PRINT FV; " to the power of "; SV; " equals "; FV^SV
100 GOTO 30
```

Now enter the RUN command to start this program so that you can see how it works. After you have entered a few numbers and understand how the program is operating, press Ctrl-C to stop the program and to get back into Amiga BASIC.

Advanced Math Functions

Amiga BASIC has many math functions that you can use directly or in a program. For example, you can use the SQR function to determine the square root of a number. To use the SQR function, type *SQR*, followed in parentheses by the number for which you want the square root. The following example finds the square root of 16.

```
PRINT SQR(16)        (RETURN)
4
Ok
```

When you use a division function, you often have a remainder that you would like expressed as an integer. For instance, when you divide 10 by 3, the solution is 3 with a remainder of 1. When you type *PRINT 10/3*, however, the result is 3.33333. If you are working with integers, you can determine the remainder by using the MOD function. The MOD function gives the remainder of two numbers that are to be divided. Here is an example:

```
54 MOD 5
4
Ok
```

Because 54 divided by 5 is 10 with a remainder of 4 (using integers only, remember), the MOD function returns a value of 4.

If you have a number that has a decimal portion you want to remove (for instance, if you want 5.23989342 to be simply 5), you can use the INT function followed by the number enclosed in parentheses. INT rounds off to the next lower integer, so even 5.99999 becomes 5. Examples of the INT function follow.

```
PRINT INT(65.238732)
65
Ok
```

```
PRINT INT(75)
75
Ok
```

```
PRINT INT(-123.43242)
-124
Ok
```

If you have a negative number that you want changed into a positive number, you can use the ABS function. Making a number positive is known in mathematics as the *absolute value*, from which the ABS command is derived. Keep in mind that a zero or a positive number is unaffected by the ABS function. Examples of the ABS function follow.

```
A = ABS(-230) : B = ABS(0) : C = ABS(50)
Ok
```

```
PRINT A, B, C
230    0    50
Ok
```

You can use the SGN function to find out whether a number is positive or negative. If the number in parentheses following SGN is negative, the computer displays a -1; if the number is zero, the computer displays a 0; if the number is positive, the computer displays a 1. The following examples illustrate.

```
PRINT SGN(-50)
-1
```

```
PRINT SGN(0)
0
```

```
PRINT SGN(5000.23423)
1
```

Although you may not use some of the advanced mathematical functions in your programs, these advanced functions can be invaluable to the person developing sophisticated math or graphics programs. The advanced mathematical functions are listed and explained in table 2.2. These functions always are followed by the number or numeric variable that is being used with the function, and the number or variable must be enclosed in parentheses.

Table 2.2
Advanced Mathematical Functions

Function	Results
ATN	Returns the arctangent, which is the angle (in radians) whose tangent equals the number you give the computer
COS	Returns the cosine of a number
SIN	Returns the sine of a number
TAN	Returns the tangent of a number
LOG	Returns the natural logarithm of a number
EXP	Raises the value of e (2.71828183) by the number you give the computer and prints the result

You can use the framework of the previous simple math program to put some of the advanced functions to use:

```
10 CLS
20 PRINT "Math Machine II, brought to you by the Amiga personal
computer"
30 PRINT: INPUT "Enter the number you want to work with: "; FV
40 PRINT "The natural logarithm of "; FV; "is "; LOG (FV)
50 PRINT "The sine of "; FV; " is "; SIN (FV)
60 PRINT "The cosine of "; FV; " is "; COS (FV)
70 PRINT "The tangent of "; FV; " is "; TAN (FV)
80 PRINT "The arctangent of "; FV; " is "; ATN (FV)
90 PRINT "The value 'e' raised to the power of "; FV; "
equals "; EXP (FV)
100 GOTO 30
```

Random Numbers

One function that at first might not seem to be mathematical is RND. This function generates a random number between 0 and 1 (which is a long decimal). You must follow the function with any positive number in parentheses. Consider the following examples of the function and their results.

```
PRINT RND(10)
^H. 3223243

PRINT RND(5)
^H. 9873829

PRINT RND(1)
. 5673920
```

No computer can generate a truly random number because the sequence that picks a number is predictable; the sequence itself is a mathematical function. Suppose that you turned on the Amiga and printed the first five numbers RND generated; if you turned on the computer a week later and did the same thing, you would get these same five numbers. The computer has a certain sequence of random numbers, and each sequence is based on a number called the *seed*. You can change the seed given to the mathematical function that generates the random numbers so that the Amiga produces a new series of random numbers. To *reseed* the random number generator, use a negative number after RND.

```
PRINT RND(-50)
. 4620339
```

If you want to find out what the last random number generated was, use a zero in the parentheses.

Although RND may seem to be a useless function at this point, you will discover many uses throughout this book. For example, RND is an excellent way to produce random graphics and sounds. Moreover, many programs, such as video games, use random numbers; for example, in certain outer space video games, the RND function is used to make a random number of aliens appear on the screen.

Because the result of the RND statement is a fairly messy decimal number, you may want the result expressed as an integer, which is easier to work with. The solution to this problem is to use the following formula:

```
VARIABLE = INT(high-limit * RND(1)) + 1
```

VARIABLE is the variable that you want the random number to be put into, and *high-limit* is the highest possible number you want generated. With this formula, after a random number is attained, the number is multiplied by the highest number you want generated. Next, the decimal part of the number is removed, and this number is increased by a value of 1. This results in a number between 1 and the high-limit you have selected. Suppose that you want to generate a random number between 1 and 50, and instead of putting the number into a variable, you prefer having the result displayed immediately. You type

```
PRINT (50 * RND(1)) + 1
35
Ok
```

You will be seeing a great deal of the RND function in Chapter 5.

Working with String Variables

Numbers aren't the only elements that can be put into variables. *Strings*, which are sets of letters and numbers, also can be put into variables called, appropriately, *string variables*. To denote a string variable, you put a dollar sign ($) after the variable name. Here are some sample string variables:

```
A$ = "Hello there. I am the Amiga computer from Commodore-
Amiga."
```

```
B1$ = "The quarterly report shows a 23% increase in sales!"
```

```
CCHI$ = "45000"
```

```
I12B4U$ = "This is a test"
```

The computer will put inside the variable exactly what is inside the quotation marks, but will not include the quotation marks themselves in the string. Notice that you can put numbers, text, symbols, and almost anything else you want inside a string. The only thing you don't want inside a string is the double quotation mark because that will make the computer "think" that you are at the end of a string.

Combined Strings

Although strings cannot be multiplied, added, subtracted, or subjected to other mathematical functions, you can use the plus sign to put strings together. Try this on your computer:

```
A$ = "Now is the time "
Ok

B1$ = "for all good men to come to the aid of their country. "
Ok

PRINT A$ + B1$
Now is the time for all good men to come to the aid of their
country.
Ok

CC$ = A$ + B1$ : PRINT CC$
Now is the time for all good men to come to the aid of their
country.
Ok
```

Notice that you made up a new string, CC$, by "adding" A$ and B1$. If you had made CC$ equal to B1$ + A$, the new string variable CC$ would have been for all good men to come to the aid of their countryNow is the time .

String Functions

Like numeric variables, string variables are supported by many functions in Amiga BASIC. The first of these, LEN, tells you the length in characters of a string. The length includes all spaces, punctuation symbols, letters, numbers, and anything else in the string, as in the following example.

```
Y$ = "The longest string in the west!"
Ok

PRINT LEN(Y$)
31
Ok
```

When a string begins with a number (or consists entirely of a number), you can *extract* this number and display it or put it into another variable. The function you use to do this, VAL, examines the first portion of the string for a number. If VAL finds a number before anything else at the beginning of the string, the program extracts that number (although the string remains intact). If a number is not the first part of the string or the entire string, VAL returns a value of zero. The following examples demonstrate the use of VAL.

```
PRINT VAL("20 years old is my age, sir")
20
Ok
```

```
PRINT VAL ("So you're 20 then, are you?")
0
Ok
```

The opposite of VAL is STR$. The STR$ function converts a number into an ASCII string. The following example illustrates.

```
NM$ = STR$(450)
Ok
```

```
Print NM$
450
Ok
```

When you want to print a single character many times, you will find the STRING$ function helpful. STRING$ creates a string that consists of a specified number of repetitions of the same character. STRING$ should be followed by two elements in parentheses and separated by a comma. The first element is a number that tells the computer how many of the characters you want, and the second is the character itself.

```
PRINT STRING$(25, "A")
AAAAAAAAAAAAAAAAAAAAAAAAA
Ok
```

```
LONG$ = STRING$(25, "*")
Ok
```

```
PRINT LONG$ + LONG$
**************************************************
Ok
```

For the second element, instead of using a character in quotation marks, you can use the ASCII value of the character you want to print. For example,

```
PRINT (20, 65)
AAAAAAAAAAAAAAAAAAAA
Ok
```

Amiga BASIC has a function, SPACE$, devoted exclusively to displaying spaces. This function works just like STRING$, except that you don't have to specify the character you are going to use because the Amiga already knows that the character will be a space. You simply specify the number of repetitions in parentheses after the command. The following example uses SPACE$ to indent the line 10 spaces:

```
PRINT SPACE$(10); "I'm over here"
          I'm over here
```

Notice that the semicolon in the PRINT statement tells the computer to display I'm over here directly after the 10 spaces. When you are using a PRINT statement, the semicolon works just like the addition sign for putting strings together. PRINT with a semicolon tells the computer, "Don't skip to the next line; just go ahead and keep printing on this line."

When you are working with a string, you sometimes may want to work with only a piece of that string. For instance, suppose that you have a string that contains the city, state, and ZIP code of a person's address (ADDR$ = "New York, NY 10020"), and you want only the ZIP code. You need to extract the last five characters of the string. You can accomplish this task with the RIGHT$ function. RIGHT$ should be followed by two elements separated by a comma within parentheses: the name of the string you are working with and the number of characters you want to extract. Using the ADDR$ example, you type

```
ZIPCODE$ = RIGHT$(ADDR$, 5)
```

The ZIP code is now stored in a string called ZIPCODE$. Keep in mind that the original string remains exactly as it was unless you alter it directly.

Amiga BASIC also has a LEFT$ command, which gets the leftmost characters out of a string. Here's an example:

```
PERSON$ = "Danny LeDude"
Ok
```

```
PRINT LEFT$(PERSON$, 5)
Danny
Ok
```

To extract a substring that is in the middle of a string, use the INSTR function. The format of that function is

    INSTR(string, beginning character, length)

String is the name of the string; *beginning character* is the number of the character you want to start with (for example, 5 would mean you want the substring to begin with the fifth character in the string you are working with). *Length* is the number of characters you want extracted from the string. Some examples of the INSTR function follow.

```
A$ = "Somewhere in the middle of this sentence"
Ok

PRINT INSTR(A$, 18, 6)
middle
Ok

PRINT INSTR(A$, 5, 5)
where
Ok
```

Using the ASCII Character Set

The Amiga computer, like all personal computers, uses the ASCII character set. ASCII, which is a system of representing computer characters with numbers, was developed to standardize information transfer from one computer to another. For example, the number for the capital letter A is 65 on the Amiga. ASCII code 65 also represents A on the Macintosh, IBM PC, Commodore 64®, TRS-80™, and most other computers. The ASCII character set ranges from 0 to 255. Your Amiga manual contains a chart that lists the ASCII code numbers with the corresponding characters.

The Amiga has two functions that deal with ASCII. The first, ASC, tells you what ASCII number corresponds to the first character you give the computer, for example,

```
PRINT ASC("A")
```

This statement causes the computer to display the number 65. Likewise, typing *PRINT ASC("Adam's Apple")* results in 65 because the first character of the string is the capital letter A.

The opposite function of ASC is CHR$, which accepts an ASCII number in parentheses and displays the ASCII character equivalent, as in the following example:

```
PRINT CHR$(65); CHR$(66); CHR$(67)
ABC
Ok
```

Creating Subroutines

You already have discovered how to create a subroutine using the GOTO command, which makes the computer jump to a specified line in the program. You can create an infinite loop by making the program continue to GOTO another line without end; in this case, you can break out of the program by pressing CTRL-C.

You can create a different type of subroutine with the GOSUB command. GOSUB also makes the computer jump to a certain part in the program; but wherever a RETURN command is issued, processing returns to the program line immediately following the GOSUB command.

```
10 REM This is a sample program demonstrating GOSUB
20 PRINT "I am the Amiga Computer. "
30 PRINT "Excuse me for a moment. "
40 GOSUB 60
50 PRINT "Thank you. " : END
60 PRINT "I just wanted to make a subroutine here. "
70 RETURN
Ok

RUN
I am the Amiga Computer.
Excuse me for a moment.
I just wanted to make a subroutine here.
Thank you.
Ok
```

In this program, the computer encounters the GOSUB statement in line 40, and processing jumps to a subroutine at line 60. When the RETURN is encountered in line 70, the Amiga returns to the point just after the GOSUB statement, in this case, line 50. The END statement on line 50 stops the program so that it doesn't execute lines 60 and 70 again. Another reason that the END statement is on line 50 is to ensure that the computer doesn't try to do another RETURN; that would cause an error because the GOSUB already has been executed and the computer wouldn't know where to RETURN to.

Counting with Your Computer

The loop is an important concept in programming with Amiga BASIC. With the loop commands, you can count in steps other than 1. Also, you can use a loop to get the program to repeat commands a certain number of times.

You can count in steps other than 1 by using the FOR and NEXT commands. For example, if you want to count from 1 to 21 in steps of 5, you could program the computer to count 1, 6, 11, 16, 21. The FOR...NEXT commands tell the computer that you want to count from one number to another number with a certain step, or increment.

What's more important is that not only can you count with FOR...NEXT, but you also can get commands to repeat a certain number of times by embedding those commands in the FOR and NEXT commands. For example, if you want to count from 1 to 10 and watch the computer count, you can RUN this simple program:

```
10 FOR I = 1 TO 10
20 PRINT I
30 NEXT
```

Line 10 tells the computer to count from 1 to 10 and to use the variable I for the counting. The PRINT statement on line 20 prints the current value of I, and line 30 completes the loop by telling the Amiga to "count to the NEXT number." This loop makes the computer go to lines 10, 20, 30, then back to lines 10, 20, 30, and so on, until the loop is finished. The output is

```
1
2
3
4
5
6
7
```

```
8
9
10
Ok
```

You can make the FOR...NEXT loop more useful by substituting a new line 20:

```
20 PRINT "The square of "; I; "is "; I * I
```

The revised program prints the square of each number.

```
The square of 1 is 1
The square of 2 is 4
The square of 3 is 9
The square of 4 is 16
The square of 5 is 25
The square of 6 is 36
The square of 7 is 49
The square of 8 is 64
The square of 9 is 81
The square of 10 is 100
```

You can change the increment with which the computer counts by following the FOR statement with STEP and the increment you want the program to use. For example, if you want the computer to count from 1 to 100 in steps of 3, you type *FOR A = 1 TO 100 STEP 3*. This statement makes the program keep looping until it reaches the value of 100, at which point processing goes on to whatever follows the loop.

To count backward, you can make the step negative. Table 2.3 shows a few sample FOR...NEXT statements and explains what each one does.

Nesting Loops

You have seen how a loop keeps repeating until completed. Now you will see how you can "nest" one loop inside another. Take a look at this example:

```
10 FOR A = 1 TO 3
20 FOR B = 1 TO 3
30 PRINT "A IS"; A; "AND B IS"; B
40 NEXT
50 NEXT
```

Table 2.3
FOR...NEXT Statements

Statement	Action
FOR I = 1 TO 10: NEXT	Counts from 1 to 10
FOR B1 = 50 TO 1 STEP -1: NEXT	Counts backward from 50 to 1
FOR HH = 700 TO 9000 STEP 20: NEXT	Counts from 700 to 9,000 in steps of 20
FOR JZZ = 10000 TO -10000 STEP -1000: NEXT	Counts backward from 10,000 to -10,000 in steps of -1,000

The loop using the B variable is nested inside the loop using the A variable. The program first encounters the A loop and makes A equal 1. Then the program encounters the B loop and makes B equal 1. When the program finds the *first* NEXT statement on line 40, the program goes back to the *most recent* FOR statement, which in this case is the statement using the B variable on line 20. After the program has counted to 3 with the B variable, the program jumps down to the NEXT on line 50 and goes back to the most recent FOR statement *that hasn't been used yet*, which is, in this case, the one using the A variable on line 10. The A variable now equals 2, and the program encounters the B loop once again and counts from 1 to 3 with B. The output looks like this:

```
A IS 1 AND B IS 1
A IS 1 AND B IS 2
A IS 1 AND B IS 3
A IS 2 AND B IS 1
A IS 2 AND B IS 2
A IS 2 AND B IS 3
A IS 3 AND B IS 1
A IS 3 AND B IS 2
A IS 3 AND B IS 3
```

When the A variable finally reaches a value of 3, the program jumps out of that loop, and the program is over. You can nest as many loops as you like, as long as you have corresponding NEXT and FOR statements for each loop.

One hint for writing FOR...NEXT statements: Follow the next statement with the name of the variable. This will clarify which NEXT corresponds with which FOR. You can modify your earlier program as follows:

```
10 FOR A = 1 TO 3
20 FOR B = 1 TO 3
30 PRINT "A IS"; A; "AND B IS"; B
40 NEXT B
50 NEXT A
```

Now you can more easily see where the FOR...NEXT loops are. You can take this a step farther by having one NEXT statement do all the work by following the NEXT with both variables:

```
10 FOR A = 1 TO 3
20 FOR B = 1 TO 3
30 PRINT "A IS"; A; "AND B IS"; B
40 NEXT B, A
```

You soon will find that loops are invaluable in programming. They can repeat a function a certain number of times and at a specified step, and they can move forward or backward in increments as small or as large as you like. For instance, *FOR I = 0 TO 1 STEP .0001* is perfectly acceptable. The real key to writing effective FOR...NEXT statements is to make the most use of the counter variable. The counter variable in a loop should not serve just to count. Instead, use the counter variable as a tool to accomplish other tasks.

Experimenting with Simple Programs

The following sample programs will help you better understand the concepts presented in this chapter. Type and RUN these programs and pay careful attention to what each line does. Practice with these simple programs can help you become a better programmer and give you the ability to create your own sophisticated programs.

The first program computes how much a person should be paid, given the hourly wage and the number of hours worked. The program first clears the screen with the CLS command. Then the program asks for the name of the worker, the hourly rate, and the hours worked so that the amount the person should be paid can be displayed. After this, the program repeats the process for the next worker.

```
5 CLS
7 INPUT "Name of Worker: "; NA$
10 INPUT "Hourly Rate: "; HR
20 INPUT "Hours Worked: "; HW
30 PRINT "Pay "; NA$; HR * HW; "dollars. "
40 GOTO 7
```

This next program accepts the starting and ending values for a FOR...NEXT loop and displays the squares and the square roots of all integers between those numbers. After the program has received the starting and ending values, it begins the FOR...NEXT loop and displays the squares and square roots. After the program is finished, it waits for any key to be pressed before running again.

```
1 CLS
5 INPUT "Enter limits: "; S, F
10 FOR I = S TO F
20 PRINT "The square of "; I; "is "; I=+^S
30 PRINT "The square root of "; I; "is "; SQR(I)
40 NEXT
50 PRINT "Press any key to do it again. "
60 IF INKEY$ = "" THEN 60 ELSE GOTO 1
```

The last program takes advantage of an array variable to store random numbers. The array goes from X(1,1) to X(4,4), so it can hold 16 numbers. As the numbers are being stored in the array, the program displays them using the LOCATE formatting command. This is a good example of how useful nested FOR...NEXT loops can be.

```
10 FOR R = 1 TO 4
20 FOR C = 1 TO 4
30 X(R, C) = INT (RND * 100)
40 LOCATE R * 2, C * 10
50 PRINT X(R, C));
60 NEXT
70 NEXT
```

Writing Your Own Programs

You now know enough about Amiga BASIC to construct some interesting programs. You might want to stop reading for a while in order to write some of your own programs. You can refer to this chapter for keywords and ideas. Once you are ready to move on to bigger and better things, you can begin Chapter 3 and learn about more advanced aspects of the Amiga BASIC language.

3
Advanced Amiga BASIC

With Amiga BASIC, you can write programs that will make certain decisions. For example, these decisions might involve comparing two numbers, checking to see whether a variable is larger than a certain number, comparing strings, or verifying the value of a variable. This chapter shows you how to write decision-making program lines, as well as shows you a number of other features of advanced Amiga BASIC.

IF Statements

Amiga BASIC's decision-making process works like this: The program performs one action if the condition of the decision is true and another action if the condition is false. For example, consider the following program line:

```
70 IF A = 5 THEN GOTO 50
```

When line 70 is executed, a decision is made. The program first checks to see whether the variable A equals 5. IF A equals 5, THEN processing will GOTO line 50. If this condition is not true (for instance, if A equals 7), processing will "slip through" to the next program line.

To use the IF...GOTO decision-making statement, you type *IF* followed by a condition; next type *THEN GOTO* followed by a line number. The line number tells the computer what line to go to if the condition is true. If the condition is false, the computer takes the only alternative action: the program goes to the next program line.

Amiga BASIC has three forms of the IF...GOTO command. They all accomplish the same task, so the one you use is your choice. The forms are

IF...GOTO <line number>

IF...THEN <line number>

IF...THEN GOTO <line number>

Within IF statements, you can specify conditions by using mathematical operators. Table 3.1 shows the kinds of mathematical decisions you can establish. These decisions apply to numeric variables and strings.

Logical Operators

In addition to mathematical operators, Amiga BASIC uses logical words to compare elements. With these logical words, you can compare more than two elements at a time. The first logical word, AND, tests whether all of a set of conditions are true. If just one condition is false, the computer interprets the result as false. Some sample statements using AND with IF...GOTO and their results follow.

```
IF 5=5 AND 7=7 AND 9=9 GOTO 100
```

All conditions are true, so processing goes to line 100.

```
IF 5=5 AND 7=6. 99 AND 9=9 GOTO 100
```

Because 7 does not equal 6.99, processing moves to the next line without making a jump to line 100.

```
IF A=5 AND 2=2 GOTO 50
```

If the variable A equals 5, both statements are true, and processing goes to line 50. If A does not equal 5, processing goes to the next line following this conditional statement.

A similar command, OR, checks to see whether any of the conditions stated are true. Only one condition needs to be true when you use OR.

```
IF 3=5 OR 6=7 OR 4=4 GOTO 30
```

Although the first two conditions are false, the last condition is true. Because at lease one condition is true, processing goes to line 30.

Table 3.1
Programming Decisions

Operator	Operation	Decision
=	Equals	Is the first variable equal to the second variable?
>	Greater than	Is the first variable greater than the second variable? With strings, the computer checks for alphabetical order to see whether the first string should follow the second. For example, DOG is considered greater than CAT because DOG comes after CAT in alphabetical order. Lowercase letters are considered greater than uppercase letters; therefore, for instance, the string *lowercase* would follow the string *UPPERCASE*.
<	Less than	Is the first variable less than the second variable? The same rules regarding strings apply, except in reverse order.
>=	Greater than or equal to	Is the first variable greater than or equal to the second?
<=	Less than or equal to	Is the first variable less than or equal to the second?
<>	Not equal to	Are the variables not equal to each other?

IF 3=3 OR 6=6 AND 4=4 GOTO 30

All the conditions are true, so processing goes to line 30.

IF 6=5 OR 87=23 OR A=9. 5 GOTO 30

If A does not equal 9.5, all the conditions are false, so processing does not go to line 30.

Other logical word commands, which follow the same pattern as AND and OR, are XOR and EQV. When you use XOR, the computer takes action only if just one of the two conditions stated is true. If both are true or if both are false, the computer does not act on the statement. When you use EQV, the Amiga takes action if the two conditions are both true or both false. Otherwise, processing goes to the next statement.

You can use the IF statement with more than just the GOTO statement. In fact, you can follow IF and a condition with just about any regular Amiga BASIC command. To use IF with another command, type *IF*, the condition or conditions you want to check, followed by the word *THEN* and the action you want taken if the final result is positive. Consider this example:

```
IF AGE < 10 THEN PRINT "You're pretty young. "
```

If the variable AGE is less than 10, the computer prints the words You're pretty young.

You also can have multiple statements on an IF...THEN line:

```
IF AGE < 10 THEN PRINT "You're pretty young. ": IF AGE < 5
THEN PRINT "In fact, you're very young!"
```

In this case, the program first checks to see whether the variable AGE is less than 10. If so, the program displays You're pretty young. and proceeds to the next IF statement; if not, processing goes directly to the next statement without displaying anything. If the variable AGE is less than 5, the program displays In fact, you're very young! Whether or not the first IF statement is true, processing proceeds to the next IF statement. These IF statements work together properly. However, you could not write statements, for example, where AGE is greater than 10 and less than 5.

The ELSE Command

Up until now, you have seen that the program will take action if a condition is true and will slip through to the next program statement if the condition is not true. With the ELSE statement, you also can tell the program to take one action if the condition is true and another action if the condition is false. Consider the following statement:

```
IF B = 5 AND TT = 63. 4 THEN PRINT "Values verified" ELSE
PRINT "Values in error. Please check again. "
```

The preceding statement causes the program to check to see whether B equals 5 and TT equals 63.4. If both conditions are met, the computer displays Values verified. However, if one or both of the conditions are not true, the program goes to the ELSE statement and displays Values in error. Please check again. The ELSE statement instructs the computer to take a specific action if the condition or conditions of the IF statement are not met.

One command similar to the IF...THEN statement is ON...GOTO. With the ON...GOTO command, you can simplify a routine such as the one that follows.

```
50 IF A=1 THEN GOTO 1000
60 IF A=2 THEN GOTO 1160
70 IF A=3 THEN GOTO 570 ELSE IF A=4 THEN GOTO 980
80 IF A=5 THEN GOTO 800
```

This program is rather cumbersome. Using the ON...GOTO command, however, you can give the same instructions in more compact form. ON...GOTO says, "If the variable stated equals 1, go to the first line number; if the variable equals 2, go to the second line number; if the variable equals 3, go to the third line number," and so on. With ON...GOTO, you can condense the preceding four lines into one simple statement:

```
ON A GOTO 1000, 1160, 570, 980, 800
```

The program checks the variable A to see whether it has a value of 1, 2, 3, 4, or 5; and processing goes to the line number that corresponds to the value of A. IF A is less than 1 or greater than 5, the program slips through to the next line. The power of ON...GOTO lies in the fact that you can list as many line numbers as you want. The more line numbers you use, the more helpful ON...GOTO is.

The command ON...GOSUB works exactly the same way as ON...GOTO, except that with ON...GOSUB, processing goes to the subroutine at the line number listed. When a RETURN is encountered in the subroutine, processing moves back to the statement immediately following the ON...GOSUB command.

The ON ERROR GOTO Command

Another command that takes action based on a certain condition is the ON ERROR GOTO command. This command should be placed at the beginning of a program if you want processing to go to a specified line number when an error is encountered. For instance, consider the following line:

```
ON ERROR GOTO 500
```

This command tells the program to go to line 500 when an error is encountered instead of displaying an error message. Here is an example of how ON ERROR GOTO can be used in a program:

```
10 ON ERROR GOTO 50
20 INPUT "What number do you want to find the square root
of"; NM
30 PRINT "The square root of "; NM; "is"; SQR (NM)
40 GOTO 20
50 IF NM < 0 THEN PRINT "There is no such thing as a square
root of a negative number. "
60 RESUME 20
```

Line 10 tells the program to go to line 50 if an error is found. In line 20, the program gets the number for which the user wants the square root. Line 30 displays the square root of the number. If all is well, the program executes the instructions in line 40 and returns to line 20. However, if an error is encountered, processing moves to line 50 to display a special error message. (The most common error is the entry of a negative number, which cannot have a square root.) The RESUME 20 in line 60 tells the computer, "I've taken care of the error—now pick up where you left off at line 20 when the error was encountered."

Screen Input

A number of commands in Amiga BASIC are devoted to getting information from the user and from the program and sending that information to the screen. These input and output commands, which are used to get and display information—are the focus of the next sections in this chapter. These commands are essential for letting a program "know" the wishes of the user and for being able to display information to the user.

The fundamental input command is, naturally, INPUT. You can use INPUT in a variety of ways in order to get both numeric and alphabetic data from the user. The simplest way to use the INPUT command is to follow it with the name of a variable:

```
INPUT A
```

This command tells the computer to wait for the user to type a number and press RETURN; after the user enters a number, the number is stored in the variable A. When this INPUT statement is encountered, the program displays a flashing cursor so that the user can type the number and press RETURN.

INPUT also can accept a string variable in the same manner, but the string variable cannot contain commas. If the user enters a string when the computer expects a number, however, an error message is displayed; if the user enters a number when the computer expects a string, the Amiga does not display an error message, but simply stores the number as a string.

If you want the user to enter a string variable called BBK$, you need to use a program line with the following statement:

```
INPUT BBK$
```

INPUT also can accept more than one variable at a time. Put the variables you want in the order you want the program to retrieve them and separate the variables with commas. For instance, if you want the program to get a string called A1$, a number to be put in the variable ILC, and another number for the variable UU5, type the following program line:

```
INPUT A1$, ILC, UU5
```

The person using the program must enter the data in the same order as the INPUT statement (that is, first a string, then two numbers); and the elements should be separated by commas. Suppose that the user inputs *HELLO, 5.6, 78.* As a result, A1$ equals HELLO, ILC equals 5.6, and UU5 equals 78. The two important requirements are that the elements be separated with commas and that the data be entered in the proper order. Otherwise, the computer displays an error message and asks the user to enter the data again.

Frequently, you may want the computer to prompt the user for specific information. You can do this in a program by using a PRINT statement followed by an INPUT statement, like this:

```
10 PRINT "Please enter your name and your age ";
20 INPUT NAME$, AGE
```

A more efficient way of writing this program is to put the prompt string (the sentence where the computer asks for the information) between the INPUT command and the variables to be entered. You can shorten the preceding example to the following:

```
10 INPUT "Please enter your name and your age "; NAME$, AGE
```

The LINE INPUT command works the same way as INPUT, except for two differences:

1. The INPUT command displays a question mark when program is waiting for input, and the LINE INPUT command displays a flashing cursor.

2. LINE INPUT accepts all the information you type, even if that information has commas, which INPUT normally will not accept; LINE INPUT takes whatever you type *as is* and puts it into a single variable.

Here is an example that uses LINE INPUT:

```
10 LINE INPUT "Enter a complete sentence for me, please: "; SENT$
Ok

RUN
Enter a complete sentence for me, please: This, my dear Amiga,
is the complete sentence I wish to type—somewhat
quickly—at this time!
Ok

PRINT SENT$
This, my dear Amiga, is the complete sentence I wish to
type—somewhat quickly—at this time!
```

Retrieving a Character with the INKEY$ Function

If you want the program to retrieve a single character, you can use the INKEY$ function. For example, you may be programming a game in which the user presses the Q key to quit the game. Stopping the game every few seconds and displaying the prompt Do you want to quit? is not practical. Instead, you can use the INKEY$ function to monitor the keyboard and take action if a certain key is pressed.

INKEY$ should be preceded by the string variable and an equal sign (=). The string variable stores the value of the key to be pressed. In the following program, the computer keeps displaying On and on until the letter E is pressed, at which time the Amiga displays until I stop.

```
10 PRINT "On and on"
20 A$ = INKEY$ : IF A$ = "E" THEN PRINT "until I stop" : END
30 GOTO 10
```

If the user presses the E key, the computer displays until I stop and ends the program at line 20. Otherwise, the program slips through to line 30, which makes processing jump back to line 10.

You may want the program to wait for an indefinite period until any key is pressed and then take action based on that key. To do this, you set up an infinite loop:

```
10 G$ = INKEY$ : IF G$ = "" THEN GOTO 10
```

The program checks to see whether G$ is a null string. A null string is a string variable with nothing in it (signified by two double quotation marks). If G$ is a null string, the program goes back to line 10.

Retrieving Data with the READ and DATA Commands

After you have established strings and numbers, you may want the program to read that information for itself. That information is called DATA in Amiga BASIC, and you can tell the computer to read the data from anywhere in the program by using the READ the DATA commands. These commands are easy to use as long as you READ string variables that are indeed strings, and numeric variables that are indeed numbers. For example, consider the following program:

```
10 READ A, A$
20 DATA 20, HELLO
```

The program first reads the number 20 into the variable A and then reads the word *HELLO* into the variable A$. Suppose that you reverse the two DATA elements:

```
10 READ A, A$
20 DATA HELLO, 20
```

The computer displays an error message because the program cannot put the string HELLO into the numeric variable A.

When you use READ and DATA, you must observe the following rules:

1. Separate with commas the elements following both the READ and DATA statements.

2. Make sure that the elements with your READ and DATA statements are in the same order as your variables; don't mix up strings and numbers.

3. Be sure to READ the same number of variables that are available in the DATA statements.

Here is a longer example of the READ and DATA commands:

```
10 PRINT "This will show the ages and relationships of 5 people and 1 dog. "
20 FOR I = 1 TO 6
30 READ NAME$, I
40 PRINT NAME$" is "I"years old. "
50 NEXT
60 FOR J = 1 TO 3
70 READ RELATIONSHIP$
80 PRINT RELATIONSHIP$ : NEXT
90 DATA Marge, 45, Bill, 47, Jennifer, 23, John, 24, Dave, 32,
Frisky the Dog, 3
100 DATA Marge is married to Bill., John is dating Jennifer.,
Dave is looking more like Frisky the Dog every day!
```

The results of this program are the following:

```
This will show the ages and relationships of 5 people and 1 dog.
Marge is 45 years old.
Bill is 47 years old.
Jennifer is 23 years old.
John is 24 years old.
Dave is 32 years old.
Frisky the Dog is 3 years old.
Marge is married to Bill.
John is dating Jennifer.
Dave is looking more like Frisky the Dog every day!
```

When the program reads a piece of data, the program "uses up" that data, so that it is not used again. As the program continues to read data, the program uses a pointer in memory to point to the next element to be read when another READ command is encountered. If you use the RESTORE command to reset the pointer, when the program is ready to read the next piece of data, the program will read the first element again. Here's a short sample program to demonstrate how RESTORE resets the program's interpretation of what piece of data is to be read next:

```
10 READ A$
20 PRINT "I read A$ again. It is: "A$: RESTORE: GOTO 10
30 DATA Element One
Ok

RUN
I read A$ again. It is: Element One
I read A$ again. It is: Element One
I read A$ again. It is: Element One
```

Screen Output

Now that you understand how to get information, both from within the program and from the user, you will examine how to send information to the screen. You are going to take a look at *output*. The first thing you need to know about output is how to clear the screen of anything that might be on it. The CLS command eliminates everything—graphics, text, and anything else—that is on the screen. You should use CLS at the beginning of every program you write because you want the screen to have a "fresh start" when the computer begins displaying information.

You already have discovered that you can use the PRINT statement to display variables, sentences, and numbers. To refresh your memory, here are some sample PRINT statements and their resulting output:

```
PRINT "This is a test"
This is a test

PRINT "If the variable A equals 5, then we'll see a"; A
If the variable A equals 5, then we'll see a 5

PRINT A, B, C, D, 10
25      43      13      43      10

PRINT "A, B, C, D, 10"
A, B, C, D, 10

PRINT 60 * 20 + 3
1203
```

The PRINT statement has some peculiarities that you should know about. First, if you put a comma between elements that you want to PRINT, the elements will be separated by spaces. Notice in the third example that because the variables and the number 10 are separated by commas, they are displayed separated from one another.

Another punctuation mark that you can use is the semicolon (;). When you follow whatever a PRINT statement with a semicolon, the computer does not move down to the next line on the screen after the program displays the information. The semicolon must be outside the quotation marks, of course, or else the character will be displayed as a semicolon. Here is an illustration of this concept:

```
PRINT "The quick red fox ": PRINT "jumped over the fence. "
The quick red fox
jumped over the fence

PRINT "The quick red fox "; : PRINT "jumped over the fence. "
The quick red fox jumped over the fence.
```

Notice that the semicolon in the second example makes the computer stay on the same line so that the second half of the sentence is not displayed on the line below.

If you don't feel like typing out PRINT all the time, you can use a question mark (?) in its place. Typing *? "Hello"* has the same results as typing *PRINT "Hello"*.

Using Variations of the PRINT Command

The PRINT command has two variations: LOCATE ( ) and PRINT USING. Each command has specialized functions. LOCATE ( ) tells the computer to print something in a specific place on the screen.

The Amiga's screen is made up of columns (which go across the screen) and rows (which go down the screen). Column 0 is the extreme left side of the screen, and row 0 is the topmost horizontal part of the screen. Column 0, row 0, therefore, is the upper left corner of the computer screen. Column 1, row 0, is just to the right of this; and column 0, row 1, is just below. As you move to the right on the computer screen, the column numbers are higher; and as you move down the screen, the row numbers are higher (see fig. 3.1).

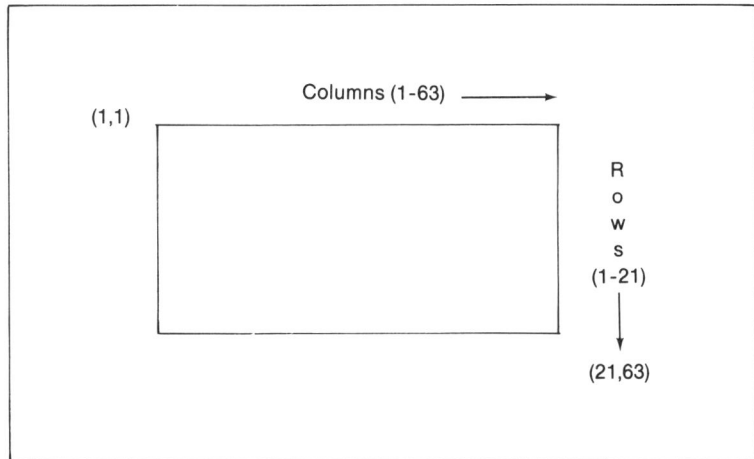

Fig. 3.1. The LOCATE command's
rows and columns on the screen.

LOCATE ( ) tells the computer to print something beginning at a
particular column and row. For example, to print the words *HI
THERE* beginning at column 5, row 3, you type

LOCATE (5, 3) : PRINT "HI THERE"

Formatting Numbers

PRINT USING is a complex statement that requires a thorough ex-
amination. Essentially, PRINT USING formats the display of numbers.
The statement uses a format string, which is a series of characters
enclosed in quotation marks. These special characters tell the computer how to print a number. You can use several different format
strings to achieve different formatting results. You may want numbers to be printed as dollars and cents, or you may want positive
and negative numbers to be printed with positive and negative signs
in front of them. PRINT USING can make your output more accurate
and professional-looking.

The most basic PRINT USING format string is the pound sign (#).
This sign tells the computer to print numbers using only a certain
number of characters. Therefore, if you use three pound signs as
your format string to format the variable N (*PRINT USING "###";
N*), the program allows N only three places. If N is larger than 999
(which means that N requires more than three places), the program
puts a percent sign (%) in front of the displayed number to show

that it is too large. If the variable N has a decimal portion, N is displayed as the next lower number. Here are some numbers and how they would appear if they were controlled by the statement

PRINT USING "###"; N

100	100
12.5	12
49.00012312	49
94556	%94556
5	5

The next format string, the plus sign (+), can be used with either a PRINT USING or just a PRINT statement. The plus sign puts the sign of a number in front of it. If the number is positive, it is preceded by a plus sign; if the number is negative, it is preceded by a negative sign. Here is what happens to numbers stored in the variable X after being displayed with the statement

PRINT USING "+###. ##"

21	+21.00
-343.23	-343.23
7	+7.00

Similar to the plus sign format string is the negative sign (-). The negative sign, however, affects only negative numbers. Another distinction is that the program puts the negative sign after the negative number; therefore, -34 is displayed as 34- and -56.23 as 56.23-.

You can use the decimal point (.) with the pound signs to specify how many digits you want after the decimal point. If the variable N equals 5.468, here are some results of various PRINT USING statements:

PRINT USING "##. #####"; N
5. 46800

> The program formats the number to include five digits following the decimal.

PRINT USING "###. "; N
6.

> The program rounds off to the next higher number because no decimals are allowed.

PRINT USING "#. #"; N
5. 5

The program rounds off as close as possible to the original number.

One format string you will use frequently when you PRINT financial data or large numbers is the comma (,). The comma formats numbers so that a comma is inserted every third place to the left of the decimal point. In order to format numbers with commas, you put a comma before the decimal point with your pound signs. For example, to display numbers with up to 10 digits, use the statement

PRINT USING "######, . ###"

Here are the results of this statement used with various numbers:

76572	76,572.000
1000000	1,000,000.000
76.345	76.345
9809823415	%9,809,823,415.000

If you want dollar signs to precede your numbers, type two dollar signs in the format string before any pound signs. Use the same PRINT USING statement you just used, except this time specify that numbers should have dollar signs displayed with them by typing the statement

PRINT USING "$$######, . ###"

867239	$867,239.000
1	$1.000
.87	$.870

You may have noticed that the numbers are not in regular right-justified columns because the numbers are of different lengths. The double asterisk format string solves this problem by making the right-most digits of the numbers line up evenly, while the portion to the left of the left digit of each number is filled with asterisks. The computer makes sure that every number fills up five spaces by adding asterisks to the left side of the number until all five positions are filled. PRINT USING "**###.#" formats the following numbers shown in the left column as they appear in the right column:

5.34	*5.34
870.2	870.2
187	**187
999.3	999.3
3	****3

To sum up the different types of format strings available with PRINT USING, table 3.2 shows the different signs and their effects.

Table 3.2
Format Strings

Sign	Name	Function
#	Pound sign	Allows a certain number of digits to be printed, indicated by how many pound signs are present
+	Plus sign	Puts a plus sign (+) in front of positive numbers
–	Negative sign	Puts a negative sign (-) after negative numbers
.	Decimal point	Specifies at what position you want the decimal point and how many digits after the decimal point should be allowed
,	Comma	Puts a comma every third place left of the decimal point
$	Dollar sign	Puts a dollar sign in front of the number
**	Asterisks	Formats the numbers so that they are right-justified

One last formatting option is that you can make the PRINT statement display a variable or text a certain number of spaces to the right by using the TAB function. By stating PRINT TAB (number), with *number* representing how many spaces to the right the computer should begin printing what follows the statement, you have an easy way to format information on the screen. For example, PRINT TAB (10) "I'm over here" prints the words I'm over here beginning at the 10th character on a line.

Advanced Features for Variables

By now you understand enough about numeric and string variables to be able to use them well. Next, you will explore two advanced features for variables: assignments and arrays. These added features in Amiga BASIC make variables more powerful and easier to use.

Assignments

One of the easiest ways to assign a number or a string to a variable is with the LET command. For example, you can tell the Amiga to LET A = 50, LET R$ = "COMPUTER", or LET UJ1 = 5. 678. When you make *assignments*, that is, when you store a number or string in a variable, the word LET is optional, so you may want to leave it out. The preceding three assignments, therefore, could be expressed as A = 50, R$ = "COMPUTER", and UJ1 = 5.678.

The equal sign (=) by itself can do more than assign a number or string to a variable. The equal sign also can be used to put one variable into another. For example, suppose that A$ equals AMIGA and B$ equals COMPUTER, and you make the following assignment:

A$ = B$

This statement makes A$ also equal COMPUTER. Both A$ and B$ have become COMPUTER, and AMIGA is no longer in memory. You can make this same type of assignment with numeric variables.

If you would rather switch the values or the strings within variables, you can use the SWAP command. Suppose that you have two string variables, X$ and Y$; and you want X$ to contain the string currently in Y$ and Y$ to contain the string currently in X$ (in other words, you want them switched). All you have to do is type

SWAP X$, Y$

Arrays

So far, you have been dealing with simple variables: A$, YY, B1, and other numeric and string variables that hold one piece of information. Another way to use variables is more efficient if you are going to be storing large amounts of data, or if you are storing data that is structured in a way that would make using simple variable names inefficient. For example, assume that you have the following chart showing how many widgets three salespersons sold during the months of April, May, and June.

Salesperson:	Mary (1)	James (2)	Darren (3)
Month:			
April (1)	47	54	23
May (2)	62	43	72
June (3)	30	77	51

Both the months and the names are numbered in order to make reference easier and to illustrate a new kind of variable: the *array*. Suppose that you want to store all these sales figures in the computer's memory. Using simple variables, you could devise different variable names to match the first letters for each month and each person's name. For example, Mary's sales in June could be the variable MJ, and James' sales in April could be JA. Your variables therefore would be MA, MM, MJ, JA, JM, JJ, DA, DM, and DJ. This is obviously an inefficient way to refer to this type of information, especially if you are working with 50 individuals over the span of 12 months.

A much easier way to work with information like this is to use an array. An array consists of a variable name followed by a certain number of elements in parentheses. In the preceding example, you are dealing with two factors: salespersons and months. These factors are known as *dimensions*. An array used to store these values is called therefore a two-dimensional array. You can have one-dimensional arrays, three-dimensional arrays, eight-dimensional arrays, or any other kind of array as long as the Amiga has enough memory to store all the information.

You call the array in the example SA (for sales), and you use numbers in parentheses to refer to the salesperson number and the month number. For example, the sales that Mary (salesperson number 1) had in May (month number 2) are stored in the array variable SA(1,2). Mary's sales in June (month 3) are stored in SA(1,3). The sales made by James (salesperson 2) in April (month 1) are stored in variable SA(2,1). As you can see from the chart that follows, the first number in parentheses is the number of the salesperson, and the second number is the number of the month. Arrays provide an efficient way of working with this information because you can store and retrieve data easily as long as you know the numbers of the salespersons and months.

Salesperson:	Mary (1)	James (2)	Darren (3)
Month:			
April (1)	SA(1,1)	SA(2,1)	SA(3,1)
May (2)	SA(1,2)	SA(2,2)	SA(3,2)
June (3)	SA(1,3)	SA(2,3)	SA(3,3)

You can assign an array variable a value just as easily as you assign a value to a regular variable. The following example illustrates the proper format.

```
A(5, 5) = 67.232
DD$(0, 0) = "THIS IS MY FIRST ELEMENT"
```

One decision you should make when you set up an array is whether you want your first element to be 0 or 1. Should A(0,0,0) or A(1,1,1) be the first element in a three-dimensional array? This choice is simply a matter of personal preference. Once you decide, you use the OPTION BASE command to tell the computer what the starting element value should be. If you want 0 to be the starting element, include OPTION BASE 0 in your program; to make the number 1 the first reference point in an array, use OPTION BASE 1.

If you are going to use an unusually large array (one that has more than 3 dimensions or more than 10 elements for each dimension), you need to use the DIM command to allocate enough memory for the array. The variables A(11), B(2,14,0), and CC$ (15) all require the DIM statement because they have more than 10 elements for at least 1 of the dimensions. A variable such as D(5,6,7,2,1) needs a DIM command because it has more than 3 dimensions. If you don't issue DIM for a large array, you will get a Subscript out of Range error message, and the computer will stop the program.

To use DIM, you type *DIM* followed by the variable name and the number of elements for which space should be allocated in memory. If you are going to have an array called XX( ), for example, which goes from XX(0,0) to XX(15,3), you would type

```
OPTION BASE 0: DIM XX(15, 3)
```

This command makes 0 the first reference point in your array and sets aside enough memory for the array. Enough memory has been allocated for the XX array to be 16 elements by 3 elements; this dimension allows the array to hold 48 numbers. You also can issue the DIM command for more than one array at a time:

```
DIM A$(12), BB(5, 5, 5), C1$(50)
```

When programming, be careful not to use the DIM statement twice for the same array. Something like DIM A(20): DIM A(30) causes an error statement because Amiga BASIC cannot set up the same array more than once. You can avoid this problem by erasing arrays that you are finished with. If you want to erase an array, use the ERASE command. To get rid of all the arrays in the preceding example, you type

```
ERASE A$, BB, C1$
```

You do not need to use parentheses when you use the ERASE command, and you can erase arrays in any order you desire. After you have created an array, you are free to use DIM to redimension the array or to do other tasks.

Program Editing

If you have tried to write any programs up to this point, you probably have made a few mistakes along the way. Prior to entering a program line (pressing RETURN), you can correct mistakes simply by pressing the BACKSPACE key to delete the error and retyping. If you already have entered a program line containing an error (the Amiga usually will indicate an error after you press the RETURN key), you either can retype the entire line or use the built-in line editor.

The editor, which is actually the List window, shows you the program so that you can go to specific parts of the program and make changes. The List window is simply an electronic means for modifying the program you have in memory. Just as if you were working with a word processor, you can change what is on the screen. You can add more information, delete certain characters, or get rid of a line or group of lines entirely. After you leave the List window and go back to the Output window to RUN the program, the modified program is stored in memory and the old one has been erased.

To get to the editor, move the mouse pointer to the List window and click the left mouse button. You can position the pointer anywhere in the window; when you click the button, the cursor appears at the location where the mouse pointer was.

You can edit a program in the List window in three ways:

1. *You can add to the program.* When the cursor is pointing to the place where you want to add information, click the left mouse button. You can add a

program line, a single character, or other information. When the cursor appears, you are ready to type your new information. You still can use the BACKSPACE key to delete characters, the arrow keys to move around the screen, and the mouse to move to a different part of the program. You do not need to be worried about mistakes because you can correct any problems in the List window. Once you are finished adding to your program, move the pointer to the Output button and click the left mouse button. Your new program now will be in memory, ready to be saved to the disk or to be RUN.

2. *You can delete something from the program.* You can use the mouse to move the cursor to the information you want to delete and then press the BACKSPACE key as often as needed. You also can move the pointer to the beginning of the information you want to delete. Then *hold down the left mouse button* while you move the cursor to the end of the text you want to delete. After you have selected this block of text (which the Amiga will display in inverse video), you can press the BACKSPACE key to get rid of the entire block.

3. *You can manipulate blocks of information.* A block, as you may have guessed, can be a group of consecutive program lines, several programs on one program line, or any other program text that is *contiguous* (is one uninterrupted block of text). When you have "blocked out" a portion of your program using the mouse as described in method 2, you can perform several activities with this block of text. You can CUT the block, which removes it from the program and stores it elsewhere in memory. You can COPY the block, which leaves it unaltered but stores it in memory for later use, perhaps in another program. Or you can *replace* the text with anything else you type. When you CUT or COPY something, you can later PASTE the text elsewhere in the program or in another program.

To CUT, COPY, or PASTE a block of text, move the pointer to Edit on the Menu Bar and select the option you want to use. If you want to replace a block of text

> with something else, begin typing the material;
> whatever you blocked off will disappear, and the new
> text you are typing will appear in its place.

Now that you have examined the keywords of Amiga BASIC, you will look at some of the features that help you polish your program. This material that follows shows you how to delete or display specific program lines.

If you want to delete a single line, you type only the line number and press RETURN; if you want to get rid of a group of consecutive lines, you type *DELETE* followed by the range you want to remove. As you can see from the examples that follow, you can use a hyphen (-) to indicate a range. For instance, *100-200* means "from 100 to 200," and *-100* means "from the beginning to 100." Be careful when you use the DELETE command; you can't bring back program lines after they have been removed.

DELETE-100

> Removes all lines from the beginning of the program up to and including line 100

DELETE 100-

> Removes all lines from and including 100 to the end of the program

DELETE 50-150

> Removes all lines from 50 to 150, inclusive

DELETE 70

> Removes line 70

The LIST command uses the same parameters as DELETE, but LIST displays the lines instead of removing them from the program. You can use LIST to display the following: (1) a single line, (2) lines from the beginning of the program to a specified line number, (3) lines from a specified line number to the end of the program, (4) lines from one line number to another line number, and (5) the entire program. For instance, *LIST 500-760* displays lines 500 through 760, inclusive. Typing only *LIST* shows the entire program. If you want scrolling to pause so that you can examine what is on the screen, press CTRL-D. To restart the scrolling, press CTRL-D again.

Disk Input and Output

This section describes the disk input and output commands. With these commands, you can save your program to disk, load a program into memory from the disk, merge two files, change the name of a file, and start running a program stored on a disk.

When you are ready to save your program to the disk, you type *SAVE* followed by the name that you want to give the program. You must be sure to enclose the file name in quotation marks. Suppose that you have completed an Amiga BASIC program that you want to call MYPROG. You type

```
SAVE "MYPROG"
```

and press the RETURN key. In a few moments, the computer finishes saving the program on the disk, and you can continue with other work.

A good practice is to save your program frequently as you are working on it. In fact, a good rule of thumb is to save every 10–20 minutes or 20 lines, whichever comes first. That way, if the computer should malfunction, a large portion of what you have worked on will be saved on the disk. If you don't save as you work, and someone trips over the Amiga's power cord a few minutes before you have finished your program, your work will be lost and cannot be recovered.

You can save a newer version of a program over an older version of the same program on the disk by using the REPLACE command. As you are developing MYPROG, for example, you can tell the computer any number of times to REPLACE "MYPROG". That command will save under that name whatever program is in memory.

Another good practice is saving the same program with different names. This method is a good idea for future debugging of your program. You can run the earlier versions of the program to see which versions of the program first demonstrate the problems.

LOAD is the opposite of the SAVE command, but the formats of the command are exactly the same. To load a program into memory from the disk, you type *LOAD* followed by the file name in quotation marks (for example, LOAD "MYPROG"). If the file is not on the disk, the computer responds with an error message.

You can load a program without wiping out the program that is in memory by using the MERGE command. (Note: Before you use the MERGE command, be sure to save to disk the program currently in memory.) The MERGE command combines two Amiga BASIC programs, as long as they don't have conflicting line numbers. To combine two programs, you must have one program in memory and then load the other one (which you will call *PROGTWO*) off the disk by typing

```
MERGE "PROGTWO"
```

You already know that the RUN command will execute whatever program is currently in memory; now you will see how you can use RUN in other ways. RUN followed by a file name automatically loads that file from disk and executes the program. For example, RUN "MYPROG" loads and runs the program MYPROG. RUN followed by a line number starts the program from that line number. The following example illustrates:

```
RUN 50
```

    Starts executing whatever program is currently in memory
    from line 50

After studying the material in this chapter, you should have an understanding of how Amiga BASIC works and how you can program in this language with a minimum of difficulty. With this knowledge, you can move on to more advanced aspects of Amiga BASIC: graphics and sounds.

4

Creating Graphics with Amiga BASIC

This chapter focuses on one particular element of the Amiga BASIC language: the graphics commands. With these commands, you can draw a variety of shapes and colors on the screen with surprising ease. Graphics commands on the Amiga computer are not only easy to use, but are much more powerful than the graphics commands of other machines because the commands execute at such a fast rate. Furthermore, the variety of colors available (4,096) and the high-resolution display make the Amiga one of the best graphics microcomputers available for the price.

About Pixels

One of the basics of graphics on the Amiga is telling the computer where on the screen you want to draw. You do this by referring to pixel coordinates. A *pixel* is the smallest thing that you can draw. A character, for example, is 8 pixels wide, and you can use more than 64,000 pixels on the Amiga. The screen is 200 pixels high and 320-640 pixels wide (depending on your monitor).

To tell the computer which pixel you are referring to, you use a two-number reference system. The first number, the *X coordinate*, indicates where the pixel is on the x-axis, which has a value of 0 on the far left and 319 on the far right. The number following the comma, the *Y coordinate*, specifies where the pixel is on the y-axis, which has a value of 0 at the top and 199 at the bottom. For example, the pixel in the top-left corner of the screen is pixel (0,0). The pixel just to the right of (0,0) is (1,0), and the pixel below (0,0) is (0,1).

As you move to the right across the screen, the X coordinate takes on a bigger value. You encounter pixels (2,0), (3,0), and (4,0), all the way up to (319,0), which is the pixel in the top right corner of the screen (see fig. 4.1).

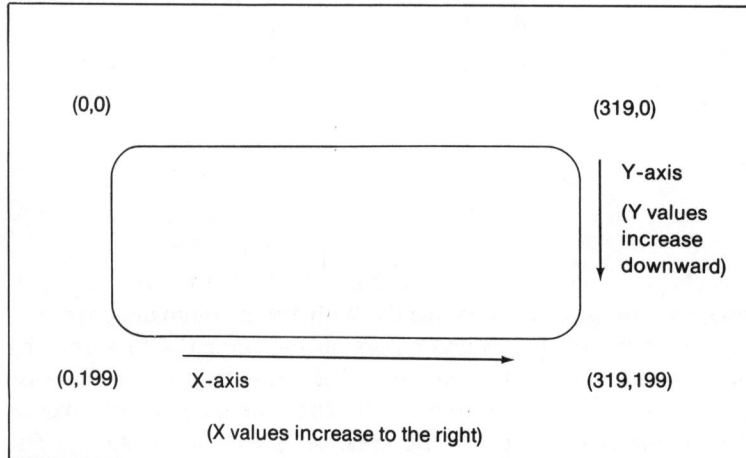

Fig. 4.1. The coordinate system.

When you move the cursor downward on the screen, the Y coordinate increases in value. You find pixels (0,1), (0,2), and (0,3), all the way to (0,199) at the bottom of the screen. Most of the pixels you will use will be somewhere in the middle of the screen—for instance, (50,50), (178,45), and (21,150).

In this chapter, you will learn about the Amiga BASIC graphics commands by examining their functions and working with sample programs. Before you begin reading about these commands, load Amiga BASIC into the computer so that you will be ready to type and run the programs. You will learn the commands most easily by typing and running them as you read through the chapter. You also will be able to modify and experiment with them so that you can continue learning on your own.

Lines and Boxes

LINE is the most fundamental graphics command! You use this command to draw a line between two pixels or to draw a box or a filled box. For example, to draw a line that begins at (20,23) and ends at (50,60), you type

LINE (20, 23) - (50, 60)

Figure 4.2 shows the result.

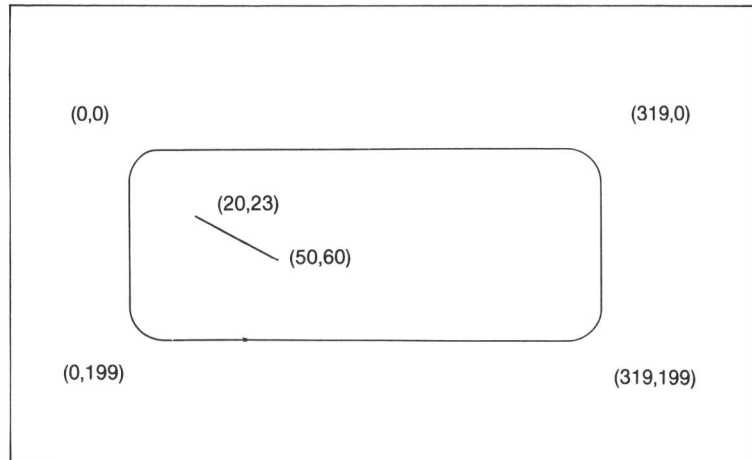

Fig. 4.2. A line created with the LINE command.

Suppose that you want to construct a triangle made up of the points (10,10), (70,10), and (40,60). You type

LINE (10, 10) - (70, 10) : LINE (70, 10) - (40, 60) : LINE (40, 60) - (10, 10)

Notice that you need to specify (10,10) twice because the Amiga doesn't automatically connect all the points. With these LINE commands, you are telling the computer: "draw from (10,10) to (70,10) to (40,60) to (10,10)." When you work with this simple command, you need to instruct the computer to draw another line back to (10,10) in order to complete the triangle.

The following program, which draws different-colored lines between changing points, shows LINE in action. If you put a comma and a number after the LINE command, the program draws the line in the color represented by the number. The following short program uses this feature. The program first clears the screen then starts the FOR...NEXT loop. This part of the program will keep changing the X value.

```
10 CLS
20 FOR X = 0 TO 160 STEP 4
```

Next, you issue a LINE command, which draws a line between these pixels: from (the present X value,160) to (0,the present X value) to (300 minus the present X value,160) to (300,the present X value). Actually, this line looks more like three lines. These unusual coordinates (which keep changing because the X variable keeps changing) achieve an interesting graphics result.

```
30 LINE (X, 160) - (0, X), RND * 3 : LINE (0, X) - (300-X, 160), RND *
3 : LINE (300-X, 160) - (300, X), RND * 3
```

Instead of using a constant number to specify the color, you use RND * 3 to generate a random color from 0 to 3. You end the program by finishing off the loop, then making the program return to line 20 in order to run again.

```
40 NEXT
50 GOTO 20
```

With a changing X value, you can create a perspective drawing. A perspective drawing consists of a series of lines connected to a vanishing point that represents "the horizon." You draw from one pixel (the vanishing point) to various pixels specified by the FOR...NEXT loop, which alters the pixels' X values. First you clear the screen and draw the line that forms the front part of your perspective drawing.

```
10 CLS
20 LINE (20, 150) - (280, 150)
```

Then you set up the FOR...NEXT loop for X. This part of the program makes the X variable go from 20 to 280 in steps of 20. Therefore, the program draws 14 lines in order to complete the perspective. You follow the loop with the LINE command and then a NEXT statement to close up the loop.

```
30 FOR X = 20 TO 280 STEP 20
40 LINE (150, 50) - (X, 150)
50 NEXT
```

Just for fun, add a COLOR statement to change the color of the pen that draws the perspective for the next loop. Although the elements of any one perspective will be a uniform color, each separate perspective will be a random color.

```
60 COLOR RND * 3
70 GOTO 20
```

Writing a Line Graph Program

Although the LINE command is simple, you can use it for many useful and complex applications. For example, you can use LINE to create line and bar graphs, sophisticated pictures, and other graphics.

The program that follows shows you how you can use LINE to construct the simple line graph shown in figure 4.3 (see color figures in center of book). The program draws a grid on the screen and then creates a random line graph on the grid. The program uses both the "old" coordinate, where the last point in the line graph was drawn, and the "new" coordinate, where the computer should draw to. You store the old coordinate value in a variable, which you will call OY (for old Y coordinate). By giving the variable a value of 40, the program begins drawing the first graph at X coordinate 0 and Y coordinate 40. To begin, you clear the screen and tell the pen to draw in white, specified by the number 1.

```
5 OY = 40
10 CLS
15 COLOR 1
```

Now you draw the grid. You use a changing X value to draw the vertical lines and a changing Y value to draw the horizontal lines. The X value goes from 20 to 280 in steps of 10; a line is drawn that extends across the screen connecting all the X coordinates.

```
20 FOR X = 20 TO 280 STEP 10
30 LINE (X, 20) - (X, 160)
40 NEXT
```

The Y variable goes from 20 to 160 in steps of 10.

```
50 FOR Y = 20 TO 160 STEP 10
60 LINE (20, Y) - (280, Y)
70 NEXT
```

Now that you have set up the grid, you can begin drawing the line graph. To distinguish the line graph from the grid, you change the COLOR to 2. This graph, as mentioned earlier, is random. As you can see in lines 90 and 110, the program draws from the old Y coordinate to a new one. Y is a random number between 20 and 160. The X variable goes from 20 to 280 in steps of 3. The FOR...NEXT loop draws the line graph on the grid; each time the FOR...NEXT loop executes, the program draws from (X,OY) to (X+2,Y).

```
75 COLOR 2
80 FOR X = 20 TO 280 STEP 3
90 Y = RND * 140 + 20
110 LINE (X, OY) - (X+2, Y)
115 OY = Y
```

Notice that the present value of Y is stored in the variable OY in line 115. You complete the loop with a NEXT statement. After the loop finishes executing, the program pauses, then returns to line 10 to draw another random graph.

```
120 NEXT
140 FOR D = 1 TO 1000 : NEXT : GOTO 10
```

Using Variables with LINE

The advantage of being able to put variables in the LINE statement is that you can use the same program to draw different figures. For instance, you can write a program that draws any cube you specify. You tell the program the size of the cube and where you want to put it. By using the LINE statement with the numbers you provide, the program can draw the cube. The first part of the program clears the screen and asks for the cube's size and coordinates.

```
10 CLS
20 INPUT "What size cube"; SZ
30 INPUT "X and Y coordinates"; X, Y
35 CLS
```

Now the program is ready to draw the cube. The front face of the cube is easy to draw because it is just a square made up of the following pixel points:

X,Y	X+SZ,Y
X,Y+SZ	X+SZ,Y+SZ

To draw the other face of the cube and the lines that connect the two square faces, you need to do a little arithmetic. In line 40 in the following program lines, the program jumps to the subroutine in line 110, which draws a square. After returning to line 40, the program changes the values of X and Y in order to draw the second face. Then the program executes the subroutine in line 110 again, which draws the second face, and sets the X and Y values back to their original values.

```
40 GOSUB 110 : X = X+SZ/3 : Y = Y+SZ/3 : GOSUB 110 : X = X-SZ/3 : Y =
Y-SZ/3
110 LINE (X, Y) - (X+SZ, Y)
120 LINE (X, Y) - (X, Y+SZ)
130 LINE (X, Y+SZ) - (X+SZ, Y+SZ) : LINE (X+SZ, Y) - (X+SZ, Y+SZ)
140 RETURN
```

To draw the lines that connect the two faces, you connect the four corresponding points on each square. You use the same arithmetic that you used to draw the squares.

```
50 LINE (X, Y) - (X+SZ/3, Y+SZ/3)
60 LINE (X+SZ, Y) - (X+SZ*4/3, Y+SZ/3)
70 LINE (X, Y+SZ) - (X+SZ/3, Y+SZ*4/3)
80 LINE (X+SZ, Y+SZ) - (X+SZ*4/3, Y+SZ*4/3)
```

Now that the cube is finished, you can print its size and coordinates. Line 100 is included as a "safety net"; this endless loop protects the cube and text from accidental destruction. If, however, you want to interrupt the program, you press CTRL and C simultaneously.

```
90 PRINT "This cube is size"; SZ; "and is located at "; X; ", "; Y
100 GOTO 100
```

The following program demonstrates how you keep one point the same for the LINE commands you are using. The program draws a "sunburst" by placing the graphics cursor in the middle of the screen and then drawing a line to another random part of the screen. The program keeps resetting the graphics cursor to the middle of the screen, so all the lines start at the same point. The result is a sunburst effect (see color fig. 4.4).

```
5 PALETTE 3, 1, 1, .13
10 COLOR 3
15 CLS
20 LINE (150, 90) - (RND*300, RND*200)
25 GOTO 20
```

The PALETTE command is discussed later in this chapter.

All the lines in this example are orange in order to make the picture look like an exploding sun. If you prefer a multicolored sunburst, delete line 10 by pressing 10 and RETURN. Then add the following line:

```
30 COLOR RND * 3
```

Screen Colors

Before you move on to more graphics programs, you should understand how to set the foreground and background colors. The COLOR command determines these colors, and it can be followed by the numbers for the foreground and background colors, For instance,

```
COLOR 1, 2
```

would set the foreground color to 1 (white) and the background color to 2 (black). The foreground color includes all the objects that you draw after you issue the COLOR command.

You can find out the color of any individual pixel with the POINT command. You either can print the number of the color at a location, for example, PRINT POINT (50,34); or you can put this number into a variable for later use, for instance, CO = POINT (50,34). If the color of the pixel at location (50,34) is Fire Engine Red, the number stored in the variable CO is 4.

Basic Boxes

The LINE command automatically draws a box when given two pixel coordinates followed by a comma, a color, and the letter B. The format for this command is

LINE (X1,Y1) - (X2,Y2), <color>, B

For example, if you want to draw a box with an upper left corner at (20,60) and a lower right corner at (290,160) using color 3, you would type

```
LINE (20, 60) - (290, 160), 3, B
```

Here are some other examples:

```
LINE (10, 10) - (20, 30), 2, B
```

Draws a box with an upper left corner of (10,10) and a lower right corner of (20,30)

```
LINE (10, 10) - (20, 30), 2, BF
```

Draws the same box as the one in the preceding example, except that this box is filled because you used BF (box filled) instead of only B

```
LINE (50, 60) - (113, 69), 1, B
```

Draws an unfilled rectangle that extends from the coordinate points (50,60) to (113,69)

You can use the LINE command in a program that alters the color of the rectangle being drawn. By drawing 50 boxes, all close to one another, you can create the illusion of a three-dimensional object made up of various colors (see color fig. 4.5). You clear the screen, set up a loop that makes X go from 1 to 100 in steps of 2, and change the color according to the current value of X. With each pass through the loop, the program draws a box. After the loop is finished, line 60 continually loops back to itself in order to preserve the picture you have created.

```
10 CLS
20 FOR X = 1 TO 100 STEP 2
40 LINE (X, X) - (X*2, X*1.5), RND*2+1, BF
50 NEXT
60 GOTO 60
```

Creating Random Graphics

RND, a command used frequently in the programs in this chapter, is the Amiga's random number generator. Using RND and a number, you can generate a random number between 0 and 1—for example, .52335, .01253, and .98431. Although RND is generally used to create unusual effects, the command also can be used to demonstrate how different components of a command operate.

You can create a program, for example, that draws random boxes on the screen. In the sample program, the coordinates of the boxes are random, and the color of each box is random as well. The use of RND statements in this program demonstrates how the random number generator works and how different numbers produce different results when used with the LINE command. First, clear the screen and generate random numbers for two different X and Y coordinates.

```
5 CLS
10 X1 = RND * 300: Y1 = RND * 200: X2 = RND * 300: Y2 = RND * 200
```

Now that you have established the coordinates, you can draw the box.

```
20 LINE (X1, Y1) - (X2, Y2), RND*3, B
```

Now you can continue the loop endlessly by making the program go back to line 10.

```
40 GOTO 10
```

Run this program and watch as the screen quickly fills up with boxes. By making one simple modification to this program, you can fill the screen with solid boxes, each of which has a random color. Enter this new line 20:

```
20 LINE (X1, Y1) - (X2, Y2), RND*3, BF
```

You can use your knowledge of the LINE command to write a bar graph program. This program is similar in many ways to the line graph program that you created earlier in this chapter. To draw the bar graph shown in color figure 4.6, you clear the screen, set the COLOR to black, and make a grid by using the same technique that you used in the random line graph program.

```
5 COLOR 1
10 CLS
20 FOR X = 20 TO 280 STEP 10
40 LINE (X, 20) - (X, 160)
45 NEXT
50 FOR X = 20 TO 160 STEP 10
60 LINE (20, Y) - (280, Y)
70 NEXT
```

Now you are ready to draw the bars that make up the bar graph. You draw the bars with COLOR set to a random number between 1 and 3; and you start at X coordinate 40 and end at X coordinate 240, drawing the bars every 20 pixels.

```
75 COLOR RND*3
80 FOR X = 40 TO 240 STEP 20
```

Next, create a random height for the bar. To do this, you set up a random value, which will be between 20 and 160, for the Y coordinate.

```
85 YY = 20 + RND*140
```

Now you can draw the bar. It will be solid and start at (X+2,YY) and end at (X+8,160). The bar, therefore, will be six pixels wide and extend from the bottom of the screen all the way to the random Y coordinate you created in line 85. You close the loop with a NEXT statement.

```
90 LINE (X+2, YY) - (X+8, 160), RND*3, BF
100 NEXT
```

Determining Values

Although the mathematics used in these programs might seem confusing to you, you should understand that many of the values used in the statements here are arbitrary. For example, no sophisticated formula was used to come up with the statement *LINE (X+2,YY) - (X+8,160)*. The statement was written with two considerations in mind: (1) that the bar should be about six pixels wide, and (2) that the bars should not run into each other. Therefore, the values X+2 and X+8 were used as the left and right sides of the bar.

The next program illustrates the art of writing good statements. The program shows that sometimes certain values are used for a particular reason.

```
10 CLS
20 FOR S = 4 TO 66 STEP 2
30 LINE (5+S, 5+S) - (280-S, 150-S), 1, BF
40 NEXT
```

This program draws 32 boxes. Each one is smaller than the last and fits inside the larger boxes (see color fig. 4.7). If the boxes were circles, they would be called *concentric* because they are all similar in size and shape and have the same center point. To achieve the effect shown in the figure, the statement *LINE (5+S,5+S) - (280-S,150-S), 1, BF* had to be devised carefully so that the boxes stay within the confines of the screen and so that the boxes all fit inside one another.

To meet these specifications, careful attention had to be paid to the values in the FOR...NEXT loop. The value of S goes from 4 to 66 in steps of 2. Therefore, the loop "passes" a total of 32 times (4, 6, 8, 10, 12, and so on to 66). The coordinate for the upper left corner, (5+S,5+S), makes the X and Y values grow larger as the loop gets closer to its end. The coordinate for the lower right corner, (280-S,150-S), grows smaller as the loop nears its end. Each box, therefore, fits inside all the others previously drawn, and all the boxes fit within the confines of the screen. The numbers used in line 30, derived after much experimentation, meet these goals.

The CIRCLE Command

Another fundamental command used to create graphics in Amiga BASIC is CIRCLE. Its format is

CIRCLE (X,Y), <radius>, <color>, <start>, <end>, <aspect>

In a CIRCLE statement, the only variables that you *must* use are the (X,Y) coordinates and the radius. The color is used just like you used it in the LINE command. The start and end options are the starting and ending points of the circle, ranging from -2π to 2π. The aspect variable, which is a number that you assign, "warps" the circle. For example, if the aspect is .44, the circle appears normal. If the aspect is .22, the shape is half as high as it is wide, so the result is an ellipse. An aspect of .88 produces an ellipse that is half as wide as it is tall.

Running the following short program will help you better understand the aspect variable. The program draws circular shapes with aspects ranging from .1 to 2 in steps of .05. The first ellipse drawn is short and wide, whereas the last ellipse drawn is tall and thin. Watch carefully to observe the effects of the aspect ratio as the program draws each new ellipse.

```
10 CLS
20 FOR A = . 1 TO 2 STEP . 05
30 CIRCLE (150, 90), 50, A
40 NEXT
```

To see the results of different X and Y coordinates, coupled with random radii, run the following program:

```
10 CLS
20 X = RND * 300
30 Y = RND * 200
40 R = RND * 30
50 CIRCLE (X, Y), R
60 COLOR RND * 31
70 GOTO 20
```

From this basic program, you easily can make modifications that will produce a number of different effects. By changing two lines, you can use the aspect ratio to produce random ellipses instead of circles. First, add a command and the letter A to the end of line 50 so that the line looks like this:

```
50 CIRCLE (X, Y), R, A
```

Now add the following new line to make the program create random aspects:

```
45 A = RND * 2
```

By putting circles on top of each other, you can create a three-dimensional cone. The trick to doing this is to make each circle successively smaller and shift away from the last circle drawn.

The next program draws not just one, but four cones, each of which spreads out from a different corner of the screen. These cones converge on each other and create a textured sphere in the middle of the screen.

```
5 COLOR 1
10 CLS
20 FOR Y = 1 TO 76 STEP 2
30 CIRCLE (Y*2, Y), Y : CIRCLE (303-Y*2, Y), Y
40 CIRCLE (303-Y*2, 166-Y), Y : CIRCLE (Y*2, 166-Y), Y
50 NEXT
60 GOTO 60
```

For those cold holiday nights, here is a program that uses the CIRCLE command to create the winter scene shown in color figure 4.8. (The PAINT command is discussed later in this chapter in the section titled "Using PAINT To Fill Shapes.")

```
5 COLOR 1
10 CLS
30 LINE (0, 120) - (319, 120)
40 CIRCLE (150, 115), 25
45 PAINT (150, 115), 1
50 PAINT (150, 125), 1
60 CIRCLE (150, 65), 21
70 CIRCLE (150, 55), 16
80 CIRCLE (145, 51), 2
81 COLOR 2 : PAINT (145, 51), 1
90 CIRCLE (155, 51), 2
91 PAINT (155, 51), 1
92 COLOR 1
95 PAINT (150, 85), 1
100 LINE (150, 55) - (160, 57)
105 LINE (150, 59) - (150, 55)
110 LINE (160, 57) - (150, 59)
115 COLOR 3 : PAINT (151, 56), 3
120 LINE (150, 55) - (150, 59)
```

```
123 COLOR 3
125 PAINT (145, 55), 1
127 PAINT (150, 65), 1
130 COLOR 2 : LINE (147, 63) - (149, 64) :
LINE (149, 64) - (152, 64) :
LINE (152, 64) - (154, 63)
135 COLOR 1
140 CIRCLE (127, 83), 7
145 PAINT (127, 83), 1
150 CIRCLE (173, 83), 7
155 PAINT (173, 83), 1
160 FOR I = 1 TO 100
170 X = RND * 319 : Y = RND * 119
180 PIXEL (X, Y)
185 NEXT
200 GOTO 200
```

CIRCLE, like the LINE command, works quickly, as you can see from running the preceding programs. Now that you have examined these commands, you are ready to move on to more sophisticated graphics functions. With the functions discussed in the rest of this chapter, you will be able to control the kinds of lines, patterns, and shapes that you draw.

Solid Shapes and Patterns

When you want to draw a shape made up of several different points, using the LINE command isn't always the most effective way to accomplish the task. Several other Amiga BASIC commands make drawing complex shapes easier: AREA, AREAFILL, and PATTERN.

Using the AREA Command

The AREA command lets you specify the points of a polygon that you want to create. Although the AREA command by itself doesn't do anything, each pair of coordinates that you give is stored in the computer's memory for later use with AREAFILL, which draws the shape. You can type the coordinates directly after the command—for example, *AREA (10,10): AREA (50,50): AREA (100,75)*. You should use AREA and AREAFILL to draw simple shapes. Watch this next simple program in action as it draws overlapping triangles of many different colors.

```
10 CLS
20 FOR I = 1 TO 3
30 X(I) = RND * 300: Y(I) = RND * 180
40 NEXT
50 AREA (X(1),Y(1)): AREA (X(2),Y(2)): AREA (X(3),Y(3))
60 COLOR RND * 3, RND * 3: AREAFILL
70 GOTO 20
```

When AREAFILL draws a figure defined by the AREA points, the figure remains on the screen until you clear it. You can take advantage of this feature by using the AREA and AREAFILL commands to create shapes that overlap each other. The result is a three-dimensional object that looks somewhat like half a pyramid.

```
10 CLS
20 FOR X = 0 TO 300 STEP 2
30 AREA (0,0): AREA (300,0): AREA (X,100): AREA (300,180): AREA
(0,180):
AREA (X,100)
35 COLOR RND * 3, RND * 3: AREAFILL
40 NEXT
```

After you run this program, try modifying it to display four colored arrows pointing to the center of the screen:

```
20 FOR X = 300 TO 0 STEP -2
30 AREA (0,0): AREA (X,100): AREA (0,180): AREA (300,0):
AREA (300-X,100): AREA (300,180)
```

By changing the coordinates that make up a shape, you can use the AREA and AREAFILL commands to create simple animation. For instance, you can create a four-point "mirror" that has two constant points and two changing points. The result is a rotation effect.

```
10 CLS
20 FOR X = 10 TO 150 STEP 2
30 AREA (X,X): AREA (150,10): AREA (160-X,110-X): AREA (10,100):
AREAFILL
35 COLOR RND * 3
40 NEXT
```

Now that the mirror has rotated in one direction, you can complete the effect by making the program loop back to line 20. This results in continuous smooth "animation."

```
50 FOR X = 150 TO 10 STEP -2
60 AREA (X, X) : AREA (150, 10) : AREA (160-X, 110-X) : AREA (10, 100) :
AREAFILL
65 COLOR RND * 3
70 NEXT
80 GOTO 20
```

Although this rotation effect is interesting, it isn't true animation
because the figure is overlapping itself. By the time the mirror has
rotated once, an abundance of shapes is concentrated on the screen.
You can change the program so that after it draws the figure each
time, the program pauses, then erases the figure. The result is something more like true animation. Add the following lines to the preceding program:

```
1 CLS : INPUT "Color of mirror"; CO
5 COLOR CO, 0
20 FOR X = 10 TO 150 STEP 3
31 FOR D = 1 TO 50 : NEXT
33 COLOR 0 : AREA (X, X) : AREA (150, 10) : AREA (160-X, 110-X) :
AREA (10, 100) : AREAFILL
35 COLOR CO
50 FOR X = 150 TO 10 STEP -3
61 FOR D = 1 TO 50 : NEXT
63 COLOR 0 : AREA (X, X) : AREA (150, 10) : AREA (160-X, 110-X) :
AREA (10, 100)
65 COLOR CO
```

Using PAINT To Fill Shapes

If you have a shape on the screen that you want to fill with a color,
you can use the PAINT command to "flood fill" that shape. A flood
fill starts painting at the (X,Y) pixel that you specify and continues
painting until reaching the boundary specified. For instance, if you
draw a circle on the screen and use the PAINT command, it paints
inside the circle until reaching its boundaries.

The PAINT command's format is

PAINT (X,Y), <color>, <border color>

The *(X,Y)* specifies the place to start painting. The *color* is the
number of the color that you want used to fill an area, and the *border
color* specifies what color the boundary of the area will be.

Keep in mind that flood fills can "leak out" just like water if the areas are not completely bounded. If you paint a circle or square in which even one pixel is missing, the paint "spills" through that leak. In other words, PAINT keeps painting until an area that is completely surrounded by boundaries is filled.

The following program draws random circles on the screen and fills them with random colors. When you run the program, be sure to notice this: When a circle begins overlapping another circle, PAINT does not go beyond the confines of the border surrounding the first circle, even if that border is partially formed by another circle that overlaps the one being painted.

```
10 CLS
20 X = RND * 300 : Y = RND * 180 : R = RND * 30
30 CIRCLE (X, Y), R
35 COLOR RND * 3
40 PAINT (X, Y), 1
50 GOTO 20
```

Painting the Amiga Bear

You can create a more complex drawing by taking the commands you have learned one step farther. The next program uses the PAINT command to draw a little bear's face. The program gives the features the appropriate colors so that the image looks just like a teddy bear. To begin the program, set the color to orange and clear the screen.

```
5 COLOR 3
10 CLS
```

Now draw the circles that make up the bear's face, eyes, and ears.

```
20 CIRCLE (150, 90), 20
30 PAINT (150, 90), 1
40 CIRCLE (130, 80), 5
45 PAINT (129, 79), 2
50 CIRCLE (170, 80), 5
60 PAINT (169, 79), 2
65 COLOR 1
80 CIRCLE (143, 85), 2
90 PAINT (143, 85), 2
100 CIRCLE (158, 85), 2
110 PAINT (158, 85), 2
```

To complete the picture, add line 120, which draws a smile on the bear's face, and line 130, which draws a nose.

```
120 LINE (145, 98) - (148, 100) : LINE (148, 100) - (152, 100) :
LINE (152, 100) - (154, 98)
130 LINE (148, 92) - (150, 90) : LINE (150, 90) - (152, 92) :
LINE (152, 92) - (148, 92)
```

Writing a program that draws a picture is sometimes difficult because you have to spend a lot of time finding the correct coordinates. If you spend enough time altering the coordinates so that the picture looks right, you will be able to expand your program to make it do other things. You will do that later in this chapter, so be sure to save this Bear Face program onto a diskette.

Patterns Created with Binary Numbers

Until now, you have been using solid patterns in the graphics you have created. You also can change these patterns so that they are not solid, but instead conform to the specifications that you provide. To understand how this is done, you first need to examine the concept of binary numbers.

The decimal system (1, 2, 3, 4, 5, . . . 10, 11, 12) is also known as *base 10*. You can create a number system out of any base, but computers primarily use *base 2* (binary) and *base 16* (hexadecimal) numbers. The binary number system involves only two digits: 0 and 1. Therefore, numbers take forms such as 10101010 and 11010111. Determining the decimal value of these numbers is not difficult because each digit's place has a specific value.

The rightmost place has a value of 1. As you move to the left, each place has a value twice as high as that of the previous place. The next place to the left, therefore, has a value of 2; the place after that, a value of 4; and so on, through 8, 16, 32, 64, and so on, depending on how many digits (places) the binary number has. Some equalities to help you understand binary numbers follow.

00000001 =   1   The only digit set to 1 is in the place with a value of 1.

00000010 =   2   The only digit set to 1 is in the place with a value of 2.

00000011 =	3	Both the 1 and 2 places are set.
10000000 = 128		The place with a value of 128 is set.
10000001 = 129		Add 128 plus 1 to get the value of 129.
10000010 = 130		Add 128 plus 2 to get 130.
10000011 = 131		Add 128 plus 2 plus 1 to get 131.

A binary digit with eight ones and zeroes is called a *byte*. A byte, therefore, is equal to eight binary digits, or *bits*.

The PATTERN Command

The Amiga uses two bytes to determine what line patterns look like. Each 1 represents a pixel that is turned on, and each 0 represents a pixel that is turned off. Therefore, the default setting of the two bytes, 11111111 and 11111111, causes the line to be solid. If one of these bytes were 11000011, a gap of four pixels would occur in each segment of the line. A very long line would be full of gaps because the two bytes represent only a specific length of line. If all the bits in these two bytes were set to 0, you would not be able to see any lines that were drawn, because all the pixels would be turned off.

Fortunately, you don't have to translate binary numbers into decimal numbers when you specify patterns. Instead, you simply can put *&B* in front of the binary pattern you want the polygon's border line or pattern element to have, and the program will do the rest. For instance, if you want the pattern's border to be made up of short dashes, you type

    PATTERN &B1100110011001100

PATTERN makes the program draw polygon borders in a specific way. The *&B* and series of ones and zeroes specify what pixels you want to turn on and off in the border.

The second part of the PATTERN command, which works on somewhat the same principle as the first part, establishes a specific kind of pattern based on binary digits. You can use PATTERN to change how a solid figure appears by changing the pattern created by an AREAFILL or PAINT command.

The PATTERN command is followed by the number used to define the border of the polygon. For instance, suppose that you want to make the upper half of a pattern solid and the lower half blank. In binary, the pattern would be the following:

1111111111111111	All 16 bits are on, making the top solid.
0000000000000000	All 16 bits are off, making the bottom empty.

If you filled an area with this pattern, the entire region would be made up of solid lines separated by blanks. Examining the large 16-bit words (a *word* equals two bytes), you can determine that the higher number is equal to 65535, whereas the lower number is equal to 0. If you wanted to put this pattern into the computer, you would type something like

```
PAT%(0) = 65535: PAT%(1) = 0
PATTERN, PAT%
```

The two numbers stored in the PAT%( ) array establish what the pattern will be like. The PATTERN command is followed by a comma (which can be preceded by a number in order to establish what the border should be like) and the array in which the pattern is stored (PAT%( )). To use more elements in the pattern, you just store more numbers in the array used with PATTERN. You do not need to tell the computer how many elements you are using.

One important rule to remember is that if you use an odd number of elements (such as 1, 3, or 5), then the program uses the next-highest even number for the number of elements in the pattern. For example, if the ONE%( ) array had only five elements and you issued the command *PATTERN, ONE%( )*, the program still would assume that the pattern has six elements. However, the sixth element would have a value of 0.

Programmed Patterns

You can see the Amiga move through different patterns by writing a program that moves increasingly from a mostly empty pattern to a solid one. With every pass of the loop, the program changes the pattern by increasing each element's value by 255. The bits in each element change according to the change in the value. Type the following program and run it to see the results.

```
10 CLS
20 FOR I = 0 TO 7 : FIRST%( I ) = 255 + F : NEXT
30 PATTERN, FIRST%
40 AREA (10, 10) : AREA (300, 10) : AREA (150, 150)
50 F = F + 255
60 IF F = 65535 THEN GOTO 60
70 GOTO 20
```

Line 60 checks to see whether the value of the elements has reached 65535, the value that indicates a solid pattern. When this value is reached, line 60 repeatedly loops back to itself so that the solid pattern remains on the screen.

For a different effect, you can program random patterns into the computer. Here is a simple way to determine what numbers should go into the first and second bytes of a word:

1. For the second byte, which consists of the rightmost eight bits of the word, you can determine which number to use with the binary-to-decimal translation method discussed earlier in the chapter. If the last eight bits of the word are going to be 10010010, for example, you can determine that the decimal equivalent is 146.

2. For the first byte, which consists of the leftmost eight bits of the word, multiply whatever decimal result you get by the number 256. You do this because the left byte has a value 256 times greater than the right byte. Therefore, even a small number such as 00000001 has a value of 256 if the number represents the left byte.

3. After you determine the values of both bytes, add the values together. The result is the value of the entire word.

4. If you want to take the easy way out, you simply can use the &B symbol to tell the computer that you want the element to be &B1001010010100101.

In the following program, eight elements make up the pattern. The odd-numbered elements are random numbers from 0 to 255. Therefore, the right sides of the words are affected, whereas the left sides remain black. The even-numbered elements have random values between 255 and 62025 (in multiples of 255), so the left sides of the words change, but the right sides stay black. An example of what the random patterns could produce follows. The resulting patterns are waves that appear to be random.

```
0000000011101011
1101011100000000
0000000011111011
1000110100000000
0000000011110000
1111100100000000
0000000000101010
0101011100000000
```

The left side of every other word changes, whereas the right side of the alternate words change. The following program demonstrates how this procedure works.

```
10 CLS
20 FOR I = 1 TO 7 STEP 2 : FIRST%(I) = RND * 255 : NEXT
30 FOR I = 2 TO 8 STEP 2 : FIRST%(I) = (RND * 255) * 255 : NEXT
40 PATTERN, FIRST%
50 AREA (10, 10) : AREA (300, 10) : AREA (150, 150)
```

An advantage of the PATTERN command is that it enables you to superimpose images in order to create interesting illusions. For example, you can create a four-element pattern in which every odd-numbered element is colored entirely on the right, and every even-numbered element is colored entirely on the left.

```
10 CLS
20 FOR I = 0 TO 3 : READ FIRST%(I) : NEXT
30 DATA 255, 65280, 255, 65280
```

You can program a second pattern that is the opposite of the preceding one by adding these lines:

```
40 FOR I = 0 TO 3 : READ SECOND%(I) : NEXT
50 DATA 65280, 255, 65280, 255
```

You can superimpose the two opposite patterns continuously so that the shape of the object being drawn does not change, but the object seems to be "vibrating" as the different patterns are switched on and off.

```
60 PATTERN, FIRST%
70 AREA (10, 10) : AREA (300, 10) : AREA (150, 150)
75 FOR I = 1 TO 100 : NEXT
80 PATTERN, SECOND%
```

```
90 AREA (10, 10) : AREA (300, 10) : AREA (150, 150)
100 FOR I = 1 TO 100 : NEXT
110 GOTO 60
```

Notice that lines 75 and 100 are inserted in order to slow down the computer. The Amiga is so fast that you must add these delay lines to achieve the proper effect. If you delete lines 75 and 100 and run the program again, you will discover that the patterns are superimposed too quickly for creating quality graphics.

Accessing and Saving Graphics

Two Amiga BASIC commands enable you to take graphic images from the screen, save them in an array, and display them later. These two commands and their formats are

GET (X1,Y1) - (X2,Y2), <array>

PUT (X,Y), <array>

You use GET to capture an image and put it into an array. To use this command, you type *GET*, then you type the X and Y coordinates of the upper left and lower right corners of the area that you want to capture. These two corners define the rectangular area of graphics that you want put into the array. Even if you are storing areas that are circular or some other shape, you still must encompass the shape in the confines of the rectangle you establish with the two corners.

After you determine which rectangular portion of the screen you want to store, you need to set up a specific amount of memory for the array. Here is the formula for determining the amount of memory required:

((width of rectangle in X pixels) * (height of rectangle in Y pixels) * 4) / 32

For instance, if you want to store an image within a rectangle with an upper left corner of (20,20) and a lower right corner of (70,40), the width is 70 - 20, or 50, and the height is 40 - 20, or 20. Fifty times 20 equals 1000, multiplied by 4 equals 4000, divided by 32 equals 125. This final number is what you would put after the DIM statement defining your array. If you were going to store this graphics image in an array called PICTR%( ), you would put the statement *DIM PICTR%(125)* somewhere near the beginning of the program. You always should set up the array before you use the GET command.

Once an image has been saved in an array, you can perform other tasks in the program until you want to display the image again. When you want to redisplay the image, you type *PUT*, then you type the X and Y coordinates where you want the upper corner of the image to appear on the screen. With the PUT command, you can put the image anywhere on the screen.

Creating Superbear

By using GET and PUT with the Bear Face program, you can create a Superbear that "flies" across the screen in a single leap. You start with the simple Bear Face program you saw earlier in this chapter:

```
5 COLOR 3
10 CLS
20 CIRCLE (150, 90), 20
30 PAINT (150, 90), 1
40 CIRCLE (130, 80), 5
45 PAINT (129, 79), 2
50 CIRCLE (170, 80), 5
60 PAINT (169, 79), 2
65 COLOR 1
80 CIRCLE (143, 85), 2
90 PAINT (143, 85), 2
100 CIRCLE (158, 85), 2
110 PAINT (158, 85), 2
120 LINE (145, 98) - (148, 100) : LINE (148, 100) - (152, 100) :
LINE (152, 100) - (154, 98)
130 LINE (148, 92) - (150, 90) : LINE (150, 90) - (152, 92) :
LINE (152, 92) - (148, 92)
```

You can change this program, which draws a bear's face, to make the bear's face move. First, set up enough memory to save the image.

```
7 DIM BEAR%(500)
```

Next, save the shape by specifying the upper left and lower right coordinates of the rectangle encompassing the bear's face.

```
140 GET (120, 70) - (180, 112), BEAR%
```

Now, move the bear's face to many random locations. The result is a multitude of faces on the screen.

```
150 PUT (RND*300, RND*150), BEAR% : GOTO 150
```

After you run this program and see the results, use the following lines to create Superbear. The program uses a FOR...NEXT loop to move the face to increasingly lower-numbered coordinates. The face moves up and to the left until it disappears beyond the screen, at which point the program repeats the process so that the bear keeps "flying" the same route.

```
150 FOR A = 180 TO 0 STEP -1 : PUT (A, A), BEAR% : NEXT
155 CLS
160 GOTO 150
```

Changing Red, Green, and Blue Color Levels

If you want to change the values that make up any color register, you use the PALETTE command, followed by the number of the color register you want to change and the three R, G, B numbers you want to change the color to. Suppose that you want color register 0 to have a red level of 10, a green level of 5, and a blue level of 12. You type

    PALETTE 0, 10, 5, 12

To see the results of the changing values for each of the three color levels, run this program for as long as you like. Displaying all 4,096 colors that are available on the Amiga takes quite a while.

```
10 FOR R = 0 TO 15
20 FOR G = 0 TO 15
30 FOR B = 0 TO 15
40 PALETTE 0, R, G, B
50 NEXT : NEXT : NEXT
```

Just Ask the Mouse

In addition to the graphics output commands, such as PUT and PALETTE, other graphics-related commands deal strictly with input. Input allows the program to accept information from the "outside world" through the mouse, keyboard, or some other device controlled by the user.

MOUSE is an input graphics command that gets information from the mouse about the position of the graphics cursor on the screen and the state of the left mouse button. The most obvious use for

MOUSE is to create a simple drawing program; the X and Y coordinates from MOUSE can be converted directly into graphics. When you use MOUSE in a program such as the one that follows, you can move the mouse to draw a picture.

```
1 CLS
5 CO = 1
6 X% = MOUSE (1) : Y% = MOUSE (2) : B% = MOUSE (0)
7 GOTO 40
20 X% = MOUSE (1) : Y% = MOUSE (2) : B% = MOUSE (0)
25 IF B% = 1 THEN CO = CO + 1 : IF CO = 3 THEN CO = 0
30 LINE (OX%, OY%) - (X%, Y%), CO
40 OX% = X% : OY% = Y%
50 GOTO 20
```

The variables X% and Y% specify where the mouse is currently pointing, and OX% and OY% indicate the mouse's "old" location; these four variables tell the computer where to draw. Pressing the left mouse button changes the color, but the variable CO (representing the color) is not allowed to go over 3.

When you run the program, moving the mouse will allow you to draw (corresponding to the movement of the mouse) on the screen. Pressing the left button will change the color of your "drawing pen."

You also can use the mouse to create shapes, as demonstrated in the following program. With this program, you can use the mouse to create boxes. First, you use the mouse to specify the upper left corner of the box.

```
10 CLS
30 X% = MOUSE (1) : Y% = MOUSE (2) : B% = MOUSE (0)
40 IF B% = 1 THEN X1% = X% : Y1% = Y% ELSE 30
```

After you push the left mouse button and put the values for the upper left corner into the variables X1% and Y1%, the program pauses to give you time to release the button. The program then waits until you press the button again, then establishes the current location of the graphics cursor at the lower right corner of the box.

```
45 FOR D = 1 TO 100 : NEXT
50 X% = MOUSE (1) : Y% = MOUSE (2) : B% = MOUSE (0)
60 IF B% = 1 THEN X2% = X% : Y2% = Y% ELSE 50
```

Finally, the program draws the box, using the coordinates established. The program then loops back to line 30 to wait for another box to be drawn.

```
70 LINE (X1%, Y1%) - (X2%, Y2%), CO, B
80 GOTO 30
```

As you may have realized, the mouse is a powerful input device. The mouse is suited especially for graphics because it can be moved in any direction with excellent accuracy. Amiga BASIC's MOUSE command is exclusively for getting input from the mouse device. By using the MOUSE (0) command, you instruct the computer to get information from the mouse. The current X-coordinate that the mouse represents will be in the variable MOUSE (1); the Y-coordinate will be in the variable MOUSE (2).

By using the LINE command in conjunction with the mouse, you can create a drawing program with only a few lines of code:

```
CHECKER:
    B = MOUSE (0)
    X = MOUSE (1)
    Y = MOUSE (2)
    LINE (OX, OY) - (X, Y), 1
    Y = X: OY = Y
GOTO CHECKER
```

For the next issuance of the LINE command, the values of X and Y again are stored in different variables (OX and OY). This is because the Amiga needs to know where the drawing pixel currently is located on the screen. While running the previous program, you can draw by moving the mouse around. Also, you can create straight lines by moving the mouse to the point where you want the line to start, holding down the right mouse button as you move the pointer to the place where you want the line to end, and then releasing the button.

With a slight modification, you can have a program that also allows you to change the color of the line being drawn:

```
C = 1
CHECKER:
        B = MOUSE (0)
        X = MOUSE (1)
        Y = MOUSE (2)
        LINE (OX, OY) - (X, Y), C
        OX = X: OY = Y
        IF B THEN C = C + 1: IF C = 4 THEN C = 0
GOTO CHECKER
```

You still can use the right mouse button to draw lines, but now you also can use the left mouse button to change colors. Moreover, by holding down the left mouse button, you can get the color of the drawing pixel to change continuously as you draw.

The next program uses both the MOUSE and the AREA commands. With this program you click the mouse button at five different points in order to define a five-pointed solid area. The FOR...NEXT loop, which uses the variable D, slows the computer so that it won't interpret one click of the mouse button as several clicks.

```
COLOR 1
CHECKER:
        B = MOUSE (0)
        X = MOUSE (1)
        Y = MOUSE (2)
        IF B < 0 THEN AREA (X, Y): NP = NP + 1: FOR D = 1 TO 750: NEXT
        IF NP = 5 THEN AREAFILL: NP = 0
GOTO CHECKER
```

Because the Amiga is such a fast machine, even BASIC programs can be used to create complex three-dimensional graphics. With this next program, you can move the mouse around the screen (while holding down the left button) and duplicate a circle hundreds of times. As you move the mouse in the direction you want the circle to be duplicated, you create a three-dimensional pattern.

```
CIRCLE (100, 100), 50
DIM P (1000)
GET (50, 50) - (150, 150), P
CHECKMOUSE:
        X = MOUSE (1)
        Y = MOUSE (2)
        B = MOUSE (0)
        IF B < 0 THEN PUT (X, Y), P
GOTO CHECKMOUSE
```

If you want just to move an element rather than duplicate it, you can use CLS to clear the screen every time the object is moved. The Amiga does this so quickly that the object seems to move smoothly without any "flickering." The following program allows you to move a cube around the screen by means of the mouse:

```
DIM P (2000)
COLOR 2
LINE (50, 50) - (150, 100), , B
```

```
LINE (75, 40) - (175, 90), , B
LINE (50, 50) - (75, 40)
LINE (150, 100) - (175, 90)
LINE (50, 100) - (75, 90)
LINE (150, 50) - (175, 40)
GET (50, 40) - (175, 100), P
CHECKMOUSE:
          X = MOUSE (1)
          Y = MOUSE (2)
          B = MOUSE (0)
          IF B < 0 THEN CLS: PUT (X, Y), P
GOTO CHECKMOUSE
```

Putting It All Together

In this chapter, you have learned the fundamentals of producing graphics with Amiga BASIC. Now you can put your knowledge to use by writing some programs that use some of the commands you know.

Moving Blocks of Graphics

The following program demonstrates the usefulness of the PUT and GET commands. It draws a random graphics picture on the screen, then allows you to use the mouse to move blocks of graphics around. First, you use random CIRCLE and LINE commands to create the graphics.

```
10 CLS
20 FOR I = 1 TO 60
30 CIRCLE (RND*300, RND*150), RND*60
40 LINE (RND*250, RND*150) - (RND*300, RND*150), RND*3, BF
50 LINE STEP (RND*300, RND*150)
55 COLOR RND*3
60 NEXT
```

After the graphics are on the screen, the program begins to monitor the mouse and waits for the button to be pressed (B% equals 1).

```
70 X% = MOUSE (1): Y% = MOUSE (2): B% = MOUSE (0)
80 IF B% <> 4 THEN GOTO 70
```

When you press the button the first time, the program is signaled that you have selected the upper left coordinate of the rectangle of graphics to be moved. The program stores those X and Y coordinates in the variables X(1) and Y(1). The program pauses so that you have time to release the mouse button. If the pause is not included in the program, the program might "think" that you are pressing the button again.

```
90 X(1) = X%: Y(1) = Y%
95 FOR D = 1 TO 200: NEXT
```

The program waits for the button to be pressed a second time. When this happens, the program stores the X and Y coordinates in the variables X(2) and Y(2) and figures out how much memory space to allocate for the array that will hold the graphics-filled rectangle.

```
100 X% = MOUSE (1): Y% = MOUSE (2): B% = MOUSE (0)
110 IF B% <> 1 THEN GOTO 100
120 X(2) = X%: Y(2) = Y%
130 DM = X(2) - X(1)
131 DM = DM * (Y(2) - Y(1))
132 DM = (DM * 4) / 16
140 DIM (DM)
```

Now the program "grabs" the shape, stores it in GRS%, and pauses again to let you release the button. For the third time, the program monitors the mouse. Pushing the left button signals the program that you want to place the graphics rectangle in the location that the mouse is currently pointing to. The PUT statement tells the program to place the shape in that location. In line 200, the program resets itself so that it can redimension the GRS% array and move another graphics rectangle.

```
150 GET (X(1),Y(1)) - (X(2),Y(2)), GRS%
160 FOR D = 1 TO 200: NEXT
170 X% = MOUSE (1): Y% = MOUSE (2): B% = MOUSE (0)
180 IF B% <> 1 THEN GOTO 170
190 PUT (X%, Y%), GRS%
195 FOR D = 1 TO 200: NEXT
200 CLEAR: GOTO 70
```

Setting Up Patterns

The next two sample programs could be a big help to you if you have trouble figuring out what numbers to use with the PATTERN command. With the first program, you can set up an eight-byte pattern by pointing the mouse at the part of the pattern that you want to fill, then clicking the left mouse button. You can turn a part of the pattern on or off by clicking the button while the arrow is pointing inside that box; clicking the button causes the box to change its state.

First, the program sets up the boxes in the same format as PATTERN will use to create the pattern: four boxes down by two across.

```
5 CLEAR
10 CLS
20 FOR Y = 30 TO 90 STEP 20
30 FOR X = 30 TO 90 STEP 40
33 LINE (X, Y) - (X+40, Y+20), 1, B
35 CO = CO + 1 : COLOR CO
37 PAINT (X+1, Y+1)
50 NEXT : NEXT
```

Because each box is a different color, when you point to a box and click the button, the program can use the POINT command to determine what box to change according to the pattern you are programming. The program also monitors the keyboard and, when you press P, jumps to line 500 to calculate the numbers for the pattern you created.

```
60 X% = MOUSE (1) : Y% = MOUSE (2) : B% = MOUSE (0)
65 A$ = INKEY$ : IF A$ = "P" OR A$ = "p" THEN GOTO 500
70 IF B% <> 1 THEN GOTO 60
80 CC = POINT (X%, Y%)
90 IF PP(CC) = 1 THEN PP(CC) = 0 ELSE PP(CC) = 1
100 FOR D = 1 TO 200 : NEXT
110 GOTO 60
```

After you specify the kind of pattern you want to create, the program does the hard work for you by calculating and printing the value of each of the four numbers that make up the pattern.

```
500 FOR I = 1 TO 7 STEP 2
510 R(I) = PP(I) * 65280 + PP(I + 1) * 255
520 NEXT
525 CLS
530 FOR I = 1 TO 7 STEP 2 : PRINT R(I) : NEXT
```

The following program uses the same idea as the first program but is somewhat more advanced. When you press P, the pattern is programmed into the computer, and the computer displays a shape that uses that pattern. The first part of the program is almost exactly like the last one:

```
5 CLEAR: CO = 0: CT = 0
10 CLS
20 FOR Y = 30 TO 90 STEP 20
30 FOR X = 30 TO 90 STEP 40
33 LINE (X, Y) - (X+40, Y+20), CO, BF
35 COLOR CO: CO = CO + 1
37 PAINT (X+1, Y+1)
50 NEXT: NEXT
60 X% = MOUSE (1): Y% = MOUSE (2): B% = MOUSE (0)
65 A$ = INKEY$: IF A$ = "P" OR A$ = "p" THEN GOTO 500
70 IF B% <> 1 THEN GOTO 60
80 CC = POINT (X%, Y%)
90 IF PP(CC) = 1 THEN PP(CC) = 0 ELSE PP(CC) = 1
100 FOR D = 1 TO 200: NEXT
110 GOTO 60
```

The next part of the program calculates the numbers for the pattern and uses the pattern to draw a box. After you press any other key but P on the keyboard, the program sets the pattern back to what it was before (solid) and goes back to line 5 so that you can try out another pattern.

```
500 FOR I = 0 TO 6 STEP 2
510 R(I) = PP(I) * 65280 + PP(I + 1) * 255
520 NEXT
525 CLS
530 FOR I = 0 TO 6 STEP 2: P%(CT) = R(I): CT = CT + 1: NEXT
540 PATTERN, P%( )
550 CLS
560 LINE (10, 10) - (200, 150), CO, B
570 A$ = INKEY$
580 FOR I = 0 TO 3: P%(I) = 65535: NEXT: PATTERN, P%( )
590 GOTO 5
```

Pick Your Polygon

Until now, the programs that included AREA commands have used the RND statement to create random polygons. The next program enables you to move the mouse and click the button at five different locations in order to create a five-pointed polygon made out of those points. With this program, you also can change both the color of the polygon (by pressing C) and the color of the border of the polygon (by pressing B). First, you specify the coordinates of the five points.

```
10 CLS
20 FOR I = 1 TO 5
30 X% = MOUSE (1) : Y% = MOUSE (2) : B% = MOUSE (0)
35 A$ = INKEY$ : IF A$ <> "" THEN GOSUB 100
40 IF B% <> 1 THEN GOTO 30
50 X(I) = X% : Y(I) = Y%
55 FOR D = 1 TO 200 : NEXT
60 NEXT
```

Next, the program draws the figure on the screen and returns to line 20 to monitor the mouse and keyboard.

```
70 AREA (X(1), Y(1)) : AREA (X(2), Y(2)) : AREA (X(3), Y(3)) : AREA
(X(4), Y(4)) : AREA (X(5), Y(5)) : AREAFILL
80 GOTO 20
```

If the program detects in line 35 that a key has been pressed, the program jumps to line 100. In the lines that follow, the program increases the value of the interior color by 1 if C is pressed and increases the value of the outline color by 1 if B is pressed. If either of these values goes above 16, the program brings the value back down to 1.

```
100 IF A$ = "C" OR A$ = "c" THEN CO = CO + 1 : IF CO > 3 THEN CO = 0
105 IF A$ = "B" OR A$ = "b" THEN OT = OT + 1 : IF OT > 16 THEN OT = 1
110 COLOR CO, OT RETURN
```

To observe another interesting animation effect, run the following program. This program places a circle on the screen and randomly increases or decreases X and Y values. First, you establish the X and Y values and draw the circle.

```
5 COLOR 2
10 CLS
20 X = 50 : Y = 50
30 CIRCLE (X, Y), 8
```

Now you set the pen color to 0 (the color of the screen) and draw the circle again in order to increase or decrease randomly both the X and Y values and to make sure that the values are within the permissible limits of the screen. Then you set the pen color back

to black and return to line 30 so that you can continue to move
the circle around.

```
35 COLOR Ø: CIRCLE (X, Y), 8
40 CX = RND * 2: IF INT(CX) = 1 THEN X = X + 2 ELSE X = X - 2
50 CY = RND * 2: IF INT(CY) = 1 THEN Y = Y + 2 ELSE Y = Y - 2
53 IF X > 300 THEN X = 300 ELSE IF Y > 180 THEN Y = 180
54 IF X < Ø THEN X = Ø ELSE IF Y < Ø THEN Y = Ø
55 COLOR 1
60 GOTO 30
```

A Drawing Program
That Uses the Keyboard

Although you have seen several times how useful the mouse can be
in programs, you should not neglect other computer components
that can be useful input and output devices. The keypad, for example,
makes an excellent drawing tool because you easily can use it to
specify upward, downward, left, right, and diagonal motion. For instance, the 8 key can specify "up"; the 2 key, "down"; the 1 key,
"down and left"; and so on.

The following drawing program uses the keypad to find out the
direction in which you want to draw. Among the other commands
included in the program are these:

"5"   Toggles the pen on and off so that you can either
         draw or simply move around the screen

"0"   Changes the color of the pen

"."   Starts the program over again. You have to press
         this key twice in order to verify that you want to
         start over.

"-"   Fills the bounded surroundings of the graphics
         cursor with a random color

You start the program by specifying what color (represented by the
variable DR) you want to use and what the X and Y coordinates of
the graphics cursor are.

```
5 DR = 1
10 CLS
20 X = 150
30 Y = 90
35 PIXEL (X, Y)
```

Now the program can begin to monitor the keyboard. Each key either alters the X and Y values or performs one of the other functions already mentioned.

```
40 A$ = INKEY$
50 IF A$ = "8" THEN Y = Y - 1
55 IF A$ = "1" THEN X = X - 1 : Y = Y + 1
57 IF A$ = "3" THEN X = X + 1 : Y = Y + 1
60 IF A$ = "2" THEN Y = Y + 1
61 IF A$ = "7" THEN X = X - 1 : Y = Y - 1
62 IF A$ = "9" THEN X = X + 1 : Y = Y - 1
70 IF A$ = "6" THEN X = X + 1
80 IF A$ = "4" THEN X = X - 1
81 IF A$ = "5" THEN IF DR = 1 THEN DR = 0 ELSE DR = 1
82 IF A$ = ". " THEN GOTO 110
83 IF A$ = "=" THEN COLOR RND * 3 : PAINT (X, Y), 1
84 IF A$ = "0" THEN DR = RND * 3
```

The program checks to see whether the X and Y values are "out of bounds" and corrects them if they are. The LINE command does the drawing. Line 100 sends the program back to the A$ = INKEY$ command so that the program can continue checking the keyboard. Lines 120 through 140 wait for you to push the period (.) key a second time in order to verify that you want to run the program again. If you press a key other than the period, the program returns to the regular drawing routine.

```
85 IF X > 300 THEN X = 300 ELSE IF X < 0 THEN X = 0
87 IF Y > 180 THEN Y = 180 ELSE IF Y < 0 THEN Y = 0
90 LINE STEP (X, Y), DR
100 GOTO 40
120 A$ = INKEY$ : IF A$ = "" THEN GOTO 120
130 IF A$ = ". " THEN GOTO 5
140 GOTO 40
```

You can add an additional feature—changeable drawing speed—to this program by making only a few alterations. First, you add the following two lines:

```
3 IN = 1
83 IF A$ = CHR$(13) THEN IN = IN + 1 : IF IN = 6 THEN IN = 1
```

Line 83 increases the value of IN (your drawing speed) by 1 if you press the RETURN key. After IN reaches 6, it goes back down to 1. Change all the occurrences of +1 in lines 50 to 80 to +IN, and change all the occurrences of *-1* in lines 50 to 80 to *-IN*. Lines 50 through 80 now should look like this:

```
50 IF A$ = "8" THEN Y = Y - IN
55 IF A$ = "1" THEN X = X - IN: Y = Y + IN
57 IF A$ = "3" THEN X = X + IN: Y = Y + IN
60 IF A$ = "2" THEN Y = Y + IN
61 IF A$ = "7" THEN X = X - IN: Y = Y - IN
62 IF A$ = "9" THEN X = X + IN: Y = Y - IN
70 IF A$ = "6" THEN X = X + IN
80 IF A$ = "4" THEN X = X - IN
```

How To Set Colors with PALETTE

The last few programs presented here will help you discover the real power of the PALETTE command, a command touched on earlier in this chapter. PALETTE enables you to access the Amiga's 4,096 colors. Although you can display only 32 colors at a time, such a variety of colors makes almost any kind of graphics possible.

Using the PALETTE command, you can randomly change the colors of colored circles.

```
10 CLS
20 FOR X = 0 TO 3
25 XX = RND * 250 + 20: YY = RND * 160 + 20
30 CIRCLE (XX, YY), 30
33 COLOR X
35 PAINT (XX, YY)
40 NEXT
60 FOR CO = 0 TO 3
70 PALETTE CO, RND*16, RND*16, RND*16
90 NEXT
100 GOTO 60
```

A Color Finder Program

The final program in this chapter is a programmer's tool that helps you "find" the one color that you are looking for out of 4,096. The following keyboard commands are used in this program (once again, the keypad is used extensively):

"1"	Raise red level.
"4"	Bring red level back to default.
"7"	Lower red level.
"2"	Raise green level.
"5"	Bring green level back to default.
"8"	Lower green level.
"3"	Raise blue level.
"6"	Bring blue level back to default.
"9"	Lower blue level.
"-"	Go back to normal colors and clear the screen.

The program fills a box on the screen with whatever color you set, and the levels for red, green, and blue appear just below the box. After you are satisfied with the color you have found, you can write down the PALETTE number so that you can use the color later in another program.

You begin this program by setting aside enough memory for the arrays you are going to use, then clearing the screen.

```
5 DIM R(15), G(15), B(15)
7 DIM RR(15), GG(15), BB(15)
10 CLS
```

The R, G, and B arrays store the current color levels of the colors you are working with. The RR, GG, and BB arrays hold the colors' default (regular) values, which are reset when the program ends.

The program reads into memory the default values of the red, green, and blue levels for the 16 different color registers.

```
20 FOR CO = 0 TO 15
30 READ R(CO), G(CO), B(CO) : PALETTE CO, R(CO), G(CO), B(CO)
35 RR(CO) = R(CO) : GG(CO) = G(CO) : BB(CO) = B(CO)
40 NEXT
50 DATA 6, 9, 15
60 DATA 0, 0, 0
70 DATA 15, 15, 15
80 DATA 15, 9, 10
90 DATA 14, 3, 0
100 DATA 15, 11, 0
```

```
110 DATA 15, 15, 2
120 DATA 11, 15, 0
130 DATA 5, 13, 0
140 DATA 0, 14, 13
150 DATA 0, 13, 15
160 DATA 7, 13, 15
170 DATA 12, 0, 14
180 DATA 15, 2, 14
190 DATA 15, 13, 11
200 DATA 12, 9, 8
210 DATA 11, 11, 11
```

Next, the program asks which color register you would like to alter, chooses that pen color, and draws the color-filled box.

```
220 INPUT "Which color do you want to change"; C
225 COLOR C
230 LINE (10, 10; 300, 150), 1
```

Like the earlier programs, this program also monitors the keypad. Values for the red, green, and blue levels are altered according to the keys pressed.

```
240 A$ = INKEY$
250 IF A$ = "7" THEN R(C) = R(C) - 1
260 IF A$ = "4" THEN R(C) = RR(C)
270 IF A$ = "1" THEN R(C) = R(C) + 1
280 IF A$ = "8" THEN G(C) = G(C) - 1
290 IF A$ = "5" THEN G(C) = GG(C)
300 IF A$ = "2" THEN G(C) = G(C) + 1
310 IF A$ = "9" THEN B(C) = B(C) - 1
320 IF A$ = "6" THEN B(C) = BB(C)
330 IF A$ = "3" THEN B(C) = B(C) + 1
335 IF A$ = "-" THEN GOTO 400
```

As usual, the program makes sure that none of the values go out of bounds.

```
340 IF R(C) < 0 THEN R(C) = 0 ELSE IF R(C) > 15 THEN R(C) = 15
350 IF G(C) < 0 THEN G(C) = 0 ELSE IF G(C) > 15 THEN G(C) = 15
360 IF B(C) < 0 THEN B(C) = 0 ELSE IF B(C) > 15 THEN B(C) = 15
```

Now the program sets the PALETTE color and prints the values.

```
370 PALETTE C, R(C), G(C), B(C)
375 LOCATE 0, 21 : PRINT R(C), G(C), B(C);
380 GOTO 240
```

At the end of the program, the values are reset.

```
400 FOR C = 0 TO 15 : R(C) = RR(C) : G(C) = GG(C) : B(C) =
BB(C) : NEXT
410 CLS
```

The programs in this chapter have illustrated how powerful just a few lines of compact programming code can be. Now that you have learned the fundamentals of programming graphics in Amiga BASIC, you can begin using more complex graphics and sounds.

5

Sounds, Music, and Speech

Until recently, the most that personal computers could offer in the way of music or voice synthesis was accessible only through complicated assembly language commands and programming tricks. Only the most experienced and knowledgeable programmers could make computers play a simple song or sound, and making a computer "say" a few intelligible words was a real accomplishment.

With the Amiga, you can create sounds, music, and speech directly through Amiga BASIC, and producing any of these three is very simple compared to methods that were formerly used. In this chapter, you will look at how to make the Amiga emit sounds, music, and words. Furthermore, you will learn how to take advantage of the Amiga's stereo sound.

You don't have to hook up a stereo to the Amiga to run the programs in this chapter. However, some of the programs do work in stereo, and you will need two speakers in order to enjoy the "dual sounds." Connecting a stereo to the Amiga is easy enough. Using a portable "boom box" stereo is recommended, but you can use a full-blown system if you like. Get two phono cables (the RCA-type plugs used to hook stereo components together) and plug one end of each into the Amiga's sound output ports (on the back of the computer, underneath the pictures of speakers). Plug the other end of each phono cable into the input port of your stereo.

Here are some tips that will save you trouble when you use the Amiga with a stereo:

1. Make sure that the plug hooked into the right speaker output of the Amiga is connected to the right speaker input of your stereo. Do the same for the left speaker.

2. Keep your stereo volume low at first, then gradually turn it up until you are satisfied with the sound level.

3. Although stereos differ, you probably will find the input port of your stereo by looking for the phono plug input labeled *Line input* or *Phono input*. If you run into trouble, check your stereo manual.

If you aren't going to use a stereo, make sure that your monitor's sound is on so that you can hear the sounds and words that the Amiga produces.

Amiga Sounds Off

If you have used the documentation and you haven't gotten good results, the information and sample programs in this chapter should help clear up your confusion. Using the tips here, which are based on practice and experience, will help you best realize the potential of the Amiga's sound.

If you have tried to make sounds with the Amiga and have been frustrated, you are not alone. Even someone who has been working with computers for years could spent a long time figuring out how to use the sound commands. You can rest assured that you will get the "true story" in this chapter. You will learn the problems that arise when you use Amiga BASIC and how to avoid them. This chapter will steer you in the right direction so that your sound programs work properly.

Aspects of SOUND

The most fundamental sound command is SOUND. You can use the SOUND command to tell the computer which voice to send a sound through, which speaker(s) to play the sound through, how long to play the sound, and what the sound's volume and pitch should be. The format of the SOUND command is

SOUND <frequency>, <duration>, <volume>, <voice>

The elements of the SOUND command are explained as follows:

<frequency>　　This can range from 20 to 15,000, with larger numbers generating higher-pitched sounds.

\<duration\>	This can range from 0 to 77, where one second equals 18.2. The higher the number, the longer the sound will last.
\<volume\>	This is the sound's volume. This element determines the volume of the sound for its entire duration, and it can range from 0 (no sound) to 25 (loudest sound).
\<voice\>	A 0 or 3 value will send the sound to the left speaker, while 1 or 2 will send it to the right speaker.

Table 5.1, reproduced from the Amiga BASIC Manual, provides a list of musical notes and their corresponding frequencies.

One of the best features of the SOUND command is that the Amiga can do other tasks while a sound is being played. On most other computers, everything else stops until the sound finishes playing. In addition, if you issue several SOUND commands, the Amiga retains them all in memory and plays them in order. However, if you send the Amiga too many SOUND commands, an Out of Workspace error occurs.

Sample Sounds

The sample programs that follow will let you hear what SOUND can do. Before you begin, make sure that your computer is in Amiga BASIC and that your stereo (or single speaker) is on.

This first program sends sounds of random volume and pitch to random channels. The program demonstrates how fast the SOUND command works. The results are interesting to listen to.

```
20 SOUND RND * 1000 + 20, 2, RND * 255, INT (RND * 3)
30 GOTO 20
```

The next program produces a rapidly descending tone. As the variable in the FOR...NEXT loop decreases in value, the tone becomes lower.

```
10 FOR I = 3000 TO 500 STEP -15
20 SOUND I, .2
30 NEXT
```

As you can guess by running these programs, you could create a whole library of sounds simply by using different pitches and

Table 5.1
Musical Notes and Their Corresponding Frequencies

Note	Frequency	Note	Frequency
C	130	A	440
C#	138	B	493
D	146	C	523 (middle C)
D#	155	D	587
E	164	E	659
F	174	F	701
F#	185	G	783
G	196	A	880
G#	207	B	993
A	220	C	1046
A#	233	D	1174
B	246	E	1318
C	261	F	1396
D	293	G	1568
E	329	A	1760
F	349	B	1975
G	392		

FOR...NEXT loops. By moving a pitch up or down (or oscillating the pitch up and down) at a certain speed, you can produce a unique tone. Try altering the FOR...NEXT loop in line 10 to see what sounds you can produce.

The Musical Computer

As mentioned earlier, you can create musical notes by using certain pitch values. The next program plays the A notes spanning an octave by using the information stored in a DATA statement.

```
5 DIM A%(8)
20 FOR P = 1 TO 8 : READ A%(P) : NEXT
30 FOR P = 1 TO 8
40 SOUND A%(P), 10
50 NEXT
60 DATA 130, 146, 164, 174, 196, 220, 246, 261
```

The program sends notes that ascend in pitch through the right channel. Change the following line so that the notes move downward in pitch through the left channel:

```
40 SOUND A%(P), 10, , 1
```

Now type the following additional line, which is almost the same as line 40 in the original program:

```
45 SOUND A%(9-P), 10, , 0
```

The notes move up in pitch in one speaker, down in pitch in the other speaker. Experiment with the program to see what different effects you can achieve with the two speakers.

To make sure that you understand the concept of stereo sound and the procedure used to create it, type the following program. The first line makes the computer send random sounds to the right speaker, and the second line sends random sounds to the left speaker.

```
10 SOUND RND * 300 + 20, 5, , 0
20 SOUND RND * 300 + 20, 5, , 1
30 GOTO 10
```

This program keeps looping back to line 10 so that the notes "bounce" back and forth between the speakers.

Cranking Your Amiga

The next program is similar to the last one, but goes a step further by modifying the volume of the SOUND commands as the program runs. The program starts off with maximum volume in one speaker and silence in the other speaker. As the FOR...NEXT loop progresses, the loud speaker grows quieter, and the once-silent speaker becomes louder. After the two speakers "switch roles," the process reverses itself so that the sound grows louder in the speaker that was silenced. This entire process keeps repeating, which creates the effect of a sound bouncing from one speaker to another and back again.

```
20 FOR V = 1 TO 255
30 SOUND 250, .3, V, 0
40 SOUND 250, .3, 256 - V, 1
50 NEXT
60 FOR V = 254 TO 0 STEP -1
70 SOUND 250, .3, V, 0
80 SOUND 250, .3, V, 1
90 NEXT
100 GOTO 20
```

Next, try a program that makes the sound grow higher in pitch in one speaker and lower in pitch in the other speaker.

```
20 FOR P = 100 TO 1000 STEP 5
30 SOUND P, 1, , 0
40 SOUND 1100 - P, 1, , 1
50 NEXT
```

You can modify this program so that all four channels are used. Remember that each speaker has two channels, so the effects you can produce with all four tones can be quite interesting. Type the following lines:

```
35 SOUND P + 500, 1, , 2
45 SOUND 1600 - P, 1, , 3
```

Take some time now to review what you have learned about SOUND. After you master this command, make some sounds of your own and work up to using two different speakers.

Music and the Amiga

You can produce real music on the Amiga in a number of ways, including using the commercial Musicraft® program, hooking up a synthesizer to your computer, or using the musical keyboard from Commodore®. In this section, you will examine one of the easiest methods: using the SOUND command. You can use the SOUND command to create notes, and you can change the notes' duration by altering the second element in the SOUND command.

The next program is an effective tool for punishing unruly children who spill drinks on your Amiga. (To see what this means, you will have to type and run the program.) The program sets up an array, P%(|), to hold the musical notes. Setting up arrays makes writing programs easier, and you probably will want to do this in all the music programs you write. After setting up an array, the program reads the pitch values for these notes into the array.

```
5 DIM P%(13)
20 FOR I = 1 TO 13 : READ P%(I) : NEXT
30 DATA 130, 138, 146, 155, 164, 174, 185, 196, 207
```

To play the notes, you set up a subroutine that sends one pitch (stored in variable P%(P1)) to one channel and the other pitch (variable P%(P2)) to the other channel.

```
500 SOUND P%(P1), 5, , 0 : SOUND P%(P2), 5, , 1
510 SOUND 14000, 1, 0, 0 : SOUND 14000, 1, 0, 1
520 RETURN
```

Now all you have to do is tell the Amiga which two notes—specified by the numbers in the variables P1 and P2—you want the speakers to play. Then you have to issue a GOSUB 500. The program stores notes 1 through 13 in the P%( ) array; therefore, the P1 and P2 variables, used in conjunction with the P%( ) array, have meaning. For example, if P1 equals 4 and P2 equals 7, then the program goes to the subroutine at line 500 and plays the pitches stored in variables P%(4) and P%(7).

Line 35 specifies the first three pairs of notes that the Amiga plays.

```
35 DATA 6, 8, 5, 8, 3, 12
```

The computer plays each pair of notes six times, pausing at line 70 before playing each pair.

```
37 FOR J = 1 TO 3 : READ P1, P2
40 FOR I = 1 TO 6
50 GOSUB 500
70 FOR D = 1 TO 300 : NEXT : NEXT
80 NEXT
```

The Amiga plays notes 1 and 13 once, pauses, plays them again, pauses, and plays them one more time.

```
90 P1 = 1 : P2 = 13 : GOSUB 500 : FOR D = 1 TO 500 : NEXT
100 GOSUB 500 : FOR D = 1 TO 300 : NEXT : GOSUB 500 : FOR D = 1
TO 300 : NEXT
```

The computer plays two more pairs of notes, pausing before playing each pair.

```
110 P1 = 3 : P2 = 12 : GOSUB 500 : FOR D = 1 TO 300 : NEXT
120 P1 = 5 : P2 = 8 : GOSUB 500 : FOR D = 1 TO 300 : NEXT
```

The program then uses the RESTORE command to reset the DATA statements so that they can be used again. Then the program goes back to line 20. The computer keeps playing the song indefinitely (until someone throws a brick at it or until you press Ctrl-C).

```
140 RESTORE : GOTO 20
```

You can use many of the elements in this program to create your own songs on the computer. Furthermore, by using the Amiga's multiple channels (sometimes called *voices*), you can create chords and complex musical pieces.

Altering the Waveform

When the Amiga produces a sound, the tonal quality of the sound is based on its waveform. The waveform, which is made up of points on a graph ranging from 127 to -128, tells the computer the nature of the sound wave.

The default waveform of the SOUND command is a sine wave, which goes from 0 to 100, back down to 0, down to -100, and back up to 0. The wave is a smooth curve; the computer stores the points that roughly describe the wave then "smooths out" what the wave should sound like based on 256 points on the curve. If the computer plays this sound wave more than once (which is likely because even playing it 50 times produces only a short beep), the wave goes up to 100, down to -100, up to 0, and then gets ready to go up to 100 again with the second wave.

By using the points from -128 to 127, you can create any waveform you like. These points are stored in an array. You can tell the computer to make your new waveform by using the WAVE command, which has the following format:

WAVE <number>, <array>

The *number* variable tells the computer which voice the sound will be played through (which can range from 0 to 3), while the *array* is the name of the integer array where the points of the graph are stored. When you determine what kind of waveform you want to produce, try to use enough points so that the computer has enough information to make a graph close to what you want; you will need at least 256 points.

The following program defines a waveform that goes from 0 to 117, from 117 to -117, and from -117 to 0. To begin, set up the waveform from 0 to 117.

```
5 DIM W%(260)
20 FOR I = 0 TO 65 : W%(I) = I * 1.8 : NEXT
```

Next, put into the array the points that go from 117 to -117 in steps of 1.8. Notice that by using the variable I from the FOR...NEXT loop in the simple formula *W%(I) = 1.8 * (130-I)*, you are using the variable to accomplish two things: to tell the computer what the array variable is and to determine the value for that point in the graph.

```
30 FOR I = 66 to 130 : W%(I) = 1.8 * (130 - X) : NEXT : FOR I =
131 to 195 : W%(I) = -1.8 * (130 - X) : NEXT
```

To complete the waveform, set up the last point on the graph, issue the WAVE command, and start the sound.

```
40 FOR I = 196 to 260 : W%(I) = -1.8 (260 - X) : NEXT
50 WAVE 0, W%
60 SOUND 2000, 25, , 0
```

This next program, which is a little less "orderly" than the last one, creates random waveforms and plays each one for you. You can hear the results of changing waveforms as different tones are produced.

```
5 DIM W%(20)
20 FOR I = 0 TO 256 : W%(I) = 127 - RND * 254 : NEXT
30 WAVE 0, W%(I)
40 SOUND 500, 10, , 0
50 GOTO 20
```

The last program that uses the WAVE command helps you develop your own waveforms. You can use the keypad to make a waveform slope up, slope down, or go directly up or down. After you make the waveform, you can tell the computer to play it. You also will be able to see the waveform represented graphically on the screen.

Begin the program by setting up the array and drawing the graph to be used to make the waveform.

```
20 DIM W%(256)
30 CLS
40 C = 0
50 COLOR 1
60 REM Set up graph for wave
```

```
70 LINE (10, 10) - (10, 138)
80 LINE (10, 74) - (250, 74)
90 LINE (250, 74) - (10, 74)
```

Now, program the computer to set up the current location of the graphics drawing pixel (at 10,74) and to begin monitoring the keyboard.

```
100 Y = 74 : OY = 74 : X = 10 : OX = 10
110 A$ = INKEY$ : IF A$ = "" THEN 110
```

If you press 6, the cursor moves right by 1 pixel, and the program increments its counter by 1 for the points on the graph (determined by the variable C).

```
120 IF A$ = "6" THEN X = X + 1 : C = C + 1
```

Next, the program checks to see whether the 9 or 3 key has been pressed. If the 9 key has been pressed, the graphics pixel moves up diagonally by 1 point. If the 3 key has been pressed, the pixel moves down diagonally by 1 point. As you are forming the graph, pixels will be left behind to indicate how it is shaping up.

```
130 IF A$ = "9" THEN Y = Y - 1 : X = X + 1 : C = C + 1
140 IF A$ = "3" THEN Y = Y + 1 : X = X + 1 : C = C + 1
```

If the 8 key is pressed, the cursor moves up 1 point vertically. The counter (C), however, is not affected because going up does not make a new point for the waveform. Pressing 8 lets you draw square waves by moving straight up, directly across, and straight down. The key to press to go straight down is 2.

```
145 IF A$ = "8" THEN Y = Y - 1 : LINE STEP (X, Y)
147 IF A$ = "2" THEN Y = Y + 1 : LINE STEP (X, Y)
```

When you want to play the sound, you press P. The program checks for either a lowercase or uppercase P.

```
150 IF A$ = "P" OR A$ = "p" THEN GOTO 200
```

Then the program makes sure that the X and Y values are within their bounds. If Y is out of bounds, the Amiga corrects it. If X is out of bounds, the computer automatically jumps to the routine that plays the sound.

```
160 IF Y < 10 THEN Y = 10 ELSE IF Y > 138 THEN Y = 138
180 IF X > 256 THEN GOTO 200
```

To determine whether a new point on the graph has been established, the program checks to see whether the variable X has changed. If the variable X has changed, this tells the program that the graphics pixel has moved over horizontally and that a new point should be put into the array. To find the value for the point on the graph, you can use the simple formula *127 - (Y - 10) * 2*. This puts the point into the array somewhere between 127 (when Y is at its low value of 10) and -127 (when Y is at its high value of 138). Notice that line 190 keeps the routine going until the program jumps to the routine that plays the sound.

```
170 IF OX <> X THEN OX = X: W%(C) = 127 - (Y - 10) * 2:
LINE STEP (X, Y)
190 GOTO 110
200 WAVE 0, W%
210 SOUND 500, 20, 255, 0
```

After the sound is played, the program erases the variables and the array W% before starting over at line 20.

Now that you have a good idea of how to create a wide variety of sounds and music, you can move on to programs that make the Amiga talk.

The Amiga Speaks

The commands involved in making the Amiga speak are simpler than those used to create sounds and music. Only two commands are used: TRANSLATE$ and SAY. They are powerful and give the computer the capability to speak with tremendous flexibility.

The first command, TRANSLATE$, translates English statements into phonetics. If you have ever tried to do this yourself, you probably realize how fortunate programmers are to have this command built into the computer. *Phonetics* are alphanumeric codes that represent basic parts of speech. For instance, the phonetic equivalent for *I am the Amiga computer* is *AY AEM DHIY AHMIY3GAH KUMPYUW3TER*. Because people inexperienced in phonetics would have a hard time figuring this out, the TRANSLATE$ command can be extremely helpful. An added feature of TRANSLATE$ is that it takes into consideration question marks, exclamation points, and other punctuation and adjusts the inflection appropriately.

To make TRANSLATE$ translate English to phonetics, you use the following format:

<string variable> = TRANSLATE$("<words>")

If you wanted to store the sentence *I am the Amiga computer* in the variable BB$, you would type

BB$ = TRANSLATE$("I am the Amiga computer")

The variable BB$ then would be equal to

AY AEM DHIY AHMIY3GAH KUMPYUW3TER

The resulting phonetic string, like any string, cannot be more than 255 characters long. If you give TRANSLATE$ something that is too long to translate into a 255-character phonetic string, the screen displays an error message. The solution to this problem is to break up the sentence into several sections.

You use the SAY command to make the Amiga say the string. SAY is much more powerful than TRANSLATE$ because you can use SAY to give the speech different qualities. These qualities are determined by numbers stored in an array. The format for SAY is

SAY (<string>)

or

SAY (<string>), <array>

An example of the most basic way to make the Amiga speak follows:

```
10 A$ = TRANSLATE$("I am the Amiga computer")
20 SAY (A$)
```

This simple program makes the computer say the sentence. However, if you know something about phonetics or simply want to try a different method, you can omit the TRANSLATE$ command and use your own phonetic string in a line. In fact, you could shorten the preceding program to

```
10 SAY ("AY AEM DHIY AHMIY3GAH KUMPYUW3TER")
```

Using your own phonetic codes gives you the capability to fine-tune the speech so that it represents more closely what you want the computer to say. Although TRANSLATE$ works only with English, if you become experienced with phonemes, you can make the computer speak in almost any language.

Voice Changes

If you want the computer to speak with its default characteristics, you do not have to use an array with the SAY command. However, if you do want to change the quality of the computer's speech, you can use an array with nine different elements. These are the elements for the HOW%( ) array:

HOW%(0)   The pitch for the voice, which can range from 65 to 320. The default is 110, but you can produce a squeaky voice by going up to 320.

HOW%(1)   The inflection value, which can be either 0 for normal inflection or 1 for no inflection (monotone). The default is 1.

HOW%(2)   The speaking rate, which can range from 40 to 400. The default is 150, but you can slow down or speed up the voice as you like.

HOW%(3)   Male (0) or female (1). The default is male.

HOW%(4)   Vocal quality, which can range from 5000 (low) to 28000 (high). The default is 22000.

HOW%(5)   Volume, which is the same as the sound and music volume. This can range from 0 to 64; the highest volume, 64, is the default.

HOW%(6)   Channel, which determines which of the 4 channels the computer speaks through. Channels 0 and 3 go to the left speaker, and channels 1 and 2 go to the right speaker. The default code is 10, which makes the computer talk through both speakers. You can determine what value to use by referring to the following codes:

0 - Channel 0
1 - Channel 1
2 - Channel 2
3 - Channel 3
4 - Channels 0 and 1
5 - Channels 0 and 2
6 - Channels 3 and 1
7 - Channels 3 and 2

8 - Any left channel
9 - Any right channel
10 - Any pair of channels
11 - Any single channel

HOW%(7)   A value of 0, which is the default, makes the program stop entirely until the computer finishes speaking. A value of 1 allows other statements to proceed while the computer is talking.

HOW%(8)   This array determines whether the program should wait for any previous SAY statements to finish (0) or begin executing immediately, regardless of other SAY statements (2). If you want the computer to stop talking, use a value of 1. The default value is 0, which makes the Amiga wait for other SAY statements to finish executing before it begins saying this particular sentence.

The sample program that follows makes the Amiga say "I am the Amiga computer" through both speakers and then begins bouncing the sentence between the left and right channels. Although the values in the DATA statement in line 40 are the default values, you are going to modify HOW%(6) to change the channel through which the sentence is spoken.

```
10 CLS
20 A$ = TRANSLATE$("I am the Amiga computer")
30 FOR I = 0 TO 8: READ HOW%(I): NEXT
40 DATA 110, 0, 150, 0, 22200, 64, 10, 0, 0
50 SAY (A$), HOW%
60 IF HOW%(6) = 3 THEN HOW%(6) = 1 ELSE HOW%(6) = 3
70 GOTO 50
```

Use the preceding program as a basis for other short programs. By modifying several different elements of the SAY array and listening to the results, you will understand the significance of those elements better. Try typing a new line 60 and running the modified program, which selects a random pitch for the voice.

```
60 HOW%(0) = 65 + RND * 255
```

Now type the following new line, which varies the rate at which the words are spoken.

```
60 HOW%(2) = 40 + RND * 360
```

The following line alters the vocal quality.

```
60 HOW%(4) = 5000 + RND * 23000
```

Now, just for fun, use all these random elements at once and listen to the different ways (some of them are hilarious) in which the Amiga says this one sentence.

```
10 CLS
20 A$ = TRANSLATE$("I am the Amiga computer")
30 FOR I = 0 TO 8 : READ HOW%(I) : NEXT
40 DATA 110, 0, 150, 0, 22200, 64, 10, 0, 0
50 SAY (A$), HOW%
60 HOW%(0) = 65 + RND * 255
62 HOW%(2) = 40 + RND * 360
64 HOW%(4) = 5000 + RND * 23000
66 HOW%(6) = RND * 12
70 GOTO 50
```

To understand how the Amiga can "interrupt" words with the HOW%(7) and HOW%(8) elements, type *DELETE 60 - 66* and add the following lines to the preceding program:

```
60 HOW%(7) = 1
65 HOW%(8) = 2
67 FOR D = 1 TO 500 : NEXT
```

A good project for you to do at this point is to create a program that lets you input all the different elements that SAY can use. After the program receives the values from you, the computer could say a sentence that you also input. Writing such a program is not difficult and will help you understand even better how the TRANSLATE$ and SAY commands work.

The Amiga and the Handicapped

Through Amiga BASIC programs, the Amiga can translate and speak what you type. This capability can be of enormous benefit for stroke victims, the handicapped, and many throat surgery patients. Never before has this capability been so affordable for so many, and this feature alone makes the Amiga *the* computer for at least 100,000 people in the United States and approximately 500,000 worldwide. Here is a simple program to illustrate this point:

```
10 INPUT "What would you like to say"; SN$
20 SAY (TRANSLATE$ (SN$))
30 GOTO 10
```

Making sounds and music on the Amiga can be a lot of fun. In fact, making sounds is usually one of the best parts of writing any program because you can produce such an amazing spectrum of tones and speech. Now you have the knowledge that you need to add these elements to your programs. Sound and music can enhance the quality of just about any piece of software, especially an action-packed game or a sound and music development system. These features can make any of your programs much more enjoyable.

6
Learning Logo

Many people regard Logo as a computer language "just for kids." When these people think of Logo, they visualize an eight-year-old moving a graphics turtle around the screen. Logo is indeed an easy language for children to learn. But TLC Logo for the Amiga can do much more than move pictures of turtles around the screen.

John Allen, president of The Lisp Company (which wrote the Logo published by The Learning Company for the Amiga) believes that Logo has not been treated fairly by software publishers. Most versions of Logo, he contends, actually are subsets of the true Logo language and do not possess the computing power of real Logo. Fortunately, The Learning Company's Logo for the Amiga incorporates the features that are absent in most other versions of the language. In fact, those familiar with Logo regard it as one of the best languages available for artificial intelligence programming on the Amiga.

Although this book doesn't show you how to tap that kind of power, you will see from the material in this chapter that in spite of Logo's simplicity, it is a useful language that both children and adults can learn to use quickly. (If you want to explore Logo's artificial intelligence capabilities, you will find the documentation that comes with the language an excellent resource.)

Logo for the Amiga is not included when you buy your computer, but it is available at an extra cost directly from Commodore. Even if you don't own Logo at this point, examine this chapter to see the benefits and structure of the language. Perhaps you will be intrigued enough to buy a copy of Logo and learn it.

The simplicity of Logo, which makes it a good programming language even for elementary school children to learn, is evident in the language's commands. Simple command words usually bring immediate, visible results. For example, if you type *FD 15* in the Logo language, a picture of a "turtle" moves forward 15 units on the screen. (The shape of the turtle actually is an arrow, but will be referred to as a turtle in this chapter.) For the beginning programmer, nothing could be easier to understand. In contrast, an assembly language statement such as *MOVE.W #NUMBER,D0 6* is cryptic, confusing, and doesn't produce any result that a programmer would notice immediately.

Turtle Graphics

Although the Logo language wasn't developed with a turtle in mind, that's what most people associate Logo with. The graphics turtle on the screen moves around at your command, drawing a line or some other shape along the way. Of course, you can use Logo for many other tasks besides drawing pictures. With Logo's mathematical and input/output commands, an integral part of the language, you can develop many other programming applications. For the most part, this chapter explores graphics, but the material also touches on all the important Logo keywords you need to know in order to create some interesting and useful programs.

Moving the Turtle

After you load the Logo language into memory, you are ready to begin programming. The most fundamental programming operation you need to know is how to move the turtle. You can move the turtle most easily with the FD, BK, LT, and RT commands. These commands move the turtle forward, backward, left, and right, respectively. For example, to draw a square that is 50 units wide, you type the following:

```
FD 50
RT 90
FD 50
RT 90
FD 50
RT 90
FD 50
```

An alternate method for drawing a square of the same size uses two different commands:

```
LT 90
BK 50
LT 90
BK 50
LT 90
BK 50
LT 90
BK 50
```

Characteristics of the Turtle

The turtle moving around the screen is named Studs, and he has certain properties when he first appears on the screen. First of all, he has a name with which you can identify him—Studs. The name is useful because Amiga Logo, unlike most other versions of the language, can have more than one turtle on the screen at once. Later in this chapter, you will learn how to use multiple turtles and how to give each of these turtles a name. For now, you will experiment with the first turtle, who for some reason was named Studs by programmers at The Lisp Company.

When Studs first appears on the screen, he is located at this position: (0,0). The turtle's position is described by this set of coordinates. You can determine a turtle's position on the Amiga's screen by imagining a horizontal x-axis extending across the screen and a vertical y-axis extending up and down on the screen. The x- and y-axes intersect in the very middle of the screen, which means that there are four equal parts to the area where the turtle can move around. The position at the center of the screen, where Studs is located initially is (0,0). If Studs moves up near the top of the screen, the value of his position on the y-axis increases; for instance, if Studs moves up 50 units from the center of the screen, his new position is (0,50). If Studs moves 100 units backward from that position, his new position is (0,-50). On the other hand, if the turtle starts at (0,0) and moves to the left 25 units on the x-axis, he is at (-25,0). If Studs then moves 50 units to the right, he ends up at position (25,0).

The directional commands that you use to move the turtle are all relative, not absolute. The destination of the turtle after an FD or

BK command depends entirely on what direction he is pointed and what distance you tell him to go.

When you first load Logo into memory, Studs has certain other characteristics. These characteristics, discussed next, are heading, visibility, pen state, turtle shape, tile shape, and ink color.

Heading

At first, Studs is facing the top of the screen; if you tell him to move forward, he moves upward. Studs' heading is measured in degrees: 0 degrees means that Studs is facing the right side of the screen; 90 degrees (the default) means that he is facing the top of the screen; 180 degrees means that he is facing the left side of the screen; and 270 degrees means that he is facing the bottom of the screen.

Essentially, the measurement in degrees begins on the rightmost point of an imaginary circle that surrounds Studs and continues counterclockwise to 359 degrees. Therefore, to point Studs downward and to the left, you could enter a heading of 225 degrees. The command used to set a turtle's heading is HD, followed by the value of the degrees. For example, to make Studs point toward 225 degrees, you would type

HD 225

Visibility

When Studs first appears on the screen, you can see him. If you want a turtle to disappear so that the turtle still can draw but cannot be seen, you type

TURTLE :HIDE

If you want the turtle to reappear, you type

TURTLE :SHOW

Pen State

You can move the turtle on the screen without having the turtle draw anything by using commands that change the pen state. If you lift "up" the imaginary pen that the turtle is holding, the turtle doesn't draw as it moves. Initially, Studs holds the pen "down," ready to draw. To bring the pen up, you type

PEN :UP

Consequently, to bring the pen back down, you type

PEN :DOWN

If you want the pen to erase pixels instead of draw them, you type

PEN :ERASE

Notice that the words used in these commands are descriptive of their functions. You will find that the words used throughout the Logo language are logical as well.

Shape of the Turtle

If you would prefer to make the turtle a different shape than the arrow, you can use the SHAPE command. You can change the arrow to any of the other shapes stored on your Logo disk. For instance, to change the turtle into an airplane, type

SHAPE: AIRPLANE

If you prefer to change the turtle back to the original arrow shape, type

SHAPE :ARROW

Tile Shape

As Studs moves around the screen, he draws a line. You can alter the shape of the "tile" that Studs is laying down with the TILE command. For example, to make Studs lay a trail of hearts as he moves, type

TILE :HEART

To bring back the regular drawing line, type

TILE :LINE

Check your Logo manual for other available turtle and tile shapes.

Ink Color

You can change the color of the tiles with the INK command. To change the color of the line (or whatever tile you are using) to blue, you type

```
INK :BLUE
```

Keywords

The beauty of the Logo language is that you can create your own keywords (user-defined words that you can use in programs). You are not restricted to words defined by the Logo interpreter. In addition, you can save these keywords and use them later in order to make complicated tasks simpler. For example, you could use a command as simple as *DOIT* or *STARS* or simply *A* to do something as complicated as draw three stars of different colors on the screen and create a triangle to connect them.

To define a particular word, you use the TO command. Suppose that you want to store a routine that draws a square in a user-defined keyword called MYBOX. You would type

```
TO MYBOX
FD 50
RT 90
FD 50
RT 90
FD 50
RT 90
FD 50
END
```

Now every time you type *MYBOX* and press the RETURN key, a box with a width of 50 is drawn.

Once you begin to define your own words, you can build on them. For instance, now that you have defined MYBOX, you can create a routine called FOURBOX, which draws a set of four squares:

```
TO FOURBOX
MYBOX
MYBOX
MYBOX
MYBOX
END
```

To repeat a command, you don't have to type the same words over and over again. In fact, Logo has some powerful commands, such as REPEAT, which makes the above definition as easy as this:

```
TO FOURBOX
REPEAT 4 [MYBOX]
END
```

Remember that when you define your own commands, you cannot use "reserved" words. That is, you cannot use the TO command in conjunction with words that Logo already uses for some particular function. For example, *TO FD* or *TO ASK* would create an error because FD and ASK are Logo *primitives*, words that the language has stored to do certain tasks.

Using Variables with Keywords

You easily can take TO a step further by using a variable in conjunction with the new keyword. Remember that a variable represents a number stored in memory. Logo recognizes variables that are preceded with a colon (:). For example, suppose that you want to write a program that draws a square of a certain size. You can store the length of each side of the square in a variable called :SIDE.

To program a keyword that supports a variable, you need to type *TO* followed by a keyword and then the variable or variables. To define a keyword that draws a square, you type

```
TO PROGSQAR :SIDE
REPEAT 4 [FD :SIDE RT 90]
END
```

Note that the END command signifies the end of a routine. Also notice that the variable SIDE always must have a colon in front of it in order to be interpreted as a numeric value. When you use the PROGSQAR routine, all you have to type is *PROGSQAR* followed by a number. For instance, typing *PROGSQAR 20* results in a square 20 units wide being drawn on the screen.

Using Multiple Variables with Keywords

You can use more than one variable with a keyword definition as long as you account for each variable when you set up the keyword.

To illustrate, define a new word called MAKERECT, which creates a rectangle with the width and height that you specify. Call the width and height :WID and :HIT, respectively. Program the routine as follows:

```
TO MAKERECT :WID :HIT
FD :HIT
RT 90
FD :WID
RT 90
FD :HIT
RT 90
FD :WID
END
```

Once the keyword is defined, you can draw a rectangle of any dimensions. For example, to draw a rectangle that is 20 units wide and 40 units high, you type

```
MAKERECT 20 40
```

As you continue to build your own keyword library, achieving results becomes easier. The most valuable aspect of defining your own keywords is that you can use those keywords to build more keywords, which in turn can be used to build more keywords. In time, with your keyword library, you will be able to produce complex results by using only one or two sophisticated commands.

Controlling the Turtle

Because FD, BK, LT, and RT are your "workhorses" for drawing, take a closer look at what these commands can do. To tell the turtle to go forward or backward a certain number of units, you specify FD or BK followed by the number of pixels that the turtle should move. For example, *FD 34* makes the turtle move forward 34 units in whichever direction it is facing. LT and RT turn the turtle a certain number of degrees left or right. A full circle equals 360 degrees. Therefore, to get the turtle to do an "about face," you simply type *RT 180* or *LT 180*.

The short program that follows uses these commands to draw a triangle.

```
TO TRIANGLE
RT 45
FD 100
LT 90
BK 100
RT 315
FD 140
END
```

Although FD, BK, LT, and RT are the commands you will use most of the time to move the turtle around the screen, you also can use many other commands available in Logo to accomplish the same purpose. For instance, F, B, L, and R move the turtle forward a certain number of pixels, backward a certain number of pixels, left 45 degrees, and right 45 degrees, respectively. You can determine the "certain number of pixels" that the turtle will move when you use the F and B commands by dividing the height of the screen (in pixels) by 4. Therefore, if the screen is 200 pixels high, the B command moves the turtle backward by 50 pixels.

Because the values of the F, B, L, and R commands are fixed, these commands don't provide as much flexibility as FD, BK, LT, and RT. However, they are useful when you want to use those fixed values. The following short program uses these fixed commands to make the turtle draw a triangle. Note that more than one command can be on a line.

```
R F
R R F
R R R F
```

You didn't use the TO command to set up a word for this routine. The computer just followed the commands directly as you typed in each line. This is the *direct* way of getting the turtle to move. The *indirect* way would be to program a keyword.

N, S, E, and W are four other Logo commands that make Studs move in a particular direction. These are absolute terms: N always points up (north); S always points down (south); E always points to the right (east); and W always points to the left (west). These commands are very helpful when you are not sure which direction the turtle is facing, but you know that you want the turtle to move in one of these four directions. With one program line, you could use these commands to make a square that is 16 pixels wide:

```
N 16 E 16 S 16 W 16
```

When you write graphics programs, you will want to work with a "clean slate." To clear the screen of all text and graphics, you can use the CS command. This command erases the contents of the screen, yet leaves the turtle in its current position and heading.

To draw sophisticated graphics, you need to have a lot of control over where the drawing arrow is and what it does. The POS command lets you specify at exactly what (X,Y) coordinate you would like the turtle to be. With this command, you can draw graphics at a specified location and move the turtle around the screen with ease. To use POS, follow the command with the X and Y coordinates, in brackets, which specify where you want the turtle to be. If you want to move the turtle to position (-50,20), for instance, you type

POS [-50 30]

If you want to send the turtle back to its original position and face the turtle north, you use the HOME command by itself.

Directional Settings

An excellent way to control the turtle is to set its direction. You can tell the turtle at what angle to point by typing *HD* followed by the number of degrees. However, you often will find in graphics programming that you need to point the turtle somewhere, but you aren't sure what the angle should be. For instance, a turtle may be in a random location, and you want to point it directly to the middle of the screen. The FACE command will solve this problem. You can use FACE to point the current turtle toward a certain point by using FACE followed by the (X,Y) coordinates in brackets that specify where you want the turtle to face. Or you can use FACE to point to another turtle by using FACE followed by the name of another turtle.

For instance, if you don't know what relation the turtle is to the middle of the screen, you can type

FACE [0 0]

to point the turtle toward the middle of the screen. If you want to point the turtle toward the coordinate (30,-65), you type

FACE [30, -65]

Likewise, if you want to point the current turtle, Studs, toward another turtle named Mack, you type

FACE :MACK

FACE is used to draw a three-dimensional figure without posing too much difficulty for the programmer in the program that follows:

```
TO PERS
CS
PEN :UP
FD 70
LT 90
FD 70
PEN :DOWN
REPEAT 4 [FD 50 RT 90]
FACE [0 0]
FD 90
FACE [-70 120]
FD 130
PEN :UP
POS [-120 70]
PEN :DOWN
FACE [0 0]
FD 134
PEN :UP
POS [-120 120]
PEN :DOWN
FACE [0 0]
FD 150
END
```

If you want to draw only one dot on the screen (as opposed to a line), you can use the DOT command. This command is useful for drawing stars, forming the eyes on a figure, or plotting the points of a graph. You should use DOT by itself to draw a dot at the turtle's current location. Make sure that the turtle's pen is positioned exactly where you want it before you use DOT.

To position the pen exactly where you want it, you can use the POS command. An alternative method is to use two other commands, which together do the same thing as POS. These are the X and Y commands. If you type *X ?* or *Y ?*, the computer prints the current X or Y location of the turtle. If you type X or Y followed by a number, the computer changes the X or Y location of the turtle to the coordinate you specify.

Special Symbols

Certain symbols used in Logo have special meanings. These are the question mark (?), the semicolon (;), and the colon (:). This section looks at each of these in turn.

Here is a very important rule of Logo: If a command that you can give absolute values to is followed by a question mark, the computer displays the current status of that command's function. Examples of such commands are X, Y, POS, HD, but not FD, BK, LT, and RT; the latter commands are relative, not absolute values. For instance, if you type *POS [50 50]*, the computer puts the turtle at location (50,50). If you type *POS ?*, however, the computer interprets this to mean "tell me what the current position of the turtle is," and the computer responds by displaying the position of the turtle.

Another helpful symbol is the semicolon (;), which is used in Logo for comments. Therefore, anything following a semicolon is ignored by the computer. Here are some examples that demonstrate both the use of the question mark and the semicolon. Assume that Logo has just been loaded and that the turtle is at position (0,0) facing north. Notice that when the X or Y command is followed by a number, the computer changes the turtle's position to that new location.

```
POS ? ; display the position
[0 0]

FD 10 ; go up 10 pixels
[0 10]

RT 90 BK 20 ; turn right 90 degrees and go backward 20 pixels
POS ?
[-20 10]

X ? Y ? ; what are the current X and Y values?
-20
10

X 10 Y 20 ; set the new turtle position to (10, 20)
POS ?
[10 20]
```

Aside from the question mark and semicolon, the colon (:) also is a very important special character. The colon indicates that a variable is being used. Here is a simple rule to follow:

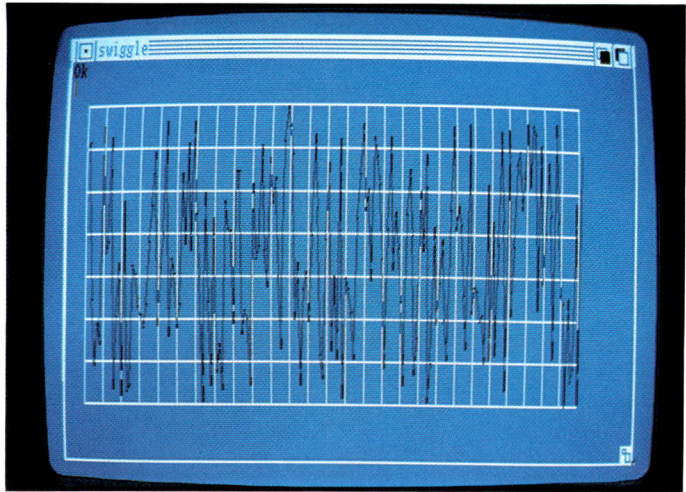

Fig. 4.3. A simple line graph.

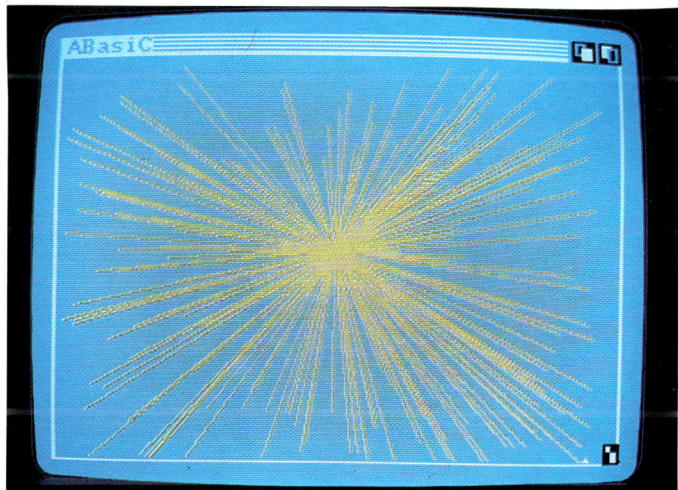

Fig. 4.4. A sunburst effect.

Fig. 4.5. A three-dimensional colored box.

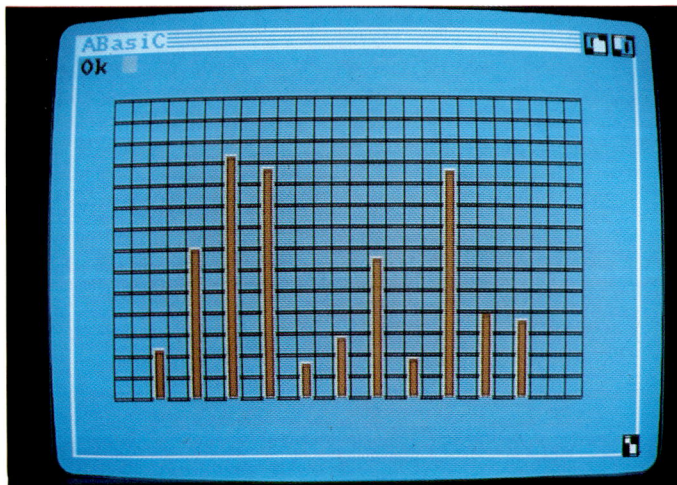

Fig. 4.6. A bar graph.

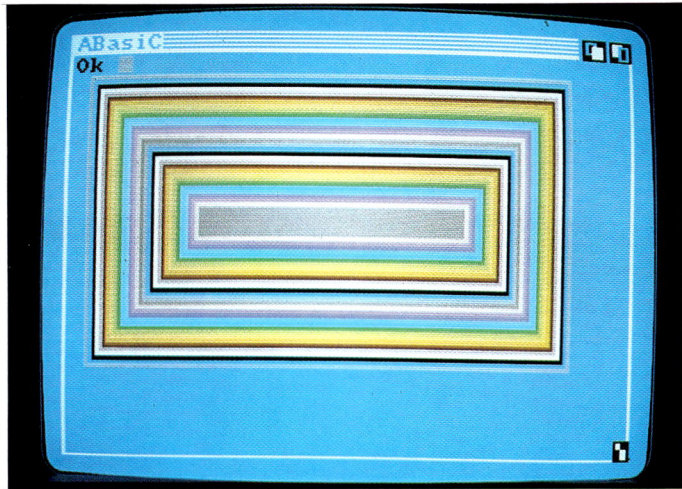

Fig. 4.7. A multitude of colored boxes.

Fig. 4.8. A computerized version of a familiar winter scene.

Fig. 10.1. A complex picture drawn easily with Graphicraft.

Fig. 10.4. The realistic three-dimensional graphics of Marble Madness.

No colon means this is an action.

Colon means this is a value represented by a variable.

You can use the question mark with the INK command to find out the current color being used to draw with, you type

INK ?

The computer responds by printing the name of the current color being used.

You also can use the INK command with a colon and the name of a color to indicate a color that you want to use. For example, to use blue, you type

INK :BLUE

You can change the background color with the PAPER command. If you follow PAPER with a question mark, the computer tells you the current background color. If you follow PAPER with a colon and a color (for instance, :WHITE, :BLACK, or :BLUE), the computer changes the background color to the one you specify.

You already have seen how the colon is used when you set up Logo keywords. You also can use the colon, for example, if you want to write a routine that gives you the square of a particular number:

```
TO SQR :NUM
:NUM * :NUM
END
```

Because it is preceded by a colon, :NUM is known to be a variable. When you use the SQR primitive, you type *SQR* followed by the number you want squared. The Amiga then prints out the square of the number.

The Screen's Boundaries

The screen is limited in size and, unless specified otherwise, the turtle may travel off the screen. You can control the movement of the turtle at the screen's boundaries with the TM command. Three different numbers can follow TM:

TM :0   The turtle can move beyond the boundaries of the screen. The screen acts as a window of a much larger size—64000 by 64000 pixels. When the turtle moves outside the boundaries of the physical screen, you can no longer see it; if you move it back into the screen area, the turtle is visible again.

TM :1   The turtle cannot move beyond the edge of the screen. The turtle simply stops, and no error occurs if you try to move beyond the boundaries.

TM :2   The turtle cannot move beyond the edge of the screen. Use this mode if you want an error to occur when the turtle tries to go beyond the boundaries of the screen.

You can control the nature of the screen itself with the GS, SS, and TS commands.

GS   Turns your screen completely into graphics mode so that no text can appear on the screen. Use this command when you are going to be drawing graphics only.

SS   Splits the screen so that a small part of the bottom of the display can be used for text while most of the screen can be used for graphics.

TS   Makes the screen work with text only. If you try to draw any graphics, you get a Non-Graphics Mode error.

Multiple Turtles

As mentioned earlier, you can have more than one turtle on the screen at one time, and you can control each turtle individually. To create a new turtle, type *HATCH* followed by a double quotation mark (") and the name of the turtle. For instance, to make another turtle, named Mark, appear on the screen, you type

HATCH "MARK

Now you have two turtles on the screen—Studs and Mark. But just because you hatch a turtle doesn't mean that the new turtle will pay attention to you. You need to decide which turtle you want to be active and tell that turtle to follow your commands. To activate a turtle, use the ASK command followed by the name of the turtle. If you want to get Mark's attention, type

ASK :MARK

After you type this command, all of your commands are sent to Mark, not Studs. You also can change the name of a turtle by using the ID command followed by the new name that you want. If Mark is the active turtle, you could change Mark's name to Tom by typing

```
ID "TOM
```

As usual, you can find out the property stored in this command by typing *ID ?*, which tells you the name of the active turtle. You can find out the names of all the turtles by typing *TF* and pressing the RETURN key.

Fundamental Programming Commands

Many keywords in Logo make programming easier and more efficient. Among these are REPEAT and FOR, DELAY, RC and RL, PRINT and its variations, PT, and HELP. The sections that follow discuss each of these commands in turn.

The REPEAT and FOR Commands

You can use the REPEAT command (mentioned earlier in the chapter) to reduce the number of programming lines you have to type. With this command, you can tell the computer to do the same operation a certain number of times. The format is

REPEAT <number> <action>

The *number* specifies how many times you want the operation performed, and the *action* is the operation itself. For example, to draw a square using only simple commands, you could type

```
TO SQUARE
FD 50
RT 90
FD 50
RT 90
FD 50
RT 90
FD 50
END
```

Or, you could make life much easier by typing

```
REPEAT 4 [FD 50 RT 90]
```

The more times you repeat a series of commands, the more useful REPEAT becomes.

When you use the REPEAT command, you must enclose within brackets whatever is to be repeated. Precede the brackets by the number of times that you want the action performed. For instance, if you want the turtle to rotate 45 degrees to the left for a total of 5 times, you type

```
REPEAT 5 [L]
```

A different version of the REPEAT command—FOR—is very similar to the FOR...NEXT commands in Amiga BASIC. The FOR command is followed by a variable name, the number you want to start with, the number you want to end with, and the commands you want acted on while the loop is executing. For instance, to make the turtle go forward 10 units and turn right 15 degrees for a total of 5 times, you could type

```
FOR "TIMES 1 5 [FD 10 RT 15]
```

Notice that the computer counts from 1 to 5 and stores the number that it is counting within the variable TIMES. Moreover, everything enclosed in brackets is repeated these five times.

The last routine could be accomplished just as easily with REPEAT. In the next program, however, FOR is clearly a more effective command than REPEAT for the routine.

```
TO SQARMAKR :NUMONE :NUMTWO
PRINTSE 'This will show the square roots of the numbers in the
range you specify'
FOR "COUNT :NUMONE :NUMTWO [PRINT :COUNT PRINT SQRT :COUNT]
END
```

When you use this routine, you type *SQARMAKR* followed by a low number and a high number that define the range of integers whose square roots you want to know. If you type

```
SQARMAKR 10 15
```

the computer displays the numbers 10 through 15 along with their square roots. Moreover, all that is enclosed in brackets is subject to the loop that goes from :NUMONE to :NUMTWO. This loop allows the function to operate properly and makes the whole routine much easier to create.

The DELAY Command

If you want the computer to pause during a routine, you can use the DELAY command followed by a number that represents how many 10ths of a second you want the Amiga to pause. You might do this, for instance, in order to show a picture on the screen for a certain amount of time. To stop the computer for a total of 10 seconds before acting on the next command in the procedure, you would type

```
DELAY 100
```

The RC and RL Commands

You have looked at the commands that make Logo do specific tasks. Now you will explore the way in which Logo gets input from the user. (A program that doesn't interact with the person using it is almost useless.) The Amiga's Logo has two commands that get information directly from the keyboard: RC and RL.

RC reads a character from the keyboard. You can determine which key was pressed by using the logic functions covered later in this chapter. After you type RC and press RETURN, the Amiga will wait until any key on the keyboard is pressed and then print the character in single quotes. Here is an example:

```
RC
A
' A'
```

The RL command, on the other hand, accepts a whole line of information from the keyboard (you must press RETURN to end the line) and stores the line as a string. For example, if you type *RL*, then press RETURN, Logo waits until you type something and press RETURN again. Logo then surrounds the string by single quotation marks and displays it.

```
RL
Hi there
' Hi there'
```

The PRINT Commands

To display something on the screen without accepting any input from the user, you can use variations of the PRINT commands. Use PRINT to display numbers and PRINTSE to display full sentences. PRINTNL has the same result as PRINT, except that each number is followed by a line feed. Here are some examples of these commands:

```
PRINT 10 PRINT 20 PRINT 30; notice on the next line that there are
no line feeds; even the question mark prompt is not forced to the
next line
10 20 30 ? PRINTNL 10 20 30
10
20
30
PRINTSE 'This is a test of the emergency broadcasting system.'
This is a test of the emergency broadcasting system.

PRINTSE [1 2 3 4 5 'Hello']
1 2 3 4 5 'Hello'
```

The PT Command

At times, you may want to examine the first line of a particular function in order to remind yourself what a certain word does. You may even want to make a habit of putting a comment on the first line of each procedure that you create. These comments can be easy references for finding out what a certain procedure does. The command that displays the first line of a function is PT. For a demonstration of how this command works, enter the following short routine.

```
TO GREETINGS
CS; This routine clears the screen and welcomes the user
PRINTSE 'Welcome to the Amiga Computer. This is the Logo
Language. "
END
```

Now issue the PT command as follows:

```
PT GREETINGS
```

The Amiga should display

```
CS; This routine clears the screen and welcomes the user
```

With PT, followed by the routine you want to check, you can quickly find out what a certain routine does as long as you have entered a comment on the first line of the routine.

The HELP Command

If you need information about one of the computer's keywords, other than one of your own, type *HELP* followed by the word you want defined. This built-in help system can save you a lot of time that you might have spent looking through documentation. Here is an example of how you could use this command:

```
HELP "HD
The Heading (In Degrees) Of The Current Turtle.
```

File Management Commands

Some commands are not meant to be used in programs because they simply help manage the files on your Logo disk. With these commands, you can save keywords and routines, load files, view a directory of all your files or of particular ones, and erase files.

Saving Files

Once you have defined a word, you may want to save it for later use. If, for instance, you had spent a lot of time perfecting a definition named SPIRAL, you could type

```
SAVE 'SPIRAL'
```

This saves SPIRAL for the future so you don't have to type it again. Later, when you want to load the word, you type

```
LOAD 'SPIRAL'
```

Displaying the Directory

After you have stored a number of routines on a diskette, you may have trouble remembering the names of every one of your routines. You can display a list of all the files on a diskette by typing

```
DIR '*'
```

or you can specify certain types of files by entering within single quotation marks the criteria for the search. For instance, to view all the files on the disk that have a .GRP extension (such as CIRCLE.GRP, SQR.GRP, and SPIRAL.GRP), you type

`DIR'.GRP'`

and something similar to the following would be displayed:

`[CIRCLE.GRP SQR.GRP SPIRAL.GRP]`

You also can specify that the names of certain files be displayed by using a wild card. If you use the question mark as a wild card, any character in the position held by the question mark will be allowed. If you use the asterisk as a wild card, up to eight characters in a row in the position held by the asterisk will be allowed. This explains why `DIR'*'` displays all the files on the disk. Here are some more examples:

If you want to display all files that begin with the letter P, you can type

`DIR'P*'`

If you want to display the files that begin with AT, you can type

`DIR'AT*'`

And, if you want to see the names of the files and words you have stored that are three letters long and the third letter is an X, you would type

`DIR'??X'`

Remember that the period (.) separates the first part of the name from the extension (the second part of the name). If you don't include the period as part of your criteria, the computer will examine only the first part of the name. A `DIR'??X'` command, therefore, would display names like LEX.123 and XXX.HI.

Erasing Files

To erase a particular file or routine that is stored on the diskette, you type *ERA* followed by the name of the file enclosed in single quotes. You can use the wild card system to eliminate more than one file at a time. (These conventions will be familiar to CP/M® users.) Here are a couple of examples:

ERA ' LEX. 123' ; this erases the file called LEX. 123

ERA ' S*" ; this erases all files that begin with the letter S

Text Commands

Even though Logo is regarded by most people as a graphics language, it also has commands that deal with text. This is fortunate, because a truly useful program interacts with the user through text.

You already have seen how the PRINT, PRINTNL, and PRINTSE text commands work (see "The PRINT Commands" section in this chapter). Another way to work with text strings is to change them from uppercase to lowercase or vice versa with the LOWER and UPPER commands. For instance, if you follow the LOWER command with a string, every character in that string becomes lowercase.

' Some of these LETTERS are UPPERCASE'
some of these letters are uppercase

Conversely, the UPPER command changes all the characters to uppercase.

UPPER ' make these letters BIG, Amiga!'
MAKE THESE LETTERS BIG, AMIGA!

Before you move on to the next text command, you should take a minute to review the ASCII system. You may remember that ASCII is the computer's set of characters that correspond to keyboard letters, numbers, and symbols. The ASCII character set ranges from 0 to 255, and each number represents a specific letter, number, or symbol. For example, the ASCII character 65 on any computer is the letter A (consequently, ASCII 66 is B).

The next text command, CH, is a character conversion command similar to the ASC and CHR$ commands in Amiga BASIC. By following the CH command with an alphanumeric character, you can find out what the ASCII code is for that character. For instance, to find out what the ASCII code is for the letter F, you type

CH "F

and the computer displays

70

Using CH with an ASCII code displays the character that corresponds to the number that you input. CH with an ASCII code performs exactly the same function as the CHR$(number) command in Amiga BASIC. Because the ASCII character set is the same for all computers, *CH 65* on your Amiga will produce an A, just as it would on any other computer equipped with Logo. The routine that follows, which is stored in the word CHRS, prints out the entire set of characters available on the Amiga by listing ASCII characters 0 through 255.

```
TO CHRS
FOR "COUNT 1 255 [CH :COUNT]
END
```

Elements and Objects

You may have noticed that Logo often uses brackets ([and]) with keywords. An important use of brackets is to set up groups of information called *objects*. Objects can contain additional information, also enclosed in brackets. Within an object, each number, character, or symbol is called an *element*.

You can use objects directly with commands, or you can store objects in variables. To demonstrate how you can use keywords to modify and extract information from objects, set up a hypothetical group of information that looks like this:

```
[1 2 3 4 5 A B C D E]
```

Now use the MAKE command to store the object in the variable TESTER. You type *MAKE* followed by the variable name and the object.

```
MAKE "TESTER [1 2 3 4 5 A B C D E]
[1 2 3 4 5 A B C D E]
:TESTER
[1 2 3 4 5 A B C D E]
```

Notice that Logo displays the object after you define it. Why? Because you typed a colon before the object name.

To find out how many elements an object contains, you use the LENGTH command. For example, if you type

```
LENGTH :TESTER
```

the screen displays 10 because the object has 10 elements. Note: If an object contains additional objects, Logo counts those subobjects as only one element. Here is an example:

LENGTH [1 2 3 [4 5]]
4

The object has only four elements. [4 5] is considered one element.

If you are going to use many of the same characters in an object, you might want to use the NEWSTR command. This command stores within a variable any number of the particular character you specify. Here is an example:

MAKE "TEST2 NEWSTR 9 ' $'
' $$$$$$$$$'

NEWSTR 9 ' $' tells Logo to put nine dollar signs within the TEST2 variable.

If you want to eliminate either the first character in an object or the first number in a group of numbers, you can use the BF (But First) command. In the three examples that follow, the input shown results in the corresponding output:

BF ' GLOVE'
' LOVE'

BF [10 9 8 7 6 5 4 3 2 1]
[9 8 7 6 5 4 3 2 1]

BF :TESTER
[2 3 4 5 A B C D E]

The BL (But Last) command works in the same manner but eliminates the last rather than the first character or number in an object or string. Here are two examples:

BL ' HIT'
HI

BL :TESTER
[1 2 3 4 5 A B C D]

The opposites of the BF and BL commands are the FIRST and LAST commands. They return the first and last elements, respectively, of an object or string. Here are some examples:

```
FIRST 'This is a test'
T

FIRST :TESTER
1

LAST 'This is a test'
t

LAST :TESTER
E

LAST [1 2 3 ['Hi there' ]]
'Hi there'
```

You can extract an element that is not at the beginning or end of an object with the NTH command. NTH represents the "Nth" element in an object. You type *NTH*, the object you are working with, and the number of the element you want returned. For instance, to extract the sixth element of :TESTER, you type

```
NTH :TESTER 6
```

Logo returns the letter A. More examples follow.

```
NTH [1 2 3 [4 5 6 7]] 4
[4 5 6 7]
TH [1 2 3 [4 5 6 7]] 2
2

NTH 'Which character do you want?" 5
'h'
```

The last two commands you should know when working with objects are FPUT and LPUT. FPUT adds whatever you specify to the beginning of a string or object; LPUT adds whatever you specify to the end. For example, suppose that you want to add the letters X Y Z to TESTER. You could type

```
FPUT "X Y Z :TESTER
```

and the result would be

```
[X Y Z 1 2 3 4 5 A B C D E]
```

To add *The End* to the end of TESTER, you could type

```
LPUT 'The End' :TESTER
```

and the result would be

[X Y Z 1 2 3 4 5 A B C D E ' The End']

Mathematical Functions

Logo supports a number of mathematical functions, simple ones as well as complex ones. The fundamental symbols that perform the functions listed in table 6.1 are +, -, *, and /. The table describes each function and gives and example of each. (The question mark is simply your prompt to type something).

Table 6.1
Logo's Mathematical Functions

Format	Description	Example
number + number	Displays the sum of numbers	? 4 + 10 14
number - number	Displays the difference between numbers	? 50 - 30. 5 19. 5
number * number	Displays the quotient of numbers	? 5 * 6 30
number1 / number2	Displays the result of n1 divided by n2	? 100 / 5 20
n1 ^ n2	Displays the result of n1 raised to the n2 power	? 4 ^ 3 64

You can use two of Logo's mathematical functions to modify a number: NEG and INT. To make a number negative, you use the NEG function. When you precede any number or variable with NEG, Logo makes that number negative, regardless of whether it was positive or negative to begin with. You use INT when you want to delete anything that follows the decimal point in a number. Here are examples of NEG and INT:

NEG 10
-10

NEG -20
-20

```
INT 5. 323215
5

INT -50
-50
```

Three more useful functions are SQRT, REM, and RN. The SQRT function, as you might guess, calculates the square root of a number. REM finds the remainder of two numbers when the first is divided by the second. And RN selects a random number between 0 and a number you specify (which can't be more than 32,767). Examples of these functions follow.

```
SQRT PI
1. 772454

SQRT 81
9

REM 10 3
1

REM 9 3
0

RN 1000
532
```

When you work with trigonometry or other programs that require the number pi (which is about 3.1415926538979), you can use Logo's built-in PI. You use PI just as you would an ordinary number, as shown in the first of the previous examples (SQRT PI).

Logo has many other trigonometric functions, all of which you use in the same way: you type the name of the function followed by the number you want to work with. Table 6.2 lists Logo's trigonometric functions and gives a description of each.

Decision-Making Commands

The "heart" of any computer language is in its capability to make decisions based on certain conditions. Logo has many more decision-making commands than Amiga BASIC. Therefore, you can program

---

Table 6.2
Trigonometric Functions

Function	Description
SIN	Determines the sine of an angle. The number you give should be in degrees.
COS	Finds the cosine of a number
TAN	Computes the tangent of an angle
ATAN	Computes the angle (in degrees) whose tangent is the number you specify
LOG	Computes the base-10 logarithm of a number
LN	Computes the natural (base-e) logarithm of a number
EXP	Raises the natural number e (2.718282) to the power you specify

---

the computer to "judge" a specific variable or value much easier with Logo than with Amiga BASIC.

The simplest decision-makers are the comma (,) and the equal sign (=), which can be used in combination with one another. You use these and other decision-making symbols to compare two values, one or both of which can be a number or variable. Logo responds with either a True or False. For instance, to find out whether the variable NUM1 is less than the number 100, you type

```
:NUM1<100
False
```

Logo returns a False, which indicates that NUM1 is either equal to or greater than the number 100. Here are six different ways that you can use decision-making symbols:

n1 > n2   Outputs True if n1 is greater than n2

n1 < n2   Outputs True if n1 is less than n2

n1 = n2   Outputs True if n1 equals n2

n1 <> n2   Outputs True if n1 does not equal n2

n1 >= n2   Outputs True if n1 is greater than or equal to n2

n1 <= n2   Outputs True if n1 is less than or equal to n2

Several Logo functions make decisions about numbers only. Here are some short explanations and examples of these functions, which are all similar.

EQ
Compares two numbers, objects, or any other comparable items

```
EQ 10 10
True
```

```
EQ "ABCD "ABCD
True
```

```
EQ [A B C D] [A B C]
False
```

```
EQ :NUM1 :NUM1
True
```

MAX
Compares two numbers and displays the larger of the two. This feature saves you time; you don't have to go through the more complicated process of comparing two numbers and programming Logo to decide which is larger.

```
MAX 10 20
20
```

```
MAX 512 :NUM2 ; assume NUM2 equals 200
512
```

MIN
Determines and prints the smaller of two numbers. MIN is the opposite of MAX.

```
MIN 10 20
10
```

```
MIN 512 :NUM3 ; assume NUM3 equals 400
400
```

MINUSP   Determines whether a number is less than zero

MINUSP 10
False

MINUSP -5
True

ZEROP   Determines whether a number is equal to zero

ZEROP 0
True

ZEROP 2
False

You also can use Logo's decision-making statements to check objects for certain conditions. For example, you can use the MEMBER command to see whether an object contains a specific element. You specify the element that you are searching for, then the object or string that you are searching within. If the object does contain the element, Logo returns the element's position; for instance, if the element is the fourth one in the object, the screen displays the number 4. If the object does not contain the element, Logo returns False. Here are some examples:

MEMBER "B [A B C]
2

MEMBER "s 'Testing'
3

MEMBER "P 'Hottub'
False

MEMBER [X Y Z] [1 2 3 [X Y Z] ABC]
4

In the last example, 1, 2, and 3 are the first three elements, and the subobject [X Y Z] is the fourth. [X Y Z] is an element in itself because it is enclosed in brackets.

You can use the ISEMPTY command check to see whether an object or part of an object is empty. Here are some examples:

ISEMPTY ''
True

```
ISEMPTY ' I AM NOT EMPTY!'
False
```

```
ISEMPTY FIRST [[ ] A B C]; note that the subobject is empty
True
```

```
ISEMPTY NTH [1 2 3 [ ] 5 6] 4; note the 4th element is empty
True
```

Logo's decision-makers also enable you to check the values of certain commands, such as HEADING, INK, and TURTLE. For example, to check the color of the ink currently being used, you type

```
( INK ?)=:BLUE
```

Logo responds True if the ink is blue; False, if the ink is any other color. The command and question mark, which must be enclosed in parentheses, ask "what is the current ink color?," and =:BLUE asks "is that color equal to blue?"

You can use ALL, a powerful decision-making command, to test the truth of two or more expressions in a single statement. The expressions that follow the command must be enclosed in brackets. If all the expressions are true, Logo outputs True. If one or more of the expressions is false, Logo returns False. Some examples follow.

```
ALL [2<10 12>7 3=3 5>3]
True
```

```
ALL [2>10 12>7 3=6]
False
```

The ANY statement, another kind of logical test, is similar to ALL. If any expression following ANY is true, Logo returns a True. If all the expressions are false, Logo returns a False. Here are some examples:

```
ANY [3=2 4>5 8=7 76<77]
True
```

```
ANY [3=3 4=4 76>1]
True
```

```
ANY [4=2 5=7 10<=1]
False
```

You may want to take a particular action if a condition is true or take an alternative action if the condition is false. The IFTRUE and IFFALSE commands allow Logo to make logical decisions based on two possible outcomes. This capability makes all the logical tests you have just learned more useful because Logo can act on an outcome, whether it is true or false. (Note: When acting on a true or false result, Logo does not display the result on the screen.)

The following program demonstrates the use of the IFTRUE and IFFALSE commands. If the value of the last test is true, Logo performs whatever action is specified in the brackets following the IFTRUE command. If the result is false, Logo skips over the IFTRUE command and its contents in brackets. The IFFALSE command makes Logo perform the action specified in brackets if the last test result is false. If the result is true, however, Logo skips to the next command line. Here is an example:

```
TO DECMAKER
MAKE "RANNUM :RN 1000
:RANNUM >500
IFTRUE [PRINTSE ' The random number is greater than 500' ]
IFFALSE [PRINTSE ' The random number is less than or equal to 500' ]
END
```

In this simple routine, Logo picks a number between 0 and 1,000 and checks to see whether the number is greater than 500. If the number is greater than 500, the message following the IFTRUE command appears. Otherwise, the screen displays the message after the IFFALSE command.

Logo's Possibilities

After studying this chapter, you should understand why Logo is an excellent language for teaching children programming. You also should get a sense of Logo's other powerful merits. If you want to explore artificial intelligence, for example, you will find The Learning Company's Logo for the Amiga an excellent introduction to the subject. In addition, learning Logo should help you to expand your computing horizons, to become more proficient in other computer languages, and to enhance your logical thinking.

7
Programming in C

The C programming language is the premier language for software development on microcomputers. Introduced by Bell Laboratories more than a decade ago, C continues to gain popularity in the programming world.

The reasons for C's popularity are many. Principal among these is the power that C provides for the programmer. The language's wide variety of operators and functions give the programmer access to the very "heart" of the computer. This power is harnessed by the functions, which are the building blocks of C programs. A C function is a self-contained program unit that performs some useful task. For example, C contains built-in functions for input and output. A programmer also can create building blocks of functions that can be used in many C programs. Once these blocks are designed and debugged, a function library can be built that speeds the process of programming considerably.

Speed in processing is a second reason for C's popularity. Aside from assembly code (which is difficult to program with), C is generally the fastest language available on microcomputers.

Languages like Amiga BASIC and Logo are interpreted languages. As the name implies, interpreted languages take a line of code and interpret that line each time it is needed. The fact that this interpretation, or translation, takes time explains the slowness of BASIC and Logo. C, on the other hand, is a compiled language. A compiled language creates (by means of a compiler) object code for the 68000 microprocessor, which is used in the Amiga. Although this one-time translation from C to Amiga may take some time, after this initial effort, the program produced is always faster than a similar interpreted program.

The third reason for C's popularity is the widespread availability of the C language for a variety of machines. Unlike Applesoft BASIC, TRS-80 BASIC, and Microsoft BASIC®, which are all limited to specific computer lines, C is a fairly portable language. This portability is useful if you are writing programs for sale and desire a larger audience for your creations.

This chapter gives you only a taste of the power of the C language. You will learn about the compilation process, in general terms, and how C is different from languages like Logo and Amiga BASIC. Then you will be taken through the steps involved in creating a C program. The first sample program, Temperature, is analyzed in detail and should reassure you that C is understandable. This analysis also points out important distinctive features of the language. Next, the chapter gives descriptions of some of the library functions available in the Amiga™ C compiler. Finally, a number of sample programs are included to give you examples of C content and form. These programs are not analyzed here, but you can enter them and experiment in order to learn some of the ways you can use the C language.

This chapter does not pretend to be a complete introduction to the C language. The best way to learn C is to find a good book on the language and use it with a C compiler and the Amiga manual. Because of the popularity of the language, C books can be found at regular bookstores throughout the country. Several excellent books and manuals are listed at the end of this chapter.

Compiling a C Program

To the programmer familiar with BASIC or Logo, C can be an intimidating language at first glance. Unlike the readily understandable READ command of BASIC or the familiar LEFT command of Logo, a typical C program may contain such items as i++ or ri.BitMap = &b. After the initial shock subsides, however, you will discover that C really is not that difficult after all.

Because C is a compiled language, you will notice another difference when you compare C to BASIC or Logo. When you are programming in Amiga BASIC or Logo, the computer monitors your lines as you enter them. If errors are found, you are told immediately. After you enter all the appropriate program lines, a request to RUN the program causes the computer to interpret your requests and perform accordingly. If you have made errors, BASIC provides an editing facility to correct them. Programming in C, however, is more indirect. As you write your program, the computer stores the information as text in a file on an Amiga diskette. In fact, the computer doesn't even recognize that you have put a C program into a file. For all the computer "knows," you might have written a letter to your grandmother!

After a C program has been entered, you tell the computer to *compile* the program. Compiling is the process by which the compiler converts the C program *source code*, the text you have entered, into *object code*, which the machine can understand. Even with a short program, this compilation process may take a few minutes. For longer programs, you might want to have this book handy for reading while you wait.

You can find several solutions to the problem of time. One solution available on many machines is to place the compiler and program source code in the machine's RAM memory, where operation is much faster than with diskettes.

A second solution is to subdivide C programs into smaller functions. Once a function has been written, compiled and debugged, it is available for use by any program. For example, the portion of the program that displays messages on the screen can be written and debugged separately from the rest of the program. After all the parts are working, they can be linked to produce a complete program.

The C Compiler from Commodore (made by Lattice, Inc.) provides a feature that makes the process of C programming more manageable. When you are using this compiler, the text editor, compiler, and linker all can be displayed simultaneously. Because the Amiga has multitasking capabilities, all of these tools can work at the same time.

Steps for Writing a C Program

Writing a C program is a four-step process. A description of each part of the process follows.

1. *Create and edit the source file*. Using the text editor, create the source code for the C program. Here you define functions, tell the computer what you want

done, and enter the required C program statements. If you find the editor supplied with the Amiga to be too primitive and you plan to spend a great deal of time with this tool, you might want to purchase a better editor. One possibility is the EMACS program, which is a free software program available through Commodore user groups.

2. *Compile the source file*. The second step of the process is the compilation of the C source code into an intermediate form usable by the linker. During this step, you are notified of any C program errors that you may have made. To correct the errors, you must return to the editor. Remember: to speed the programming process, you can create small portions of your program independently. After you have compiled an error-free program, the computer produces an object file for use by the linker.

3. *Link the object files with the library*. To produce a working program, you must integrate the object files (created with the compiler in step 2) with the library functions (such as the functions for input and output). In this step, the linker takes your program object files and combines them with the necessary library functions to produce a working program. Unfortunately, a working program is not necessarily a correctly working program; hence, the next step.

4. *Debug the program*. Once a program is created, it must be tested to ensure that all of it works as intended. In the debugging stage, you discover the little (or big) problems that must be corrected. From here, you return to the editor where you correct any mistakes and begin the process of program creation again.

Several C editors and compilers are on the market for the Amiga. An excellent editor/compiler is from a company that markets C compilers for everything from the Commodore 64 to the Amiga. The Aztec C package is available from Manx Software Systems (P. O. Box 55, Shrewsbury, NJ 07701). The package is available in three versions: personal ($199), developer ($299), and commercial ($399). The first is too limited to be recommended, but the developer and commercial versions are excellent products. They were used in developing the programs for this chapter.

A Simple Example

The easiest way to illustrate that C is not as intimidating as you might fear is by presenting a sample C program. The sample shown here is a well-known program that prints Fahrenheit and Celsius temperature values. This program, which is presented fairly early in the "standard" C language book, Kernighan and Ritchie's *The C Programming Language*, is a simple example of C operation.

The Temperature program that follows counts from 0 to 300 in steps of 20 degrees and displays the corresponding values for Fahrenheit and Celsius.

```
/*
 * This program prints Fahrenheit and Celsius degrees from 0
 * to 300 in steps of 20
 */

main ()
{
        int lower, upper, step;
        float fahr, celsius;
        lower = 0;                 /* Lower limit of temperature */
        upper = 300;               /* Upper limit */
        step = 20;                 /* Increment */
        fahr = lower;              /* Begin at lower limit */
        while (fahr <= upper) {  /* Begin while loop */
                celsius = (5.0 / 9.0) * (fahr - 32.0);
                printf ("%4.0f   %6.1f\n", fahr, celsius);
                fahr = fahr + step;      /* Get next temperature */
                }                        /* End while loop */
}                                        /* End program */
```

Features of C Programs

Before you examine the program lines in detail, you can learn from this program several important features of C. These distinctive characteristics apply to all C language programs.

1. All C programs must contain a function called main( ).
   This function serves as the starting point for execution.

2. All C statements end with a semicolon.

3. C statements may be grouped within curly braces ({ }).
   For example, the contents of the while loop begin
   with the opening brace and end with the closing brace.

4. Comments are marked off from the rest of the program
   by a combination of the slash and asterisk characters
   (/* for beginning and */ for ending).

5. C programs may be indented (as with the while loop)
   to increase readability. While not required, good
   indentation and layout makes programs look neater and
   makes them easier to modify and debug.

Analysis of the Program Lines

With these preliminaries out of the way, you now can examine the
Temperature program a few lines at a time.

The program begins with a comment that tells you what the program
is designed to do. In this case, the program is supposed to print
Fahrenheit and Celsius temperature values.

```
/*
 * This program prints Fahrenheit and Celsius degrees from 0
 * to 300 in steps of 20
 */
```

his program, like all C programs, must contain a call to the main( )
function. This is the starting point for execution of the program.
The empty parentheses tells you that the main function expects nothing else to be supplied for its operation. The opening brace after
main( ) signifies the beginning of the function (and in this case, the
entire program).

```
main ( )
{
```

Unlike BASIC, where variables can be created "out of the blue," C
requires that variables be *declared* before they can be used. The
next two lines declare five variables for use by the program. Three
of these variables (lower, upper, and step) are declared to be integers (int); the other two variables (fahr and celsius) are de-

clared to be floating-point numbers (float). Note that program lines that declare variables always end with a semicolon.

```
int lower, upper, step;
float fahr, celsius;
```

The next three lines of the C program *initialize* the lower limit, upper limit, and step value for the program. The fourth statement sets the variable fahr as the value of lower (that is, zero). Note that comments may be placed on program lines.

```
lower = 0;      /* Lower limit of temperature */
upper = 300;    /* Upper limit */
step = 20;      /* Increment */
fahr = lower;   /* Begin at lower limit */
```

The next C statement uses the while command to create a loop. The program will loop through the bracketed commands while fahr is less than or equal to the value of upper, which is 300. (At the bottom of the while loop, fahr will be incremented by the value of step, which is 20.) The opening brace marks the beginning of the while loop.

```
while (fahr <= upper) {        /* Begin while loop */
```

The while loop contains three statements. The first of these is simply an instruction to calculate the corresponding value of Celsius (in the C program, celsius) from the specified Fahrenheit temperature (fahr).

```
celsius = (5.0 / 9.0) * (fahr - 32.0);
```

The next statement in the while loop handles the printing of the Fahrenheit and Celsius temperature values.

```
printf ("%4.0f   %6.1f\n", fahr, celsius);
```

The printf command is a call to a C function that performs the formatted printing operation. Unlike the main( ) function, which does not have any values within its parentheses, printf seems to have everything but the kitchen sink between the parentheses. The %4.0f and the %6.1f tell the C program to print fahr and celsius (respectively) with four digits and no decimal places (%4.0f) and with six digits and one decimal place (%6.1f). The spaces between the two items will be reproduced on the output line so that the Fahrenheit and Celsius values will be separated. The funny-looking \n" tells the Amiga to move to the next line after the program has printed the Fahrenheit and Celsius values.

The last three lines of the program increment the counter for the while loop, complete the while loop, and signal the end of the main( ) function.

```
        fahr = fahr + step;     /* Get next temperature */
    }                           /* End while loop */
}                               /* End program */
```

This is a good time to note that with indenting you easily can see that the first closing brace applies to the while loop, and the second refers to the initial opening brace after the main( ) function.

Library Functions

In C, all functions except main( ) are library functions. These functions are stored in a library and can be accessed by any program at any time. This concept greatly increases the flexibility and usefulness of the C language. Some of the more frequently used library functions, explained in the sections that follow, have to do with input and output and with strings and data types.

Input and Output Functions

Any programming language must provide some means of communicating with the outside world. BASIC uses INPUT and PRINT statements to accomplish this task. C uses the functions printf, scanf, gets, and puts for input and output.

The printf and scanf Functions

In C, all formatted input (from the keyboard) and output (to the screen) is handled by a set of function calls. Input is controlled by the scanf function, and output is accomplished by the printf function. These functions are shown in the following lines along with their generic argument lists.

```
scanf (format, exp1, exp2, ...)     standard input

printf (format, exp1, exp2, ...)    standard output
```

A format string consists of text to be printed or matched. This text contains *format specifiers*, which determine the appearance and types of the data. In the Temperature example, the format string is

%4.0f   %6.1f\n". The expressions (exp1 and exp2) are fahr and celsius.

A format specifier has this form:

%[-][W][.P][l]<conversion character>

The elements of the format specifier are as follows:

-	Forces left-justification (in printf only)
W	Width in characters (leading 0 means padding with zeros)
P	Precision (decimal places). In the example, celsius is printed with one decimal place.
l	Specifies long integer or double

A *conversion character* controls how the data itself is printed. Here are the conversion characters along with their definitions:

Character Definition

d	Signed decimal integer
u	Unsigned decimal integer (printf only)
x	Unsigned hexadecimal integer
h	Unsigned hexadecimal short integer (scanf only)
o	Unsigned octal integer
c	Single character
s	Null-terminated string
f	Fixed-point notation for float or double
e	Scientific notation for float or double (printf only)
g	Use either %e or %f, whichever is shorter (printf only)

In the Temperature program, you can see where the variable celsius was printed as a %6.1f value. From the preceding lists, you can see that C was supposed to print a floating point number with one digit to the left of the decimal point.

The gets and puts Functions

The gets and puts functions work with strings of data. The function gets receives a string from the keyboard; puts displays a string. Actually, both functions operate with pointers, but the effect is the same: the function either "gets" or "puts" strings. Details of these operations can be found in any good C programming book.

Math Functions

Unlike BASIC, which has many math features, C itself has only addition, subtraction, multiplication, and division. The features needed for more complicated math operations are contained in a library file that you can include in your programs when needed. To include a file in your program, you use a statement like this:

```
#include    <intuition/math.h>
```

The Lattice C library contains a complete set of trigonometric functions. The functions along with their definitions follow. r is measured in radians.

Function	*Definition*
x = sin (r);	Sine of r
x = cos (r);	Cosine of r
x = tan (r);	Tangent of r
x = acos (r);	Arccosine of r
x = asin (r);	Arcsine of r
x = atan (r);	Arctangent of r
x = atan2 (y, r);	Arctangent of y divided by r
x = cosh (r);	Hyperbolic cosine of r
x = sinh (r);	Hyperbolic sine of r
x = tanh (r);	Hyperbolic tangent of r

The <intuition/math.h> library also contains logarithmic and exponential functions. Here is a list of those functions with their definitions:

Function	Definition
x = exp (t);	Exponential function e^t
x = sqrt (t);	Square root of t
x = log (t);	Logarithm (base-e) of t
x = log10 (t);	Logarithm (base-10) of t
x = pow (t, y);	Computer t to the y power; t^y

Finally, the Lattice C math library has a random number generator that generates a random integer between 0 and any number up to the maximum integer allowed on the Amiga.

```
x = rand( );
```

Strings and Other Data Types

Like any computer language, C uses a variety of data types besides numbers. The most commonly used data types are *characters* and *strings*. The library functions available with the Lattice C Compiler (and virtually all C compilers) allow the programmer to manipulate and copy strings within a program. Some of these functions are explained in the sections that follow. For complete details on these and other C functions, consult the documentation supplied with your C compiler.

The strlen Function

The strlen function calculates length of a string (in this case, string s) in characters. The format is

```
length = strlen (s);
```

The strcmp Function

The strcmp function compares the length of two strings (designated as s1 and s2). The format is

```
x = strcmp (s1, s2);
```

where s1 and s2 are the strings to compare. The function returns the following values based on the comparison:

Return Value	String Contents	Example
negative	s1 < s2	"Mary" < "Terry"
zero	s1 = s2	"Tim" = "Tim"
positive	s1 > s2	"zebra" > "yak"

The strcpy Function

The strcpy function copies one string to another. The string s2 is copied to the string s1:

```
strcpy (s1, s2)
```

The stpchr Function

You use the stpchr function to find a specific character in a string. In the following example, the string s is searched for the character specified by c and the location is returned. If s = Amiga and c = m, the value of pt is 2 because *m* is the second letter in *Amiga*.

```
pt = stpchr(s, c)
```

The strcat and strncat Functions

The strcat and strncat functions concatenate (join) specified strings. The first function (strcat) concatenates two strings, and the second (strncat) concatenates only a specified number of characters. In the examples, if s1 = Commodore, s2 = Amiga, and s3 = Amiga computer, either of the following commands will produce the string s4 (Commodore Amiga):

```
s4 = strcat(s1, s2)

s4 = strncat(s1, s3, 5)    /* Takes the first 5 characters
                              of "Amiga computer"  */
```

Sample Programs

Now that you have studied the basics of the C programming language, you are ready to look at some sample programs for the Amiga. All of the programs that follow have been tested with the Lattice C Compiler published by Commodore. If you have C available on your Amiga, enter the programs and experiment with them. This will give you a clearer idea of how C works and help you decide whether you want to learn more about this language.

Window Maker

The first sample program, called Window Maker, uses the built-in Amiga routines to create a window on the video screen. The upper-left corner of the window will be at coordinates (20,20) and the initial dimensions will be 300 by 100. Maximum (640 by 200) and minimum (100 by 20) dimensions are specified for the window. You cannot use the mouse to make the window exceed these dimensions. Window Maker demonstrates the power of both the C language and the Amiga.

```c
/* This is how you open a new window */

#include <exec/types.h>
#include <intuition/intuition.h>

struct IntuitionBase *IntuitionBase;
int *OpenLibrary(), *OpenWindow();

main() {
        struct NewWindow NWind;
        struct Window *wind;

        /* Open the intuition library */
        IntuitionBase =
                (struct IntuitionBase *)OpenLibrary("intuition.library", 29);
        if (IntuitionBase == NULL) {
                printf("Can't open library\n");
                exit(0);
        }
        NWind.LeftEdge = 20;
        NWind.TopEdge = 20;
        NWind.Width = 300;
        NWind.Height = 100;
        NWind.DetailPen = 0;
        NWind.BlockPen = 1;
        NWind.Title = (UBYTE *)"This is my window" ;
        NWind.Flags = SMART_REFRESH | ACTIVATE | WINDOWCLOSE | WINDOWDRAG
                | WINDOWSIZING | WINDOWDEPTH;
```

```
NWind.IDCMPFlags = CLOSEWINDOW ; /* Report if window is closed */
NWind.Type = WBENCHSCREEN;
NWind.FirstGadget = NULL;
NWind.CheckMark = NULL;
NWind.Screen = NULL; /* Use Workbench screen (default) */
NWind.BitMap = NULL;
NWind.MinWidth = 100;
NWind.MinHeight = 20;
NWind.MaxWidth = 640;
NWind.MaxHeight = 200;

if ((wind = (struct Window *)OpenWindow(&NWind)) == NULL) {
        printf("Can't open window\n");
        exit(0);
}

/* Wait until user closes the window */
Wait(1 << wind->UserPort->mp_SigBit);

CloseWindow(wind);
exit(1);
}
}
```

Simple Sprite

One of the functions available on the Amiga generates *sprites*. These
are multicolored graphic figures that can be created, changed, and
moved around the screen. The following program creates a simple
sprite, which you can move around the screen. Press the U, D, L,
and R keys to move the sprite up, down, left, and right, respectively.
Press Q to exit from the program.

```
/*
 * Simple Sprite
 *
 * Enter u, d, l, or r to move sprite up, down, left, or right.
 * To quit, enter q. Note that character input is buffered, so
 * you eventually must press RETURN.
 */
```

```
#include <exec/types.h>
#include <exec/exec.h>
#include <graphics/gfx.h>
#include <graphics/sprite.h>
#include <hardware/dmabits.h>
#include <hardware/custom.h>
#include <hardware/blit.h>

struct SimpleSprite sprite;
UWORD sprite_data []=
{
        100, 100,                       /* Position */
        0xff00, 0xff00
        0xff00, 0xff00,
        0xff00, 0xff00,
        0xff00, 0x00ff,
        0xff00, 0x00ff,
        0xff00, 0x00ff,
        0xf0f0, 0xff00,
        0xf0f0, 0xff00,
        0xf0f0, 0xff00,
        0xffff, 0xffff,
        0xffff, 0xfff,
        0xffff, 0xffff
};

struct GfxBase *GfxBase;

main ()
{
        int c, sp;

        GfxBase = Openlibrary("graphics.library", 0);
        if (GfxBase == NULL) {
            printf ("no lib");
            exit (0);
        }
        if ((sp = GetSprite(&sprite, -1)) == -1) {    /* Get any sprite */
            printf("No sprite!!!");
            exit (0);
        }
```

```
sprite.x = sprite.y = 100;
sprite.height = 12;

ChangeSprite(0, &sprite, sprite_data);

while (1) {
        switch (c = getch()) {
                case 'q' :
                  break;
                case 'l' :
                  MoveSprite(0, &sprite, sprite.x - 1, sprite.y);
                  break;
                case 'r' :
                  MoveSprite(0, &sprite, sprite.x + 1, sprite.y);
                  break;
                case 'u' :
                  MoveSprite(0, &sprite, sprite.x, sprite.y - 1);
                  break;
                case 'd' :
                  MoveSprite(0, &sprite, sprite.x, sprite.y + 1);
                  break;
        }
        if (c == 'q' ) {
                FreeSprite(sp);
                break;
        }
    }
}
```

Copper Processor Disassembler

In the Amiga, the Copper processor is the video microprocessor. It can be monitored by looking at the program counter (the PC) while a program is executing. The PC is essentially the Amiga's pointer to the Copper processor. The Copper Processor Disassembler program allows you to move forward and backward in memory by pressing the semicolon (;) and colon (:) keys, respectively. You can examine the contents of a memory location by pressing the slash (/) key. You can go to any location in memory by typing P followed by the desired memory location. Finally, if you want to "hunt" for something in memory, you type H, followed by the number of words

you want to search for and then the specific words. All in all, the
Copper Processor Disassembler is a most interesting program for
examining any part of the Amiga's memory.

```
/*
 * Copper List Disassembler
 *
 * PRESS:              RESULT:
 *    '/'              Disassemble instructions at PC
 *    ';'              Increment PC and disassemble
 *    ':'              Decrement PC and disassemble
 *    'p'              Set the program counter
 *    'h'              Enter hunt mode
 *    's'              Print address of current copper list
 *    '='              Enter a word into memory at current address
 *    'q'              Quit the program
 * In hunt mode, enter number of words you want to search
 * for, then enter the words one by one. To toggle ROM
 * search, enter a negative number as the number of bytes.
 * (Without the ROM search, only the RAM will be searched.)
 * To quit hunting, enter zero as number of bytes.
 */

#include <exec/types.h>
#include <graphics/gfxbase.h>
#include <graphics/view.h>
#include <graphics/copper.h>

void hunt();
int *OpenLibrary();

struct IntuitionBase *IntuitionBase;
struct GfxBase *GfxBase;

main()
{
        struct View *View;
        unsigned short i, j, *p, *pc;
        char c[3];
        int k;
        UWORD *clist;
        IntuitionBase =
                (struct IntuitionBase *)OpenLibrary("intuition.library", 0);
```

```
        GfxBase = (struct GfxBase *)OpenLibrary("graphics.library", 0);
        if (GfxBase == NULL || IntuitionBase == NULL) {
                printf("Can't open library.\n");
                exit(0);
        }
        p = 0;
        while (1) {
                printf(">");
                scanf("%s", &c);
                switch(c[0]) {
                case ':':
                        pc -= 2;
                        goto doline;
                case ';':
                        pc += 2;
                case '/':
doline:
                        p = pc;
                        printf("%06x:", p);
                        i = *p++;
                        j = *p++;
                        printf(" %04x %04x   ", i, j);
                        if ((i & 1) == 0) {    /* MOVE */
                                printf("MOVE #%04x,%03x ", j, i);
                        }
                        else {
                                if ((j & 1) == 0)
                                        printf("WAIT");
                                else
                                        printf("SKIP");
                                printf(" HP:%02x VP:%02x  HE:%02x VE:%02x BD=%x ",
                                        (i >> 1) & 0x7f, (i >> 8),
                                        (j >> 1) & 0x7f, (j >> 8) & 0x7f,
                                        (j & 0x8000) && 1
                                        );
                        }
                        break;
                case '=':
                        printf("%06x: %04x ", (int)pc, *pc);
                        scanf("%x", &k);
                        *pc = (short)k;
                        break;
```

```c
                        case 'p' :
                                printf("PC=");
                                scanf("%x", &pc);
                                break;
                        case 's' :
                                clist = GfxBase->ActiView->LOFCprList->start;
                                printf("CList is at %06x\n", (int)clist);
                                break;
                        case 'h' :
                                hunt();
                                break;
                        case 'q' :
                                exit(1);
                                break;
                        }
                }
        }

        void hunt()
        {
                static short *ptr, *tmp, i = 1, word[16];
                static int j, k, n, f, skip = 0;

                while (1) {
                        j = 0;
                        printf("\nHUNT:");
                        scanf("%d", &f);
                        if (f == 0)
                                return;
                        if (f < 0) {
                                skip = ~skip ;
                                printf("ROM search ");
                                if (skip)
                                        printf("off");
                                else
                                        printf("on");
                                continue;
                        }
                        while (f--) {
                                printf("? ");
                                scanf("%x", &n);
                                word[j++] = (short)n;
                        }
```

```
                     for (ptr = (short *)0; ptr < (short *)0x40000; ptr++) {
                             tmp = ptr;
                             for (k = 0; k < j; k++)
                                     if (*tmp++ != word[k])
                                             goto notfound;
                             if (ptr!= word)
                                     printf(" %06x", (int)ptr);
notfound:

                             if ( !skip ) {
                                     tmp = ptr + 0xf80000;
                                     for (k = 0; k < j; k++)
                                             if (*tmp++ != word[k])
                                                     goto notfound2;
                                     printf(" %06x", 0xf80000 + (int)ptr);
notfound2:

                                     tmp = ((short *)0xfc0000) + ptr;
                                     for (k = 0; k < j; k++) {
                                             if (*tmp++ != word[k])
                                                     continue;
                                     }
                                     printf(" %08x", (int)ptr + 0xfc0000);
                             }
                     }
             }
             return;
}
```

Blitter Screen

In addition to sprites, another Amiga graphics function is the *blitter*
operation. This function is used in the Blitter Screen program to fill
the entire screen with a pattern. The screen is in 320-by-200 res-
olution mode and will be filled using three different *planes* of graphics. These planes make up the colors that will be displayed on the
graphics screen.

```
/*
 * Program Bitmap
 * This program creates a 320-by-200 bitmapped screen with 3 bitplanes.
 * After they're up, the blitter will fill the screen with a pattern.
 */

#define DEPTH 3                          /* Number of bitplanes */
#define WIDTH 320                        /* Horizontal resolution */
#define HEIGHT 200                       /* Vertical resolution */

#include <exec/types.h>
#include <exec/exec.h>
#include <graphics/gfx.h>
#include <graphics/view.h>
#include <graphics/rastport.h>
#include <hardware/dmabits.h>
#include <hardware/custom.h>
#include <hardware/blit.h>

struct Custom custom;
struct GfxBase *GfxBase;

main()
{
        struct View v;
        struct ViewPort vp;
        struct RasInfo ri;
        struct BitMap b;
        struct ColorMap cm;
        int n, i, x, y;
        UWORD *w;
        static UWORD color[] = {                /* 3 planes, 8 colors possible*/
                0x000, 0x888, 0x444, 0xfff,     /* Shades of gray */
                0x00f, 0x0f0, 0xf00, 0x707      /* Some colors */
        };

        static UWORD tilemap [DEPTH] [16] = {
                {
                        0x3838, 0x3838, 0xfffb, 0xfffb,
                        0xfffb, 0x0038, 0x3838, 0x3838,
                        0x3838, 0x3838, 0xfbff, 0xfbff,
                        0xfbff, 0x3800, 0x3838, 0x3838
                },
```

```
          {
                  0x1414, 0x1414, 0x0014, 0xffd7,
                  0x0014, 0xffd7, 0x1414, 0x1414,
                  0x1414, 0x1414, 0x1400, 0xd7ff,
                  0x1400, 0xd7ff, 0x1414, 0x1414
          },
          {
                  0, 0, 0, 0, 0, 0, 0, 0, 0, 0, 0, 0, 0, 0, 0, 0
          }     /* 16 zeros here */
};

for (i = 0; i < DEPTH; i++) {    /* Allocate enough memory for bitmap */
        if ((b.Planes [i] =
                (PLANEPTR)AllocMem(WIDTH * HEIGHT * DEPTH / 8,
                MEMF_CLEAR)) == NULL) {
                printf("Out of memory!  Try using fewer planes.\n");
                exit (0);
        }
}


/* Open graphics library */
GfxBase = (struct GfxBase *)OpenLibrary("graphics.library", 0);
if (GfxBase == NULL) {
        printf("Can't open graphics library.\n");
        exit(0);
}
InitView(&v) ;          /* Initialize View structure with default values */
v.ViewPort = &vp;       /* Link View and Viewport structures */

InitBitMap(&b, DEPTH, WIDTH, HEIGHT);   /* Set up Bitmap structure */

ri.BitMap = &b;         /* Link Bitmap to RasInfo structure */
ri.RxOffset = 0;
ri.RyOffset = 0;

cm.Type = 0;                    /* Type zero means UWORD color array */
cm.ColorTabl color;             /* Point to color array */
cm.Count = 8;

InitVPort (&vp);                /* Initialize default ViewPort values */
vp.ColorMap = &cm;              /* Give ViewPort some specs */
vp.Dwidth = WIDTH;
vp.DHeight = HEIGHT;
```

```
vp.Next = NULL;
vp.RasInfo = &ri;

MakeVPort (&v, &vp);          /* Create intermediate Copper List */
MrgCop (&v);                  /* Merge Copper List */
LoadView (&v);               /* Use new Copper List */
ON_DISPLAY;                  /* Enable display */
/* Transfer tile image to top left of screen */
for (n = 0; n < DEPTH; n++)
        for (w = (UWORD *)b.Planes [n], i = 0; i < 16; i++) {
                w += (WIDTH / 16)
                *w = tilemap [n] [i];
        }
        /* Copy tile all over screen */
        for (x = 0; x < WIDTH / 16; x++)
                for (y = 0; y < HEIGHT / 16; y++)
                        BltBitMap(&b, 0, 0, &b, x * 16, y * 16, 16, 16,
                                0xc0, 0xff, 0);
}
}
```

Mandelbrot Explorer

Unlike BASIC, the C programming language can be used to go to the "heart" of the Amiga. Because of this "low-level" capability, C can access information from a variety of sources, including the mouse. With the Mandelbrot Explorer program, you can move the mouse to a certain location on a screen full of graphics and "zoom in" on a particular spot. This program highlights the power and speed of C in comparison to a language like BASIC. This C program runs in just a few minutes, and a BASIC version takes six hours to run.

```
/* Mandelbrot Explorer
 *
 * This program explores the mandelbrot set. x1 x2 and y1 y2 are the
 * real and imaginary boundaries, respectively. After initial
 * boundaries are entered, new boundaries (zoom) can be found by
 * placing the mouse in the desired location and pressing the left
 * button.
 *
```

```
 * To exit the program, move the mouse to the upper left side of the
 * screen, then press the left button. Then, you can save the screen
 * that was just created by answering the computer's questions.
 * Later, if you want to view the same plot, just run this program
 * and answer 'y' when the computer asks, "Do you want to see an old plot?"
 * Then enter the name of the previously saved plot file.
 *
 * Try these values for x1 x2 y1 y2:
 *      -2.00  0.50  -1.25  1.25     Most of the plot can be seen.
 *      -0.30  0.30  -1.10 -0.50     Zoom in to see part of it.
 *       0.00  0.30  -0.80 -0.50     Zoom in further.
 *       0.12  0.16  -0.70 -0.59     Even further. Wow! It's beautiful.
 */

#include <exec/types.h>
#include <intuition/intuition.h>
#include <graphics/gfxmacros.h>
#include <stdio.h>    /* For Lattice, it's <lattice/stdio.h> */
#include <libraries/dos.h>

PLANEPTR AllocRaster();

struct IntuitionBase *IntuitionBase;
struct GfxBase *GfxBase;

#define HEIGHT 200       /* Vertical resolution */
#define WIDTH  320       /* Horizontal resolution */
#define DEPTH  5         /* Number of bit planes */

#define XSIZ   WIDTH
#define YSIZ   HEIGHT

#define NCOLORS 64        /* Number of colors in colormap */

#define CMBITS 6          /* Log2 of NCOLORS */
#define CMSIZ  (1<<CMBITS)

#define NBITS  26
#define BSIZ   ((double)(1<<NBITS))

#define bd(x)  ((int)((x) * BSIZ))

int *OpenLibrary();
```

```
struct sh {
        unsigned short hi;
        unsigned short lo;
};


int x1, y1, x2, y2;
int dx, dy, rdx, rdy, pdx, pdy;
double rx1, ry1, rx2, ry2;



main()
{
        register int i, x, y, px, py, color;
        struct IntuiMessage *message, *GetMsg();
        struct RastPort *rp;
        struct ViewPort *vp, *ViewPortAddress();
        struct Window *Window, *OpenWindow();
        struct BitMap bm;
        struct Screen *Screen, *OpenScreen();
        static struct NewScreen NewScreen = {
                0, 0, WIDTH, HEIGHT, DEPTH, 0, 1, NULL,
                CUSTOMSCREEN | CUSTOMBITMAP,
                NULL, NULL, NULL, NULL
        };
        static struct NewWindow NewWindow = {
                0, 0, WIDTH, HEIGHT, 0, 1, CLOSEWINDOW | MOUSEBUTTONS,
                ACTIVATE | SMART_REFRESH | WINDOWCLOSE,
                NULL, NULL, NULL, NULL, NULL, WIDTH, HEIGHT, WIDTH,
                HEIGHT, CUSTOMSCREEN
        };
        char str[10], name[80];

        printf("\Do you want to see an old plot? (y/n) ");
        scanf("%s", str);
        if (*str == 'y') {
                printf("\nEnter filename:");
                scanf("%s", name);
        }
        else {
                printf("x1 x2 y1 y2 -> ");
                scanf("%lf %lf %lf %lf", &rx1, &rx2, &ry1, &ry2);
```

```
            x1 = bd(rx1);
            x2 = bd(rx2);
            y1 = bd(ry1);
            y2 = bd(ry2);

            dx = x2 - x1;
            dy = y2 - y1;
            pdx = dx / SIZ;
            pdy = dy / SIZ;
}


IntuitionBase =
        (struct IntuitionBase *)OpenLibrary("intuition.library", 0);
if (IntuitionBase == NULL)
        exit(FALSE);


GfxBase = (struct GfxBase *)
        OpenLibrary("graphics.library", 0);
if (GfxBase == NULL)
        exit(FALSE);


InitBitMap(&bm, DEPTH, WIDTH, HEIGHT);
for (i = 0; i < DEPTH; i++)
{
        bm.Planes[i] = (PLANEPTR)AllocRaster(WIDTH, HEIGHT);
        if (bm.Planes[i] == (PLANEPTR)NULL) {
                printf("Out of memory.\n");
                exit(FALSE);
        }
}
NewScreen.CustomBitMap = &bm;
if ((Screen = (struct Screen *)OpenScreen(&NewScreen)) == NULL)
        exit(0);


NewWindow.Screen = Screen;
if ((Window = (struct Window *)OpenWindow(&NewWindow)) == NULL)
        exit(FALSE);


rp = Window -> RPort;
vp = ViewPortAddress(Window);


SetDrMd( rp, JAM1);        /* Set draw mode to JAM1 */
```

```
        LoadColors(vp);          /* Load color map for this viewport */

        if (*str == 'y' ) {
                fileRW(&bm, 'r', name);
                Wait(1 << Window->UserPort->mp_SigBit); /* Wait for a message */
                CloseWindow(Window);
                CloseScreen(Screen);
                exit(TRUE);
        }
Start:
        printf("%d %d %d %d %d %d\n", x1, y1, x2, y2, dx, dy);
        SetRast( rp, 0 );        /* Initialize entire rastport to color 0 */
        for (py = 0, y = y1; py < YSIZ; py++, y += pdy)
                for (px = 0, x = x1; px < XSIZ; px++, x += pdx) {

                        if (Window->UserPort->mp_SigBit) {   /* a message? */
enter:
                                message = GetMsg(Window->UserPort);
                                if (message->Class == MOUSEBUTTONS) {
                                        ReScale(message->MouseX,
                                                message->MouseY);
                                        goto Start;
                                }
                                else if (message->Class == CLOSEWINDOW) {
                                        WBenchToFront();
                                        printf("\nShould I save this plot for \
future viewing? (y/n) ");
                                        scanf("%s", str);
                                        if (*str == 'y') {
                                                printf("\nEnter filename:");
                                                scanf("%s", name);
                                                fileRW(&bm, 'w', name);
                                        }
                                        CloseWindow(Window);
                                        CloseScreen(Screen);
                                        exit(TRUE);
                                }
                        }
                        color = mandel(x, y);
                        Color(rp, color, px, py);

                }
```

```
            Wait(1 << Window->UserPort->mp_SigBit); /* wait for a message */
            goto enter;
}

mandel(ax, ay)
int ax, ay;
{
            register int zx, zy;
            register int wx, wy, mag;

            int iter, color;

            iter = zx = zy  = wx = wy = mag = 0;

            while (mag <= (4 << NBITS) && iter < NCOLORS) {
                    iter++;

                    zy <<= 1;
                    zy = bmul(zx, zy);
                    zy += ay;

                    zx = ax;
                    zx += wx;
                    zx -= wy;

                    wx = bmul(zx, zx);
                    wy = bmul(zy, zy);
                    mag = wx;
                    mag += wy;
            }
            color = ((iter << CMBITS) / COLORS) & (CMSIZ - 1);
            return scale(color);      /* Just a little more color resolution */
}

bmul(a, b)       /* 64-bit multiply with built-in right shift NBITS */
int a, b;
{
            register unsigned short alo, blo;
            register unsigned short ahi, bhi;
            register int z;

            int sgn;
```

```
        sgn = a ^ b;

        a = (a >= 0) ? a : -a;
        b = (b >= 0) ? b : -b;

        alo = ((struct sh *)(&a))->lo;
        ahi = ((struct sh *)(&a))->hi;

        blo = ((struct sh *)(&b))->lo;
        bhi = ((struct sh *)(&b))->hi;

        z = (((unsigned)(alo*blo)) >> NBITS)
                + (((unsigned)(alo*bhi + ahi*blo)) >> (NBITS - 16))
                        + (((unsigned)(ahi*bhi)) << (32 - NBITS));

        return ((sgn >= 0) ? z : -z);
}


Color(rp, color, x, y)     /* Get color of crayon, and draw pixel */
struct RastPort *rp;
SHORT color, x, y;
{
        SetAPen( rp, color);
        WritePixel( rp, x, y);
}


LoadColors(vp)            /* Set up color map */
struct ViewPort *vp;
{
        register int n;
        register int r, g, b;

        n = 0;
        for (r = 0; r < 16; r += 8) {
                for (g = 0; g < 16; g += 4) {
                        for (b = 0; b < 16; b += 4) {
                                if (n > 32) return(TRUE);
                                SetRGB4( vp, n, r, g, b );
                                n++;
                        }
                }
        }
}
```

```
ReScale(mx, my)     /* Scale new coordinates */
WORD mx, my;
{
        double cx1, cx2, cy1, cy2;
        cx1 = (double)((mx - 40) / SIZ * (rx2 - rx1)) + rx1;
        rx1 = cx1;
        cx2 = (double)((mx+40) / SIZ * (rx2 - rx1)) + rx1;
        rx2 = cx2;
        cy1 = (double)((my - 40) / SIZ * (ry2 - ry1)) + ry1;
        ry1 = cy1;
        cy2 = (double)((my+40) / SIZ * (ry2 - ry1)) + ry1;
        ry2 = cy2;

        x1 = bd(cx1);
        x2 = bd(cx2);
        y1 = bd(cy1);
        y2 = bd(cy2);

        dx = x2 - x1;
        dy = y2 - y1;
        pdx = dx / SIZ;
        pdy = dy / SIZ;

}


/* Reuse the 32 colors for more definition. As the mandelbrot quantity
 * reaches 32, the colors start over. If very small numbers are to be
 * used for x1, x2, y1, and y2, then NCOLORS should be increased.
 */
scale(colors)
int colors;
{
        int sc;

        sc = colors / 2;
        return colors - sc * 32;

}
```

```
/* General purpose load/save routine for bitmaps
 *
 * bm is a pointer to your BitMap structure.
 * c ='r' for load and 'w' for save.
 * Note: you might want to save the current colors as well.
 */

fileRW(bm, c, name)
struct BitMap *bm;
char c, *name;
{
        FILE *fp, *Open();
        int len, plane, bytes, mode;

        if (c == 'r')
                mode = MODE_OLDFILE;
        else if (c == 'w')
                mode = MODE_NEWFILE;
        else {
                printf("\nInvalid I/O mode");
                return 0;
}
if ((fp = Open(name, mode)) == NULL) {
        printf("\nCant open %s", name);
        return 0;
}
bytes = (bm->BytesPerRow)*(bm->Rows);
for (plane = 0; plane <  bm->Depth; plane++) {
        if (c == 'r')
                len = Read(fp, bm->Planes[plane], bytes);
        else
                len = Write(fp, bm->Planes[plane], bytes);
        if (len != bytes) {
                printf("\nError in I/O to file %s", name);
                Close(fp);
                return 0;
        }
}
Close(fp);
return 1;
}
```

Mouse Function

The Mandelbrot Explorer program introduced you to the mouse; the Mouse Function takes the use of the mouse one step farther. The Mouse Function monitors the x and y coordinates of the mouse position on the screen. The function can be useful as a component of a larger drawing program or in a program that uses the mouse's position to make choices. Note that the function is not a complete program because the lines contain no main( ) function; instead, the Mouse Function would be used in a larger program to monitor mouse activity. The Mouse Function also checks the mouse button. The function returns a value of zero (0) if the mouse button has not been pressed and the mouse has not moved. If the mouse button has been pressed, a -1 is returned. If the mouse has moved but the mouse button has not been pressed, a 1 is returned.

```
/* Mouse Function
 *
 * This function updates absolute x and y coordinates of the mouse.
 * Before calling mouse() in your program, you must call initmouse().
 * Initmouse needs to be called only once. Subsequent calls to mouse()
 * will update global variables 'x' and 'y'. You must call mouse() at least
 * 50 to 60 times a second. mouse() should be part of an interrupt routine
 * that gets called every screen refresh (60 times a second).
 * mouse() returns zero if the mouse has not moved since the last call and
 * the left button is not currently pressed, otherwise it returns -1
 * for button pressed, and 1 for not pressed.
 */

#include <exec/types.h>

#define MAXX 319     /* Mouse maximum and minimum allowable values */
#define MINX 0
#define MAXY 199
#define MINY 0
#define abs(x)  (((x)<0)?(-(x)):(x))

WORD x, y;        /* Mouse x and y coords */
char oldx, oldy;  /* Used by mouse func */

initmouse(xi, yi)
WORD xi, yi;
```

```
{
        WORD r;

        x = xi;
        y = yi;
        r = *((WORD *)0xdf000a);
        oldx = (char)r;
        oldy = (char)(r >> 8);
}

mouse()          /* Get new mouse location; return 0 if no change. */
{
        WORD r;
        register WORD dx, dy;
        register char newx, newy;
        char button;

        r = *((WORD *)0xdf000a);
        newx = (char)r;
        newy = (char)(r >> 8);
        dx = (WORD)(newx - oldx);
        dy = (WORD)(newy - oldy);
        button = (*((unsigned char *)0xbfe001)) & 0x40;
        if ( dx == 0 && dy == 0 && button )
                return 0; /* No movement, no button */
        if (abs(dx) > 127) {
                if (dx < 0)
                        dx += 0x100;
                else
                        dx = 0x100 - dx;
        }
        if (abs(dy) > 127) {
                if (dy < 0)
                        dy += 0x100;
                else
                        dy = 0x100 - dy;
        }
```

```
         x += dx;
         y += dy;
         if (x > MAXX)
                 x = MAXX;              /* Range check */
         else if (x < MINX)
                 x = MINX;
         if (y > MAXY)
                 y = MAXY;
         else if (y < MINY)
                 y = MINY;
         oldx = newx;
         oldy = newy;
         if (button)
                 return 1;   /* Button has not been pressed */
         return -1;          /* Fire! */
}
```

New Screens

The first example in this section, Window Maker, creates a new
window on the Amiga. The New Screens program creates a new
screen on the Amiga. The screen created uses the Topaz font, has
80 characters per line, uses normal text style, and displays "Hello
there!" as the title of the screen. In addition, sprites, dual playfields,
high-resolution, and an interlaced display are all possible with this
new screen. Notice that all this is accomplished with only 59 lines
of C program code!

```
/* Here's how you open a new screen */

#include <exec/types.h>
#include <intuition/intuition.h>

struct IntuitionBase *IntuitionBase;
int *OpenLibrary(), *OpenScreen();

main()
```

```
{
        static struct TextAttr font = {
                (UBYTE *)"topaz.font",    /* Font name */
                TOPAZ_EIGHTY,    /* Eighty-column size */
                FS_NORMAL,       /* Normal font style */
                FPF_ROMFONT
        };

        static struct NewScreen Nscr = {
                0,    /* Not implemented, set to zero for upward compatibility */
                0,    /* Top of screen */
                320, /* 320 for lores, 640 for hires */
                200, /* 400 for interlaced, 200 for noninterlaced */
                2,    /* Number of colors = 2 ^ Depth   (in this case, 2^2=4) */
                0,    /* Color register number for gadgets, titlebar, etc. */
                1,    /* Color register number for block fills. */
                SPRITES, /* We want to use sprites. Other flags that
                                * may be set are:
                                * HIRES for high resolution display
                                *     (640 pixels across)
                                * INTERLACE for interlaced display
                                * DUALPF for two playfields
                                * HAM for hold and modify mode
                                */
                CUSTOMSCREEN, /* Type of screen. If you have your own bitmap
                                    * also set the CUSTOMBITMAP flag.
                                    * See CustomBitMap below.
                                    */
                &font, /* text font */
                (UBYTE *)"Hello there!", /* Title of the screen */
                NULL, /* Pointer to linked list of gadgets */
                NULL, /* Point to your own BitMap structure if you want
                            * to use your own display memory.
                            */
        };

        struct Screen *screen;

        IntuitionBase =
                (struct IntuitionBase *)OpenLibrary("intuition.library", 29);
        if (IntuitionBase == NULL) {
                printf("Can't open library");
                exit(0);
        }
```

```
screen = (struct Screen *)OpenScreen(&Nscr);
if (screen == (struct Screen *)NULL ) {
        printf("Can't open new screen.\n");
        exit(0);
}
}
```

Mouse Sprite

Up to this point, you have used sprites and the mouse independently.
The Mouse Sprite program moves a sprite around the screen at the
command of the mouse. Instead of using the U, D, L, and R keys,
you now can move the sprite with the mouse. Notice that Mouse
Sprite uses the Mouse Function shown in an earlier example. One
of the strengths of C is that functions can be written and debugged
and then used repeatedly.

```
/*
 * Simple Mouse Sprite
 *
 * Move the sprite around using the mouse
 */

#include <exec/types.h>
#include <exec/exec.h>
#include <graphics/gfx.h>
#include <graphics/sprite.h>
#include <hardware/dmabits.h>
#include <hardware/custom.h>
#include <hardware/blit.h>
#define abs(x)  (((x)<0)?(-(x)):(x))

WORD x, y;          /* Mouse x and y */
struct SimpleSprite sprite;
UWORD sprite_data[] =
{
        100, 100,   /* Position */
        0xff00, 0xff00,
        0xff00, 0xff00,
        0xff00, 0xff00,
        0xff00, 0x00ff,
```

```
        0xff00, 0x00ff,
        0xff00, 0x00ff,
        0xf0f0, 0xff00,
        0xf0f0, 0xff00,
        0xf0f0, 0xff00,
        0xffff, 0xffff,
        0xffff, 0xffff,
        0xffff, 0xffff
};

struct GfxBase *GfxBase;
int *OpenLibrary();

main()
{
        int c, sp;

        GfxBase = (struct GfxBase *)OpenLibrary("graphics.library", 0);
        if (GfxBase == (struct GfxBase *)NULL) {
                printf("no lib");
                exit(0);
        }
        if ((sp = GetSprite(&sprite, -1)) == -1) { /* Get any sprite */
                printf("No sprite available.\n");
                exit(0);
        }
        sprite.height = 12;             /* 12 lines high */

        ChangeSprite(0, &sprite, sprite_data);

        initmouse(10, 10);

        while (1) {
                while (!(c = mouse()));  /* Get new mouse coordinates */
                if (c == -1) {           /* If the left button is pressed, */
                        FreeSprite(sp);  /* free the sprite */
                        exit(1);         /* and quit. */
                }
                MoveSprite(0, &sprite, x, y);
        }
}
```

```
#define MAXX 319     /* Mouse maximum and minimum allowable values */
#define MINX 0
#define MAXY 199
#define MINY 0

char oldx, oldy;   /* Used by mouse func */

initmouse(xi, yi)
WORD xi, yi;
{
        WORD r;

        x = xi;
        y = yi;
        r = *((WORD *)0xdf000a);
        oldx = (char)r;
        oldy = (char)(r >> 8);
}

mouse() /* Get new mouse location; return 0 if no change. */
{
        WORD r;
        register WORD dx, dy;
        register char newx, newy;
        char button;

        r = *((WORD *)0xdf000a);
        newx = (char)r;
        newy = (char)(r >> 8);
        dx = (WORD)(newx - oldx);
        dy = (WORD)(newy - oldy);
        button = (*((unsigned char *)0xbfe001)) & 0x40;
        if (dx == 0 && dy == 0 && button)
                return 0; /* No movement, no button */
        if (abs(dx) > 127) {
                if (dx < 0)
                        dx += 0x100;
                else
                        dx = 0x100 - dx;
        }
```

```
        if (abs(dy) > 127) {
                if (dy < 0)
                        dy += 0x100;
                else
                        dy = 0x100 - dy;
        }
        x += dx;
        y += dy;
        if (x > MAXX)
                x = MAXX;               /* Range check */
        else if (x < MINX)
                x = MINX;
        if (y > MAXY)
                y = MAXY;
        else if (y < MINY)
                y = MINY;
        oldx = newx;
        oldy = newy;
        if (button)
                return 1;   /* Button has not been pressed */
        return -1;          /* Fire! */
}
```

Blitter with the Mouse

The Mouse Bitmap program integrates the Mouse function with the
Blitter Screen program. After the screen fills with a pattern, you can
use the mouse to move the object on the screen. The mouse starts
at coordinates (100, 140), as established by the #define command.

```
/* Mouse Bitmap
 *
 * This program creates a 320-by-200 bitmapped screen with 3 bitplanes.
 * Then the blitter fills the screen with a pattern.
 * Finally, a mouse-controlled object appears.
 */

#define DEPTH 3      /* Number of bitplanes */
#define WIDTH 320    /* Horizontal resolution */
#define HEIGHT 200   /* Vertical resolution */
```

```
#define MAXX (WIDTH-16)       /* Mouse maximum and minimum allowable values */
#define MINX 0
#define MAXY (HEIGHT-16)
#define MINY 0

#define XINIT 100     /* Start the mouse at 100, 140 */
#define YINIT 140
#define abs(x)  (((x)<0)?(-(x)):(x))

#include <exec/types. h>
#include <exec/exec. h>
#include <graphics/gfx. h>
#include <graphics/view. h>
#include <graphics/rastport. h>
#include <hardware/dmabits. h>
#include <hardware/custom. h>
#include <hardware/blit. h>

WORD x, y;    /* Mouse x and y */

struct Custom custom;
struct GfxBase *GfxBase;
int *OpenLibrary(), *AllocMem();

main()
{
        struct View v;
        struct ViewPort vp;
        struct RasInfo ri;
        struct BitMap bm, shipBM, bufrBM;
        struct ColorMap cm;
        int n, i;
        WORD ox, oy;
        UWORD *w;
        static UWORD color[] = {     /* With 3 planes, 8 colors are possible */
                0x000, 0xaaa, 0x555, 0xfff,  /* Shades of gray */
                0x5, 0xa, 0xf00, 0xf   /* Red and shades of blue */
        };
```

```
static UWORD tilemap[DEPTH][16] = { /* Define the pattern of tiles */
        {
                0x3838, 0x3838, 0xfffb, 0xfffb,
                0xfffb, 0x0038, 0x3838, 0x3838,
                0x3838, 0x3838, 0xfbff, 0xfbff,
                0xfbff, 0x3800, 0x3838, 0x3838
        },
        {
                0x1414, 0x1414, 0x0014, 0xffd7,
                0x0014, 0xffd7, 0x1414, 0x1414,
                0x1414, 0x1414, 0x1400, 0xd7ff,
                0x1400, 0xd7ff, 0x1414, 0x1414
        },
        {
                0, 0, 0, 0, 0, 0, 0, 0, 0, 0, 0, 0, 0, 0, 0, 0
        }
};
static UWORD bufrMap[DEPTH][16], shipMap[DEPTH][16] = { /* Define ship */
        {
                0xfffe, 0xfffc, 0xfff8, 0xfff0,
                0xffe0, 0xffc0, 0xff80, 0xfe00,
                0xfe00, 0xff80, 0xffc0, 0xffe0,
                0xfff0, 0xfff8, 0xfffc, 0xfffe
        },
        {
                0x8000, 0xc000, 0xe000, 0xf000,
                0xf800, 0xfc00, 0xfe00, 0xff80,
                0xff80, 0xfe00, 0xfc00, 0xf800,
                0xf000, 0xe000, 0xc000, 0x8000
        },
        {
                0xffff, 0xffff, 0xffff, 0xffff,
                0xffff, 0xffff, 0xffff, 0xffff,
                0xffff, 0xffff, 0xffff, 0xffff,
                0xffff, 0xffff, 0xffff, 0xffff
        }
```

```
};  /* Blue pyramid */

for (i = 0;  i < DEPTH;  i ++) {    /* Allocate enough memory
                                     * for the bitmap
                                     */
        bm.Planes[i] =
                (PLANEPTR)AllocMem(WIDTH * HEIGHT * DEPTH / 8,
                        MEMF_CLEAR);
        if (bm.Planes[i] == (PLANEPTR)NULL ) {
                printf("Out of memory! Try using fewer planes. \n");
                exit(0);
        }

        /* Make plane pointers point to the shape we defined */
        shipBM.Planes[i] = (PLANEPTR)shipMap[i];
        bufrBM.Planes[i] = (PLANEPTR)bufrMap[i];
}
/* Open the graphics library */
GfxBase = (struct GfxBase *) OpenLibrary("graphics.library", 0);
if (GfxBase == (struct GfxBase *)NULL) {
        printf("Can't open graphics library. \n");
        exit(0);
}

InitView(&v);     /* Init the view structure with default values */
v.ViewPort = &vp; /* Link the view and viewport structures */
InitBitMap(&bm,  DEPTH, WIDTH, HEIGHT); /* Set up the BitMap
                                         * structures
                                         */
InitBitMap(&shipBM,  DEPTH,  16,  16);
InitBitMap(&bufrBM,  DEPTH,  16,  16);

ri.BitMap = &bm;    /* Link the main BitMap to RasInfo structure */
ri.RxOffset = 0;
ri.RyOffset = 0;

cm.Type = 0;            /* Type zero means UWORD color array */
cm.ColorTable = (APTR)color; /* Point to the color array */
cm.Count = 8;

InitVPort(&vp); /* Init default ViewPort values */
```

```
vp.ColorMap = &cm;   /* Give the ViewPort some specs */
vp.DWidth = WIDTH;
vp.DHeight = HEIGHT;
vp.Next = NULL;
vp.RasInfo = &ri;

MakeVPort(&v, &vp); /* Create an intermediate Copper list */

MrgCop(&v);      /* Merge the Copper list */

LoadView(&v);   /* Use the new Copper list */

/* Transfer tile image to top left of screen */
for (n = 0; n < DEPTH; n++)
        for (w = (UWORD *)bm.Planes[n], i = 0;
                i < 16; i++, w += (WIDTH / 16))
                *w = tilemap[n][i];

/* Copy the tile all over the screen */
for (x = 0; x < WIDTH / 16; x++)
        for (y = 0; y < HEIGHT / 16; y++)
                BltBitMap(&bm, 0, 0, &bm, x * 16, y * 16,
                        16, 16, 0xc0, 0xff, 0);

ox = XINIT;
oy = YINIT;
BltBitMap(&bm, ox, oy, &bufrBM, 0, 0,
        16, 16, 0xc0, 0xff, 0); /* Save background */
initmouse(XINIT, YINIT); /* Init the mouse routine */
while (1) {  /* Reset the machine to stop the prog */
        ox = x;
        oy = y;
        while (!mouse()); /* Get new mouse coords */
        WaitTOF(); /* Avoid as much flicker as possible
                    * by timing the drawing
                    */
        BltBitMap(&bufrBM, 0, 0, &bm, ox, oy,
                16, 16, 0xc0, 0xff, 0); /* Restore bkg */
        BltBitMap(&bm, x, y, &bufrBM, 0, 0,
                16, 16, 0xc0, 0xff, 0); /* Save background */
        BltBitMap(&shipBM, 0, 0, &bm, x, y,
                16, 16, 0xc0, 0xff, 0); /* Draw ship */
}
}
```

```
char oldx, oldy; /* Used by mouse func */

initmouse(xi, yi)
WORD xi, yi;
{
        WORD r;

        x = xi;
        y = yi;
        r = *((WORD *)0xdf000a);
        oldx = (char)r;
        oldy = (char)(r >> 8);
}


mouse()  /* Get new mouse location, return 0 if no change */
{
        WORD r;
        register WORD dx, dy;
        char newx, newy;

        r = *((WORD *)0xdf000a);
        newx = (char)r;
        newy = (char)(r >> 8);
        dx = (WORD)(newx - oldx);
        dy = (WORD)(newy - oldy);
        if (dx == 0 && dy == 0)
                return 0; /* No movement */
        if (abs(dx) > 127) {
                if (dx < 0)
                        dx += 0x100;
                else
                        dx = 0x100 - dx;
        }
        if (abs(dy) > 127) {
                if (dy < 0)
                        dy += 0x100;
                else
                        dy = 0x100 - dy;
        }
```

```
x += dx;
y += dy;
if (x > MAXX)
        x = MAXX;           /* Range check */
else if (x < MINX)
        x = MINX;
if (y > MAXY)
        y = MAXY;
else if (y < MINY)
        y = MINY;
oldx = newx;
oldy = newy;
return 1;
}
```

More Information about C

If this chapter has whetted your appetite for C, you may want to purchase the Lattice C Compiler. Other C compilers for the Amiga are being developed and no doubt will be announced and advertised in the magazine *AmigaWorld*.

In addition to a compiler, you will need a book on the C programming language. Here is a list of recommended books:

Harbison, Samuel, and Guy Steele. *C: A Reference Manual.* Engelwood Cliffs, N.J.: Prentice-Hall, 1984.

Kernighan, Brian, and Dennis Ritchie. *The C Programming Language. Engelwood Cliffs, N.J.: Prentice-Hall, 1978. This book is considered the definitive text on the C language.*

Kochan, Steven. Programming in C. New York: Hayden, 1983.

Purdum, Jack. *C Programming Guide.* Indianapolis: Que Corporation, 1983.

Traister, Robert. *Going from BASIC to C.* Engelwood Cliffs, N.J.: Prentice-Hall, 1985.

In addition to a C compiler and a book for learning the C language, the developer's books from Commodore are recommended for serious Amiga programming. The set of developer's books contains the *Amiga ROM Kernal Manual* (two volumes), *AmigaDOS User's Manual*, and the hardware manual. This documentation explains the details of Amiga programming. The *ROM Kernal Manual* explains the 350 functions built into Kickstart and used to create animation sequences, stereo sound, and the other audiovisual capabilities of the Amiga. These routines can be accessed from assembly language or from C. These manuals are packed with information for taking full advantage of the power resident in the Amiga. Who knows . . . with C and the Amiga, you may even develop commercial software for sale.

Conclusion

Of the three languages described in this book, C is the most powerful, the most flexible, and the fastest. Of course, these features come at a price. The C language is also the most difficult to learn because of the variety of syntax rules, functions, and library capabilities it offers. Combined with the powerful capabilities of the Amiga, C is the language of choice for gaining access to these features.

8
Using AmigaDOS

The Amiga's Workbench satisfies most people's needs for operating the computer. With Workbench, you can perform essential computing tasks such as determining what files are on a disk, starting programs, and copying files from one disk to another. Workbench differs from the operating systems on most other microcomputers (except the Macintosh), because Workbench, for the most part, uses graphics instead of text. You use the mouse to tell the computer what you want to do, and the computer displays information in the form of icons.

As you become more experienced in using your Amiga, you may want its operating system to do more. For example, you may notice that although you save Amiga BASIC programs to a diskette, Workbench does not display the names of these programs when you examine that diskette's window. Also, you may prefer to use the keyboard, which is the "key" to more conventional disk operating systems such as MS-DOS®, rather than use the mouse. That is, you may prefer typing your commands instead of moving icons around the screen.

Fortunately, this kind of operating system is built into the Amiga's software. The system is called AmigaDOS, also known as CLI (Command Line Interface). DOS, as you may have guessed, is an acronym for disk operating system. AmigaDOS accepts commands typed directly from the keyboard and acts on them. This chapter examines how to access AmigaDOS and explains what its more important commands can do for you.

Accessing AmigaDOS

To access AmigaDOS, you turn on the Amiga, insert the Kickstart diskette, and then insert the Workbench diskette when the Amiga tells you to do so. After you open the Workbench window, select the Preferences icon and look for the part labeled CLI Yes No. Move the mouse so that the pointer is directed at the Yes box, and click the button so that the CLI choice section displays Yes. Now click the box called Save to tell the Amiga that you want CLI to be available from now on.

When the Workbench window reappears, double-click the System drawer and wait for that window to open. Notice now that a CLI icon is on the screen. Opening that icon accesses the Command Line Interface.

Using Directories

AmigaDOS can give you many kinds of information. Most of the time, the information you are going to need from the operating system is directory data. A *directory* is an alphabetically ordered list of files on a diskette. To display a directory, you use the DIR command.

To help you organize files on your disks, AmigaDOS has borrowed a concept used by many other operating systems: hierarchical directories. Some other operating systems that use this method to segregate files are UNIX™, MS-DOS, PC DOS, and Apple ProDOS®. *Hierarchical directories* simply means that each disk can have more than one directory, and that each directory can hold programs, data files, *and* additional directories. These additional directories can hold more files and more directories.

The easiest way to think of hierarchical directories is to visualize an upside down tree. The main or starting directory, which every disk has, is called the *root* directory. The root directory can hold files or additional directories, called *subdirectories*. Each subdirectory is like a tree branch. While a disk can have only one root directory, any branching directory can hold as many additional branches (subdirectories) as you like (as long as the disk has enough free space to hold the additional directories). Because every subdirectory can trace its "heritage" back to the root directory, a hierarchy of directories is established.

To put the concept of hierarchical directories into practice, imagine that you have a diskette called Diskone, which contains various Amiga BASIC programs as well as Amiga BASIC itself. You can group these programs into three categories: music, graphics, and utilities (which help programmers in their work).

Instead of using one large directory for all these programs, you can create four directories for Diskone. Think of the main directory as the tree's root and three subdirectories as branches, each with a name. Imagine that each program is a leaf with a name. The root holds the three smaller branches as well as a leaf called Amiga BASIC. Each of the three branches—labeled Music.Progs, Graphics, and Utilities—contains several leafs.

All the branches and leaves are closed to begin with. When you open the root (that is, examine the root directory), you find a leaf called Amiga BASIC and the names of the three smaller branches (the subdirectories). If you open any of the smaller branches (that is, examine a subdirectory), you see the leaves that those branches hold.

The purpose of a hierarchical directory system is to help organize the files on your disk. Most files can be categorized, and putting related groups of files in easily identifiable directories makes sense. Consider another example; assume that a disk contains files that have the following names:

WP Program
Financial Data
Picture 1
Database
Picture 3
Draw Machine
Picture 2
Essay
Term Paper
Mailing List

Quickly finding a specific file in this list would not be easy. And if this disk had 50 files, finding one particular file would be even more difficult. Arranging these files under subdirectories helps organize your data and make it easier to find. You might use subdirectories to arrange the preceding list of files something like this:

```
Word Processing.dir
    WP Program
    Essay
    Term Paper
Graphics.dir
    Draw Machine
    Picture 1
    Picture 2
    Picture 3
Data.dir
    Database
    Financial Data
    Mailing List
```

You can break down this list of files still further. Take the file called Mailing List as an example. You could divide this file into several files that represent different regions of the United States and create a subdirectory to store those files. Your revised list would look like this:

```
Word Processing.dir
    WP Program
    Essay
    Term Paper
Graphics.dir
    Draw Machine
    Picture 1
    Picture 2
    Picture 3
Data.dir
    Database
    Financial Data
Mailing.dir
    South
    North
    East
    West
```

As you can see, you can organize the many files on your disk to account for a variety of applications. Now that you have an idea of how you might organize your files and what a root directory and subdirectories are, you will look at how you can create and manipulate directories.

Using the DIR Command

The simplest way to list a directory is to type DIR and press RETURN. The system then displays the names of the files and subdirectories in the directory you are working with. As is the case with almost all AmigaDOS commands, the DIR command has a number of variations. They are as follows:

DIR <directory name>

If you want to list the files in a specific directory, use this format. For example, to list the names of files stored under Music.Progs, you type *DIR Music.Progs*. Remember that listing the files in a main directory is not necessarily the same as listing all the files on a disk. To list the names of files in a subdirectory, you type *DIR* and the subdirectory's name.

DIR OPT A

This format of the DIR command tells AmigaDOS "I want to list the DIRectory, and I want to exercise the OPTion to list *all* the subdirectories." This command displays every file name on a disk. The names of files stored under subdirectories are indented to show that they would otherwise not be on the main directory list.

DIR OPT D

This format lists only the names of the subdirectories on a disk. For example,

```
1> DIR OPT D
Music.Progs (dir)
Graphics (dir)
Utilities (dir)
1>
```

DIR OPT I

To display file names one at a time, use this format. A question mark appears after each file name, which indicates that AmigaDOS is waiting for your next command. Here are the commands you can issue:

RETURN   Display the next file name.

Q   Quit the listing.

E   Display the names of files in this directory.
           (Issue this command only if a directory is being
           displayed, of course.)

B	Back up to the previous directory level. For example, if you are at the first subdirectory level, this command moves you up to the main directory level.
D	Delete this directory if it contains no files.
DEL	Delete this file.
T	List the contents of this file on the screen. To stop the listing, press CTRL and C simultaneously.
?	Display the available options.

The following example demonstrates the use of the DIR OPT I command:

```
1> DIR OPT I
    Music.Progs (dir) ? E <RETURN>
                Bach.Bas ? <RETURN>
                Rock.Bas ? ? <RETURN>
    B=BACK/S; DEL=DELETE/S; E=ENTER/S; Q=QUIT/S: B <RETURN>
    Graphics (dir) ? <RETURN>
    Utilities (dir) ? Q <RETURN>

1>
```

What follows is a sample session that demonstrates how some of the other formats of the DIR command are used. The semicolon identifies a comment, which the Amiga ignores. In the sample sessions in this chapter, use the information following semicolons for your own reference. The 1> is the AmigaDOS prompt, which indicates that the system is ready to receive the next command.

```
1> DIR; this is the "root" directory
    Music.Progs (dir)
    Graphics (dir)
    Utilities (dir)
    Amiga BASIC

1> DIR Music.Progs; this lists the subdirectory Music.Progs
    Bach.Bas
    Rock.Bas
    Shock.Bas
```

```
1> DIR OPT A; this tells the computer to list all the files
      Music.Progs (dir)
            Bach.Bas
            Rock.Bas
            Shock.Bas
      Graphics (dir)
            Cube.Bas
            Perspect.Bas
            Sinewave.Bas
      Utilities (dir)
            Assem.Bas
            Editing.Bas
            Hexcode.Bas
      Amiga BASIC

1> DIR OPT D
      Music.Progs (dir)
      Graphics (dir)
      Utilities (dir)

1> ; end of sample session
```

When you use the DIR command, keep in mind that you are not limited to only one series of subdirectories under the root directory. You can create as many directories within directories as the Amiga's memory allows. To move down to the next level of directories, you use the slash mark (/). For example, if a subdirectory called Music.Progs (dir) had a subdirectory called Classics (dir), you could find out what files the Classics subdirectory contained by typing

```
1> DIR Music.Progs/Classics
```

The slash mark tells the system to move down one level from the Music.Progs subdirectory to the Classics subdirectory.

You can specify the disk drive you are referring to when you use DIR (and many other AmigaDOS commands) by using the expressions df0: and df1:. These expressions specify disk drive zero (the internal drive) and disk drive one (the external drive, if you have one), respectively. For example, to display the directory for the external disk drive, you type

```
DIR df1:
```

Using the LIST Command

The LIST command is a sophisticated version of DIR. LIST by itself displays information about files and directories on the disk drive and directory you are using. This information includes the file's name and size, any protection that the file may have, and the date and time that the file was last revised. If you used LIST with Diskone, the screen would display something similar to the following:

```
1> LIST
Directory ":" on Friday Feb-14-86
Music.Progs     Dir              rwed 25-Nov-85  21:23:02
Graphics        Dir              rmon 23-Nov-85  21:23:02
Music.Progs     Dir              rsat 21-Nov-85  21:23:02
Amiga BASIC            65234     rmon  10-Mar-85 10:53:02
Amiga BASIC.info       1320      rmon  10-Mar-85 10:05:23
2 files-3 directories-170 blocks used
```

You can use the LIST command in many other ways. If you type *LIST* and a file name, the screen displays information about that file only. If you type LIST and a directory name, the screen displays information about all the files in that directory. You also can use LIST in combination with the following DATE command options:

NODATES

This option does not display the dates that indicate when the files were created. Here is an example:

```
1> LIST NODATES
Directory ":" on Friday Feb-14-86
Music.Progs     Dir              rwed
Graphics        Dir              rmon
Music.Progs     Dir              rsat
Amiga BASIC            65234     rmonep
Amiga BASIC.info       1320      rmon
2 files-3 directories-170 blocks used
```

SINCE <date>

This option displays the files created since the date you specify. You can specify the date in a number of ways: by typing it in DD-MMM-YY format, by typing the day of the week (such as *TUESDAY*), or by typing *TODAY* or *YESTERDAY*.

UPTO <date>

This option is similar to SINCE, but displays the files created on or before the date you specify. Here is an example:

```
1> LIST UPTO 23-Nov-85
Directory ":" on Friday Feb-14-86
Graphics            Dir            rmon   23-Nov-85  21:23:02
Music.Progs         Dir            rsat   21-Nov-85  21:23:02
Amiga BASIC              65234      rmon   10-Mar-85  10:53:02
Amiga BASIC.info         1320       rmon   10-Mar-85  10:05:23
2 files-2 directories-155 blocks used
```

QUICK

This option used with the LIST command works just like DIR:. The screen displays only the file and directory names.

Creating Subdirectories

Many commands discussed up to this point in this chapter can work with subdirectories. But before you use those commands with subdirectories, you need to know how to start one. The AmigaDOS command to start a subdirectory is MAKEDIR. The format is

  MAKEDIR <subdirectory name>

Here are some examples of the MAKEDIR command:

```
1> MAKEDIR Games ; this makes a directory called Games
```

```
1> MAKEDIR Basicprogs/Games ; this makes a subdirectory
called Games under the directory called Basicprogs
```

```
1> MAKEDIR df1: Basicprogs/Games ; on disk drive 1, this makes
a subdirectory called Games under the directory
called Basicprogs
```

Using the CD Command

Another command that you use with directories is CD (change directory). To change the directory you are working with—for instance, to move down a level to the next subdirectory—you type *CD* and the name of the directory you want to access. If you type *CD* and press RETURN, the computer tells you which directory you

are working with. If you type *CD* and a slash (/), the computer
moves up one level to the next highest directory in the hierarchy.
For example, suppose that you are working with Diskone. Here is
what you would do to move down one directory level, then back
up to the main directory:

```
1> CD; this will tell you that you are at the main directory
level
(SYS:) SYS:

1> CD df0:Utilities; now you move down one level to the
Utilities directory

1> DIR; let's see what's in this directory
      Assem. Bas
      Editing. Bas
      Hexcode. Bas

1> CD; where are you now?
SYS: Utilities

1> CD /; now you will move up a level

1> CD
SYS:

1>
```

Setting the Time and Date

Storing the current date and time in AmigaDOS can help you keep
track of when you created and updated certain files. You use the
DATE both to find out the date and time, and to set it. When you
type *DATE*, the system displays the day of the week, date, and
time—for example, Monday 23-Dec-85 09:52:10. Because the Amiga
doesn't have a built-in calendar and battery, this information will
not be accurate unless you set it every time you turn on the computer. If you don't set it, the system assumes that it's the same day
and time as when DATE was last set. Here are the other formats for
the DATE command:

DATE DD-MMM-YY

By typing DATE and the date (in the day-month-year format), you can set a new calendar date. The month should be the three-character representation of the month's name (Jan, Feb, Mar, Apr, May, Jun, Jul, Aug, Sep, Oct, Nov, or Dec), and the day and year should each be two digits long. For instance, to specify the date August 23, 1986, you type

```
1> DATE 23-Aug-86
```

If the date has the correct week but not the correct day, you type DATE, then the correct day (for example, *DATE Wed*). To specify either the day after or day before the current day, you type *DATE Tomorrow* or *DATE Yesterday*, respectively.

DATE HH:MM

To set the time, you type *DATE* followed by the hours and minutes (separated by a colon). If either the hours or minutes is a single digit, be sure to make the first digit a zero. For instance, if the time is 9:03, type *DATE 09:03*. After 12:59 p.m., you need to use army time, the 24-hour system that adds 12 hours to hours after 12:59 p.m. For example, 4:30 is 16:30 in army time. When you read this 24-hour format, you subtract 12 from the hours indicated (for example, 21:23 is 9:23 p.m.).

Displaying AmigaDOS Information

You can use the INFO command to display information about the current disk operating system. When you type *INFO*, the screen displays the maximum size of each disk, the amount of used and unused disk space, the number of errors that have occurred, and the status of each disk:

```
1> INFO
Mounted disks:
Unit  Size  Used  Free  Full  Errors  Status      Name
DF0:  880K  1425  333   81%   0       Read/Write  Workbench  1.1
1>
```

Displaying a Message

You can use the ECHO command, which is similar to the PRINT statement in Amiga BASIC, to display information on the screen. For example, you could use this command to display a message that notifies you that the computer has accomplished a certain task. Although this capability may not be useful to you right now, you will find it very handy when used within DOS command sequences. ECHO displays whatever you enter within quotation marks after the command. Here is an example:

```
1> ECHO "This is a test"
This is a test
1>
```

Changing the Prompt

With the PROMPT command, you can change the AmigaDOS 1> prompt. You type *PROMPT* followed by the new prompt in quotation marks. To switch back to the more familiar 1>, you type *PROMPT "1> "*. Here is a sample session:

```
1> PROMPT "Ready when you are -> "
Ready when you are -> ECHO "I like my old prompt better"
I like my old prompt better
Ready when you are -> PROMPT "1> "
1> ECHO "There we go"
There we go
1>
```

Listing Files

To list an entire file on the screen, you use the TYPE command followed by the name of the file:

    TYPE <file name>

If you want the listing to include line numbers (1, 2, 3, 4 . . .), you type

    TYPE <file name> OPT N

To print the file as hexadecimal numbers, you type

    TYPE <file name> OPT H

The TYPE command is useful when you want to survey the contents of a particular file. Here are some examples:

```
1> TYPE Simple.Bas
10 Rem This is one simple program
20 Print "Testing"
30 GOTO 10
```

```
1> TYPE Simple.Bas OPT N
1  10 Rem This is one simple program
2  20 Print "Testing"
3  30 GOTO 10
```

```
1> TYPE Simple.Bas OPT H
0000: F5802200  000AAF20  54686973  20697320   .."....This is
0010: 6F6E6520  73676D70  6C652070  726F6772   one simple progr
0020: 616D0080  11000140  AC202254  726F6772   am.....@."Testi
0030: 6E672200  800C0000  AC202254  00000A00   ng"......"T....
0040: 00000                                     ...
```

Identifying Errors

Two more AmigaDOS commands that provide you with information are WHY and FAULT. WHY tells you why the last error occurred, and FAULT tells you what specific error codes mean. Although AmigaDOS displays a brief message when something goes wrong, you still may not understand why a command failed. The WHY command provides a more detailed explanation of what went wrong. On the Workbench, an error code number is displayed when an error occurs. To find out what particular error code numbers represent, you type *FAULT* followed by the error number(s). Look at the following examples:

```
1> COPY HI TO BY
Cannot open hi for input - object not found
```

```
1> WHY
The last command did not set a return code
```

```
1> FAULT 203 213
Fault 203: object already exists
Fault 213: disk not validated

1>
```

Working with Diskettes and Files

The sections that follow show you how to set up and manipulate the information stored on your diskettes so that you can manage the Amiga's disk storage better. You will learn how to format and name diskettes, how to create working diskettes, how to back up you diskettes, how to copy and rename your files, how to add comments to file names, how to delete files and directories, and how to merge and protect files.

Formatting and Naming Diskettes

When you purchase a double-sided, 3.5-inch diskette for your Amiga, the diskette won't work until you format it. With every microcomputer that uses diskettes, you must format the diskettes in order to customize them to the computer's specifications. The command for this task is FORMAT, and you issue the command as follows:

FORMAT DRIVE <drive number> NAME <diskette name>

The drive number, either df0: or df1:, specifies the drive that contains the diskette you want to format. For example, to format the diskette in drive 1 (df1:) and to name the diskette Disktwo, you type

```
1> FORMAT DRIVE DF1: NAME DISKTWO
```

Before you use FORMAT, be sure that you do not need any of the information on the diskette you are formatting. Using FORMAT destroys all the information on a diskette.

For the sake of organization, the name you give a diskette should be different from the names you give other diskettes. Names can have from 1 to 30 characters. If a name consists of more than 1 word—that is, if the name has any spaces—be sure to put quotation marks around the name, as in the following example:

```
1> FORMAT DRIVE DF1: NAME "Music Disk One"
```

Creating Work Diskettes

You already may have discovered that you can reset your computer with the CTRL and two Amiga keys only if certain disks are in the internal drive. Resetting the computer is called *rebooting*. With a disk such as Workbench, you can reboot the Amiga so that the Workbench screen appears and you are ready to go. However, some disks, such as the Extras disk, won't boot without other disks. You must load the Workbench disk before you can insert the nonbootable disk.

If you want your formatted diskette to be "bootable" so that you don't have to insert Workbench before you can access the programs on the diskette, you can use the INSTALL command. You type *INSTALL* followed by the name of the disk drive you are using (df0:, df1:, df2:, or df3:), and the Amiga does the rest. For instance, the following command makes the formatted diskette in drive 0 bootable.

```
1> INSTALL df0:
```

If you are not happy with the name you have given a diskette, you can use the RELABEL command to change the name. You type *RELABEL*, the number of the drive holding the diskette, and the diskette's new name. You have the option of preceding the drive number with the word *DRIVE*, and the name of the diskette with the word *NAME*. Either of the following two command statements changes the name of the diskette in drive 1 to Newdisk:

```
1> RELABEL df1: "Newdisk"
```

```
1> RELABEL DRIVE df1: NAME "Newdisk"
```

Making Backup Diskettes

One of the most important rules to follow when using any computer system is *keep plenty of backups*. If a diskette is destroyed or damaged, and you don't have a backup copy of it, the information on the diskette is gone forever. So make a copy of each original diskette in case something goes wrong with it.

To back up a diskette, you type *DISKCOPY*, the FROM drive number and the TO drive number. Remember that all the information on the diskette you are copying to will be erased. The information on the diskette you are copying from will remain intact. Formatting the diskette you are copying to is not necessary; the DISKCOPY command does that for you automatically.

If you follow the entire DISKCOPY command with the word NAME and a name in quotation marks, the system assigns that name to the diskette you are copying to. Here are some examples of DISKCOPY commands:

```
1> DISKCOPY FROM DF0: TO DF1:
```

This command copies the information on the diskette in drive 0 to the diskette in drive 1.

```
1> DISKCOPY FROM DF1: TO DF0: NAME "Music Backup"
```

This command copies the information on the diskette in drive 1 to the diskette in drive 0, and names the diskette in drive 0 Music Backup.

```
1> DISKCOPY FROM DF0: TO DF0:
```

This command copies the diskette in drive 0 to another diskette. If you have only an internal drive, you use this command to back up your diskettes. The Amiga will guide you through the process of inserting your source and destination diskettes.

Copying Files

To copy individual files, you use the COPY command. This command copies a file or directory to another file or directory. If you copy one directory to another directory, the system copies all the files in that directory to the other directory. If you are copying only one file, the system copies it to whatever directory you are using.

If you use the word ALL with the COPY command, the system copies all the files, including those in the subdirectories, to the directory you are working with. Here are some sample COPY commands:

```
1> COPY FROM Bach.Bas TO :BachMusic
```

This command makes a copy of the Bach.Bas program and stores it in the current directory under the name BachMusic.

```
1> COPY FROM Bach.Bas TO :MusicProgs/BachMusic
```

This command makes a copy of the Bach.Bas program and stores it in the MusicProgs directory under the name BachMusic.

1> COPY TO df1:UTILITIES

This command copies all the files in the current directory to the directory called Utilities in disk drive 1.

1> COPY df0: TO df1: ALL

This command copies all the files, including those in subdirectories, from disk drive 0 to disk drive 1.

1> COPY df1: to df0: ALL QUIET

This command copies all the files, including those in subdirectories, from disk drive 1 to disk drive 0. Because the QUIET option is used, the Amiga does not display each file name as the system copies it.

Renaming Files

After you make a copy of a file or directory, you might want to change its name. You might want to change a name, for instance, because you have thought of a more appropriate name. You use the RENAME command to change file and directory names. The format of the command is

RENAME FROM <name> TO <name>

The first *name* is the old name, and the second *name* is the new name. Here are some examples:

1> RENAME Oldname Newname

This command changes the file's name from Oldname to Newname.

1> RENAME FROM Oldname TO Newname

This command does the same thing as the preceding example. The words FROM and TO are optional.

1> RENAME FROM Utilities TO "Programmer Aids"

This command gives the directory called Utilities the new name Programmer Aids. Notice that because the new name consists of two words, quotation marks are used.

Adding Comments to File Names

You can add comments to file names in order to remind you of information such as revision dates, programmer name, and other important facts. These comments can be displayed when you examine a diskette's contents with the LIST command. To add a comment to a file name (which is displayed only with LIST, not DIR), you type *FILENOTE*, the name of the file, *COMMENT*, and the comment. Use quotation marks around any comments that include spaces. Here are some examples:

1> FILENOTE Shock. Bas COMMENT "This is some pretty shocking music"

1> FILENOTE Hexcode. Bas COMMENT Translator

1> FILENOTE FILE Perspect. Bas COMMENT "Version 3. 6 by Tim Knight - draws a perspective in many colors"

Notice that quotation marks are not used around the comment in the second example because the comment does not contain any spaces. In the third example, note that the word FILE before the file specified is optional.

Deleting Files and Directories

To erase files or directories that you no longer need (and to free up valuable disk space), you use the DELETE command. DELETE has a variety of options that make it very flexible; the easiest way to use the command is to type *DELETE* and the name of the file you want to erase. You can delete as many as 10 files at a time as long as you use spaces to separate each file name. For example, if Music.Progs is your current directory, you can use the following command to delete all three of that directory's programs:

1> DELETE Bach. Bas Rock. Bas Shock. Bas

You must delete all the programs within a directory before you can delete the directory itself. That is, you cannot use the DELETE command to erase a directory if the directory contains programs.

The options that you can use with DELETE are ALL, which deletes all the files in any subdirectories, and QUIET, which prevents the computer from displaying any file(s) being deleted. Here are some examples:

1> DELETE df1: ALL

This command removes all files in subdirectories on drive 1.

1> DELETE df1: ALL QUIET

This command does the same thing as the preceding command but does not list each file being deleted.

Merging Files

Sometimes you may want to combine several files into one larger file. Suppose that you have two text files called Act 1 and Act 2, and you want to combine them into a new file called Play. You type

1> JOIN "Act 1" "Act 2" AS Play

You can combine as many as 15 files to create a new file. Be sure to type the word *AS* before the new file name.

Protecting Files

When you use the LIST command to examine files, you will notice a single character just before the date. That character indicates the file's protection status. Most files will have an r before them, indicating that they can only be read. The file protection status symbols are the following:

r   The file can only be read.

w   The file can only be written to.

d   The file can only be deleted.

e   The file can only be executed.

PROTECT is the command that gives a file a specific protection status. You type *PROTECT*, the file name, and the protection status character(s). If you omit one of the protection status characters, the system knows not to perform the action that the missing character represents. Suppose that you type

1> PROTECT Editing. Bas rwd

These status characters make Editing.Bas a file that can be read, written to, or deleted, but not executed. However, suppose that you type

1> PROTECT Editing. Bas rwe

The d option is not included in the status characters. Therefore, you cannot accidentally delete Editing.Bas.

Moving Beyond the Basics

This chapter has examined all the commands that you need in order to back up disks, copy programs, protect your files, and perform simple DOS operations. If you are satisfied that these AmigaDOS commands are all you need to know, go on to Chapter 10 to read about different uses for your Amiga. However, if you want to get involved in the more complex task of creating the AmigaDOS command sequences that make the system perform functions for you automatically, then read the next chapter carefully. That chapter describes many of AmigaDOS's more powerful commands.

9

Advanced AmigaDOS

When you first begin using a computer, you may think that it is operating at maximum efficiency and that "keeping up" with such an amazing machine might be a difficult task. However, as you become more experienced at using a computer, you may begin to think that it is lagging behind you.

The problem isn't in the machine's capability to process commands; many computers, including the Amiga, operate at very high speeds. The problem is that if you type DOS commands one at a time and use the same sequences of commands frequently, you might begin to think that DOS is an inefficient way to communicate with a computer.

You can increase DOS's efficiency with command sequences. *Command sequences* are an ordered series of commands that the computer carries out after receiving a couple of command words through the keyboard. This chapter on advanced AmigaDOS commands explores windows, command sequences, and other AmigaDOS features that can increase efficiency.

Using Multiple Windows

In AmigaDOS each window is independent of the others, so you can run different programs and functions simultaneously by moving from one window to another. You just point the mouse to whatever window you want to work with and press the left mouse button.

To open a new window, you use the NEWCLI command. You can customize an AmigaDOS window by giving it a name, moving it, and changing its size. You can make these specifications by using the following format of the command:

NEWCLI CON:<x-coordinate>/<y-coordinate>/<width>/ <height>/<title>

For example, you could type

1> NEWCLI CON:10/30/60/50/"Number Two"

A new window appears with its upper left corner at (10,30), a width of 60 pixels, and a height of 50 pixels. The name Number Two appears at the top of the window. (Remember to put quotation marks around the name if it includes spaces.)

To get out of an AmigaDOS window, you type *ENDCLI*. If you have only one window left, ENDCLI exits AmigaDOS, so be careful when you use this command.

Building Command Sequences

The following sections introduce commands that you can use to build command sequences that will increase AmigaDOS's efficiency. You will learn the commands for AmigaDOS's built-in editor, the special AmigaDOS commands for sequences, and the commands for decision-making with AmigaDOS.

The Editor's Commands

AmigaDOS has a built-in editor that you can use to create text files. Although describing the editor in detail could fill a book in itself, this section provides the basic information that you need to know in order to create files.

To create a file, you type *ED* followed by a file name. For example, if you type *ED TASKONE*, the system creates a file called TASKONE and accesses the editor immediately. Then you can go ahead and type your text.

Once you have accessed the editor, you can use all of the following commands:

Cursor keys	Move the cursor up, down, left, or right
BACKSPACE	Deletes the last character typed

RETURN	Moves the cursor to the next line (below the one the cursor is presently on)
TAB	Moves the cursor to next tab position
CTRL-A	Inserts a line (when you want to add more text)
CTRL-B	Deletes a line
CTRL-D	Scrolls the text down (if you want to see text that is currently "above" the screen)
CTRL-E	Moves the cursor to the top or bottom of the screen. This command is a toggle; the first time you press CTRL-E, the cursor moves to the top of the screen, and the second time you press CTRL-E, the cursor moves to the bottom of the screen, and so on.
CTRL-F	Switches the case of the character on which the cursor is located. Uppercase becomes lowercase, and vice versa.
CTRL-G	Repeats the line that was just typed
CTRL-H	Deletes the last character typed; has the same effect as the BACKSPACE key
CTRL-I	Moves the cursor to the next tab position
CTRL-O	Deletes one word at the cursor's location
CTRL-R	Moves the cursor to end of the previous word
CTRL-T	Moves the cursor to the beginning of the next word
CTRL-U	Scrolls the text up
CTRL-V	Redraws the entire screen
CTRL-Y	Deletes everything from the cursor's location to the end of the current line

A number of other commands also are available through AmigaDOS's built-in editor. To use any of the following commands, you first need to press the ESC key. When the cursor appears at the bottom of the screen, you can enter any one of the following commands. After you enter the command, you must press RETURN in order for the computer to recognize the command.

B	Moves the cursor to the bottom of the file
BF <"string">	Searches backward through the text for the string that you specify. For example, to look for the word ECHO, you type *BF "ECHO"*.
CE	Moves the cursor to the end of the current line
CL	Moves the cursor one position left
CR	Moves the cursor one position right
CS	Moves the cursor to the beginning of the line
D	Deletes the current line
F <"string">	Searches forward through the text for the string that you specify
J	Joins the line that contains the cursor with the following line
LC	Distinguishes between uppercase and lowercase when searching for a string. (Unless you use this command, the system doesn't distinguish between uppercase and lowercase characters; it simply looks for a particular sequence of letters.) You enter this optional command before you enter the search command.
M <n>	Moves the cursor to the *n*th line number. For example, to move to line 5, you type *M 5*.
N	Moves the cursor to the beginning of the next line
P	Moves the cursor to the beginning of the previous line
Q	Quits without saving anything
S	Splits the line at the cursor's current location

SA	Saves text to disk
SL <n>	Sets the left margin to position *n*
SR <n>	Sets the right margin to position *n*
ST <n>	Sets the tab to position *n*
T	Moves the cursor to the top of the file
U	Undoes changes made to the current line
UC	Ignores differences in uppercase and lowercase when searching for strings. You enter this command before you enter the search command.
X	Exits the editor and saves the text to disk

Commands for Sequences

Although the editor has many uses, the scope of this chapter covers only how to use the editor for AmigaDOS. The material that follows shows you how to use the AmigaDOS commands with the editor to create a command sequence file, and then how to use that file as a way to issue many commands at once.

The following brief example gives you a general idea of how a command sequence file works. Access the editor by typing *ED TESTER*. Then type the following:

```
DIR
ECHO "That's all, folks!"
```

Now type *ESC* and then press the X key in order to exit the editor and save this file.

Now you have a file called TESTER that contains the commands DIR and ECHO. To start executing the commands in a file, you use the EXECUTE command. In this case, you type

```
DIR EXECUTE TESTER
```

The system displays the disk's directory and, at the bottom of the screen, the message `That's all folks!`

When you use the editor, you are not restricted to using only the AmigaDOS commands covered in Chapter 8. Other commands make AmigaDOS function like a simple programming language.

SKIP and LAB are two commands that you can use together in order to make the EXECUTE command skip to different parts of the text. For instance, suppose that you want to create the following text file called TEST2:

```
ECHO "We're going to start now"
LIST
CD :MusicProgs
LIST
SKIP OVERHERE
DISKCOPY df0: to df1:
LAB OVERHERE
CD :
ECHO "I'm glad we got around that DISKCOPY command!"
```

After you press ESC, X, and RETURN, the system saves this file as TEST2. Here's what would happen if you used this file with the EXECUTE command:

```
1> EXECUTE TEST2
We're going to start now
(The listing of the root directory would be here.)
(The listing of the MusicProgs directory would be here.)
I'm glad we got around that DISKCOPY command!
1>
```

The CD : command in the TEST2 file makes the system return to the root directory after executing the commands. You can enter any AmigaDOS commands in a file to EXECUTE. This procedure is an excellent way to put complex, frequently used routines in an easy-to-access file that you can run by giving one short command.

Here are four other sample EXECUTE files that you might find useful:

1. This program places on the screen two new windows, each with a different prompt.

```
ECHO "Here are two new windows"
PROMPT "2> "
NEWCLI "CON: 40/40/200/50/Window Two"
PROMPT "3> "
NEWCLI "CON: 150/100/210/100/Window Three"
PROMPT "1> "
ECHO "All done!"
```

2. This program changes the name of the diskettes in each drive.

```
ECHO "The disk in drive one will be called DiskOne"
ECHO "The disk in drive two will be called DiskTwo"
RELABEL df0: "DiskOne"
RELABEL df1: "DiskTwo"
ECHO "I'm done."
```

3. This program displays information about a diskette.

```
ECHO "Full information for disk in drive zero:"
LIST
INFO
ECHO "End of listing"
WAIT 5 SECS
```

4. This program formats the diskette in drive 1, names it Music Backup, and copies the files from a directory called Music in drive 0 to drive 1.

```
ECHO "Source: Drive 0/Destination: Drive 1"
FORMAT DRIVE DF1: NAME "Music Backup"
COPY DF0:Music TO DF1:Music ALL QUIET
ECHO "Backup complete."
```

The kinds of files that you should concentrate on creating are those that contain command sequences that you find yourself using frequently. The purpose of the editor and the command sequences is to save you time when you perform routine DOS operations.

Decision-Making Commands

You may remember that Amiga BASIC uses the IF...THEN command to determine whether a condition is true or false and then act on that decision. If you are programming a command sequence in AmigaDOS, you can use the IF command to check a condition and execute commands based on whether that condition is true or false.

You can follow IF with any one of the following conditionals:

WARN

WARN checks to see whether the error code number is greater than or equal to 5. For instance, if Error 103 occurs, and a command sequence contains an IF WARN statement, then the system interprets the condition as true and executes whatever commands follow IF.

ERROR

ERROR does the same thing as WARN, except that the system interprets the condition as true only if the error code is greater than or equal to 10.

FAIL

FAIL works like WARN and ERROR, but checks to see whether the error code is greater than or equal to 20. If Error 14 occurs, the IF statement doesn't register that the condition was true.

<"text"> EQ <"text">

The EQ keyword works with IF to determine whether two pieces of text are the same. The system checks only to see whether the letters correspond; it does not distinguish between uppercase and lowercase letters. Therefore, the system would interpret IF "AMIGA" EQ "amiGA", IF "TEST" EQ "test", and IF "Word" EQ "Word" as true statements and proceed to execute the commands immediately following the IF statement.

EXISTS

EXISTS makes sure that a specific file exists. By following IF EXISTS with the name of a particular file, you can make the system check to see whether that file is on the diskette that you are using.

The IF command works with any of the preceding keywords in the context of a command sequence only. You can't use IF directly from AmigaDOS.

The IF command can take several different and useful forms. The most basic way to use IF is to follow it with a condition and the word ENDIF. For instance, the following command sequence (which must be accessed through the EXECUTE command) checks to see whether an error code greater than or equal to 10 has been issued. If so, the screen displays a message.

```
IF ERROR
ECHO "You blew it, Alfalfa. "
ENDIF
```

You use the ENDIF statement to tell the system where the IF part of the sequence stops. If the condition tested is false, the system executes all the commands between IF and ENDIF. Therefore, you will want to be sure to put an ENDIF after the condition being tested, at the place where you plan to resume the command sequence. Here is a simple rule that you can follow: Type ENDIF in your command sequence after you type the commands that should be used if a condition is true. The format for this kind of sequence is as follows:

IF <condition being tested>
<commands to be executed if the condition is true>
ENDIF

The IF...ELSE...ENDIF sequence is somewhat more complex. Like the IF...THEN...ELSE in Amiga BASIC, this sequence tells the system to execute certain commands if a condition is true and to execute others if a condition is false. If a condition is true, the system acts on the commands between IF and ELSE. If the condition is false, the system executes the commands between ELSE and ENDIF. For instance, the following routine determines whether a file called Term Paper is on a diskette.

```
IF EXISTS Term Paper
TYPE Term Paper
ECHO "That was quite a paper!"
ELSE
ECHO "Keep looking."
ENDIF
```

If Term Paper is on the diskette, the system types the whole file and displays That was quite a paper!. If the file is not on the diskette, the screen displays Keep looking.

You can use more than one IF in a sequence. Just like nested FOR...NEXT loops, nested IF...ENDIF (or IF...ELSE...ENDIF) statements can be useful in complex routines. When two IF...ENDIF statements are nested, the first IF refers to the last ENDIF, and the second IF refers to the first ENDIF. This arrangement may be confusing, so here is an example to show how it works:

```
IF EXISTS "Santa Clara"
IF EXISTS "University"
ECHO "The files SANTA CLARA and UNIVERSITY are both on this
diskette. Congratulations."
ENDIF
ENDIF
```

The program checks to see whether the file called Santa Clara is on the diskette. If the file is not found, the program moves past the last ENDIF statement (the one that corresponds to the first IF) and ignores everything that was skipped over. However, if Santa Clara *is* on the diskette, the program jumps to the next IF statement to see whether University is also on the diskette. If the file is not found, the program skips to the first ENDIF, proceeds to the second ENDIF, and then executes whatever follows. If the file named University is found, the screen displays the message following the ECHO command.

Making Errors Useful

When a command sequence is running, an error may occur that could cause a problem. Some errors are so serious that the sequence should stop running so that you can find out what's wrong. Other errors might not be important for a particular sequence.

To tell the system to exit a command sequence if errors occur, you use the FAILAT command. FAILAT, when followed by a positive integer, tells AmigaDOS: "Get out of this command sequence if you encounter an error with a code greater than or equal to the number following FAILAT." Suppose that you put the following at the beginning of a command sequence:

```
FAILAT 15
```

This tells the system to stop the sequence if the system encounters error 15, 16, 17, and so on. But if the system encounters error 14, 13, 12, or anything else with a code less than 15, the sequence should not stop.

If you type FAILAT without a number, the system tells you what the current "tolerance level" is for errors. The initial value is 10. Therefore, if you want the command sequence to stop based on a different error code level, you should use FAILAT with a specified number.

A command that you can use with FAILAT is QUIT. QUIT prints the error code that you specify if the command sequence encounters an error. For instance, the following program checks to see whether any errors occur that have a return code of 25 or greater. If the system encounters an error, the system stops and displays error code 20:

```
FAILAT 25
IF ERROR
QUIT 20
ENDIF
```

QUIT, which is similar to the END statement in Amiga BASIC, stops the command sequence immediately. If you do not follow QUIT with an error code that you want displayed, the system stops the command sequence and does not display any error code.

Searching for Text

To find a particular piece of text on a diskette, you do not have to look through all your files with the TYPE command. A much more efficient method is to use the SEARCH command, a built-in AmigaDOS function. SEARCH examines the files on a diskette and displays any lines in any files that contain the text you specify. SEARCH does not distinguish between uppercase and lowercase letters; SEARCH displays the text regardless of its case.

You can use several different formats with the SEARCH command. The simplest way to search is to type *SEARCH* followed by the text you are looking for. If the text consists of more than one word (that is, if the text has a space), put quotation marks around the text. The SEARCH command by itself checks only the files in the directory that you are working with. If you type *SEARCH* and you type *ALL* after the specified text, the system searches the entire diskette.

Here are some examples of the SEARCH command:

```
SEARCH 37500
```

This command looks for the number *37500* in the files in the current directory.

```
SEARCH "37500 dollars" ALL
```

This command looks for *37500 dollars* in every file on the diskette.

To examine the diskette in a particular drive, you use *dfo:* or *df1:*. For example, to search drive 1 (the external drive) for a file called Compiler, you type

```
SEARCH df1: "Compiler" ALL
```

Making the System Pause

Whether you are using the editor or working with AmigaDOS alone, you can make the system pause by using the WAIT command. This command stops the system for a specific amount of time or until a particular hour. Here are the various formats you can use with the WAIT command:

> WAIT <number of seconds you want the system to pause> SEC

> WAIT <number of minutes you want the system to pause> MIN

To make the system wait until a certain hour, you type

> WAIT UNTIL <the hour>

Here are three examples:

WAIT 5 SEC

This command makes the system pause five seconds.

WAIT 3 MIN

This command makes the system pause three minutes.

WAIT UNTIL 20:30

This command makes the system wait until 8:30 p.m.

After you begin forming patterns in the way in which you use AmigaDOS, you will probably know what kinds of self-executing files you should create to save time. For example, WAIT is useful in a sequence that displays information on the screen and then pauses to give the user time to read the message.

Making AmigaDOS Work for You

AmigaDOS gives you much flexibility in the handling of the information stored on your files and diskettes. You should study and use the operating system commands carefully at first because, if used incorrectly, they can ruin your diskettes. As you become more experienced with AmigaDOS, you will find many new doors open to you. Using the features of AmigaDOS, you can explore assembly language programming, perform complex file manipulation tasks, and protect your diskettes and files from damage and unauthorized use.

10
Amiga at Work and Play

Now that you are nearing the end of this exploration of the Amiga, you can begin to reflect on what you have learned. You have seen how to program in Logo and Amiga BASIC, and you have studied the fundamentals of the C language. You also have taken a thorough look at the graphics and sounds capabilities of the Amiga.

All this knowledge is good because it helps you better understand the potential of the Amiga. However, if you still are asking yourself the question "What good is my computer?" this last chapter should help you find the answer. This chapter investigates that question by exploring what the Amiga can do to make your life easier, more productive, and more enjoyable.

Word Processing

One of the best ways you can use any computer is for word processing. A word processor is a computer program with which you enter, print, and save text (such as letters, resumes, and even chapters for a book about the Amiga). You can think of a word processor as a magic typewriter: you can alter, add, delete, and enhance text as you like until you are ready to have the computer print the final version on paper. Naturally, a word processor can perform all the regular functions of a typewriter: you can type words and numbers from the keyboard and get a printed copy (*hardcopy*) when you are finished, just as you can with a typewriter.

The advantage of word processing on a computer is that while you are typing, nothing is actually printed on paper. Because your words are electronic, you have all the advantages of electronics. You can erase letters and words, move blocks of text, save and retrieve your text files, print the text in special typefaces, and do all sorts of other tasks that are difficult or impossible with a typewriter. With a word processor, you can happily throw away your correction fluid. A word processor can perform the functions of a typewriter so much better than a typewriter that you will wonder how you ever got along without a personal computer in the first place.

The word processor that Commodore-Amiga offers is Textcraft® from Arktronics Corporation (520 East Liberty Street, Ann Arbor, MI 48104). This package has a list price of $99 and should be available at an Amiga dealer near you.[1] Textcraft is especially easy to learn because it provides help throughout the program; 21 different 1-minute tutorials help you get out of any jam. Note, however, that the program is slow in loading the different features.

The real power of Textcraft is that it performs all the formatting functions for you. When you start Textcraft, you can choose one of the ready-to-use templates (the forms in which you can create documents), or you can instruct the computer to start with a blank form. Textcraft will align the addresses properly in a business letter, give you space for bibliographies in a term paper, or emphasize certain parts of your resume. In short, Textcraft handles the framework so that you can concentrate on the content of your document.

Textcraft consists of six templates: a business letter, a memorandum, a technical report, a business report, a term paper, and a resume. Each template provides considerable "hand holding" that makes the program easy to use. The resume form, for example, lets you enter your name, address, the style of the resume you want (chronological, analytical, or functional), and your preference as to whether your resume should emphasize your education or your work experience. On the business letter template, you enter the form of address (such as Mr., Mrs., Ms., or Dr.) for the sender and the recipient; the names and addresses of the sender and recipient; the typist's initials; the date; the recipient(s) of any carbon copies; the format (full-block or semi-block); and the number of enclosures, if any. The term-paper template even has a special screen devoted to the title page; the prompts request such information as the title of the report, the subtitle, the name of the student, the date, and the course name. These quality templates, which few other word processors contain, make the software a very good value.

---

1. Prices given in this chapter were correct at the time the book was written, but may be subject to change.

With a word processor, you can alter, add, delete, and enhance text to your liking until you are ready to have the computer print out the final version on paper. Here are some of the features of the Textcraft word processor that can help you perform these tasks:

Insertion: To add an extra character, word, sentence, or whole section of text, you can move the cursor to the desired point and insert the text. As you insert the extra text, the rest of the document moves over to make room for the additional information.

Deletion: If you get rid of part of the document (even just one character), the word processor keeps the rest of the document looking as good as it was before.

Search and Replace: Suppose that you have a 10-page document and you realize that you may have misspelled the possessive pronoun *its* as *it's*. Because you don't want this all-too-common error marring your paper, you can tell the computer to search for the word *it's*. The program will go to the first occurrence of *it's* and stop. You also can instruct the computer to search for certain pieces of text and replace them with the new text. In this case, you could tell the Amiga to change every *it's* to *its*. When you are searching and replacing or simply searching for text, you can specify words, sentences, or any text up to 255 characters long.

Block Moves: You sometimes may decide that a block of text would be more appropriate in another part of your document. Textcraft lets you remove an entire block of text and place it somewhere else.

Formatting: To make your document look just the way you want, you can change the spacing and alignments, center or justify the text, switch from 60- to 80-column mode, number pages, and change typefaces (such as bold, italic, underline, superscripts and subscripts, or any combination of these). The term *justify* simply means that the right margin of the text, as well as the left, is even rather than ragged. You may notice in magazines and books that the text is justified; that is, both edges of the text are lined up. The computer justifies text by adding space between words so that all the lines are the same length. Justification of text can help you achieve a professional look.

File Commands: One of the most important advantages of using a word processor is that you can save and load your files. If you ever have turned in a long paper or mailed a letter that was later lost, you will understand how valuable this feature is. With a computer, you can load the old file back into memory and print the document again.

Another advantage of being able to save and load files is that you can modify and enhance a document easily over as long a period of time as necessary. To do so, you need only to load the file into the computer when you are ready to work with that document. This high-tech advantage has a flip side, however, because a computer can just as easily "eat" a document by "bombing" when you are in the middle of typing something or by malfunctioning and perhaps destroying more than one of your disk files. The way to protect yourself against these kinds of catastrophes is not only to save frequently as you go along, but also to keep backup copies of diskettes that contain documents. This point cannot be emphasized enough; remember this and you can avoid losing valuable files and many hours of time.

Textcraft makes excellent use of the Amiga's windows, color graphics, and mouse. The cursor keys move the cursor around the document; and when used with the SHIFT key, they move the cursor to the corresponding edge of the screen. The function keys can be used to indicate that you need help or to select certain Preferences; function keys F5 through F10 are represented by icons. Table 10.1 lists the function keys, their icons, and their functions.

Table 10.1
Textcraft Function Keys

Key	Icon	Function
F5	Pencil	Move the text cursor
F6	Scissors	Delete text
F7	Camera	Copy text
F8	Paste Jar	Paste text
F9	Paint Brush	Change the format of text
F10	Style Brush	Change the type style

Word processing is an outstanding use for any personal computer, especially for the Amiga with its easy-to-use Textcraft word-processing program. Even if you type just a few letters a month and a long paper now and then, a word processor is well worth the expense. You will be amazed to find out how efficient you can be.

Telecommunications

Telecommunications is the system in which computers send and receive information to and from other computers by means of an ordinary telephone. For personal computer owners, this capability means that a wealth of information, news, and friends are within your reach.

To communicate with the outside world, a computer needs a device that connects the computer to a telephone. This device is called a *modem*, and with it you can communicate with other personal computers, large mainframe computer databases, and nationwide bulletin board services.

The rate at which you can send and receive information with your modem is measured in binary digits (bits) per second. If your modem can send or receive a certain number of bits within one second, the modem is operating at that particular baud rate. For example, a modem that transmits 1,200 bits every second is a 1200-baud modem, and 2,400 bits per second transmission is possible with a 2400-baud modem.

The modem available from Commodore-Amiga, the 1200 RS®, is a 1200-baud modem that sells for $395. A more sophisticated device is the T-modem™, which sells for $695 from Tecmar (6225 Cochran Road, Solon, OH 44139). A T-modem can operate at 300, 1200, or 2400 baud and features a sophisticated design that is appropriate for business users.

Communications with Other Personal Computers

Before you decide whether you should purchase a modem for your Amiga, you would be wise to consider the possibilities that are available with a modem. One way to use a modem is to communicate directly with another personal computer owner. You "chat" with each other by typing on your keyboards, and you can send and receive public domain programs. Public domain programs are programs that are legal to distribute to others; these are unlike copyrighted programs, which should be purchased in a store. (Illegally selling or giving a copyrighted program to someone is called software piracy. That topic is examined later in this chapter.)

The process of electronically sending and receiving information is not complicated. The *host computer* (the one sending the information) transmits information to its modem. The modem then translates the characters, letters, symbols, and other information into a harsh sound composed of pulses that represent the bits of information being transmitted. This sound is sent over the telephone line, which keeps the signal intact until it reaches the modem receiving the information. That modem then translates the sound back into the characters, letters, and symbols that appear on the screen of the computer receiving the information.

Bulletin Board Services

A computer that is equipped with a modem can communicate directly with any other computer that has a modem. However, most people involved in computer communications prefer to call bulletin board services or large mainframe databases like The Source℠ or CompuServe®.

A bulletin board service (BBS) is usually just a personal computer equipped with a modem and special software. Unattended by an operator, the service receives calls and serves as a host to whoever is calling. A BBS can store and retrieve messages, upload (receive) and download (send) programs, and do just about anything else involved with the transmission of data from one computer to another.

Calling a BBS or any other system is simple enough: you dial the number, wait for the high-pitched tone, then switch your modem to "receive." At that point, data will begin appearing on your screen. This information will tell you where the BBS is located, who the system operator (SYSOP) is, and what the bulletin board's purpose is. A menu then will appear on the screen. Table 10.2 lists and explains some of the frequently used menu options.

Bulletin board services are located all over the United States. Table 10.3 gives the telephone numbers of some BBSs in major cities. One of these is probably relatively close to you. By using the command

Table 10.2
BBS Menu Options

Letter	Option	Result
B	Bulletins	Displays the bulletins currently on the system. Bulletins, which are entered by the SYSOP, announce club meetings, birthdays, special events, and so on.
D	Download	Allows you to retrieve a program from the BBS. You can save the program on a disk for later use.
E	Enter a message	Leaves a message for everybody (ALL) or for one person. A message to ALL can be read by anyone, but a message to a particular person is accessible only to that person, who will be "flagged" (notified that a message is waiting) the next time the person logs on to the system.
G	Goodbye	Tells the host computer you want to hang up
H	Help	Accesses BBS instructions on how to use the system
O	Other systems	Displays the telephone numbers of other systems
R	Retrieve a message	Lets you get a message addressed to you or a series of messages intended for everybody
S	Summarize messages	Displays the whole library of messages and their subjects so that you can scan the list to decide what messages you want to read
T	Talk with SYSOP	Allows you to send messages to the SYSOP and read what is typed back. This sort of conversation is great typing practice and, although slower than talking, is a great deal of fun.

| U | Upload | Gives the system a program for its files |
| X | Expert user | Makes the system recognize you as an expert user who can be given very brief commands instead of long descriptions. Use this command after you are confident about using the BBS and its commands. |

that will print out other systems' phone numbers, you probably can find quite a few bulletin boards near enough to keep your phone costs low. On some BBSs, all 1,500+ systems are listed, but probably about 15 percent of these are no longer around or have changed their phone numbers.

Table 10.3
Locations of Some BBSs

City	Phone
Atlanta, Georgia	(404) 953-0723
Belmont, California (devoted to Amiga users!)	(415) 595-5452
Cambridge, Massachusetts	(617) 354-4682
Chicago, Illinois	(312) 337-6631
Dallas, Texas	(214) 634-2668
Denver, Colorado	(303) 759-2625
Houston, Texas	(713) 977-7019
Los Angeles, California	(213) 349-5728
Manhattan, New York	(212) 245-4363
Miami, Florida	(305) 821-7401
Portland, Oregon	(503) 646-5510
San Francisco, California	(415) 552-8924
Shreveport, Louisiana	(318) 631-7107
Washington, D.C.	(703) 281-2125

Bulletin boards are an inexpensive way to have fun with computer communications, as long as you are calling local services. You can make friends with the SYSOP and with the regular users of the system, get some good public domain software, and establish an efficient "mail system" with other modem-equipped computer users. Remember, though, that long distance calls and "message units" for calls to locations in your area code quickly can make this pastime an expensive one.

The Source and CompuServe

To make more practical use of your modem, you can try one of the large systems that offer newspaper stories, airline schedules, the latest news and weather, research databases, and even mail-order catalogs on-line. These systems can be used by thousands of people at the same time and offer an enormous amount of information, which you can access with your Amiga and a modem.

These large systems have disadvantages, however. Some have start-up fees (like The Source at $100), and all charge for the time you are on the system, usually from $6 to $25 per hour. In addition, the response rate of large time-sharing services is usually slower than the response of a BBS because you are one of many people sharing the same system. Finally, the incredible variety of interesting features of these systems is enough to make most people burn more time and money on-line than they should.

Generally speaking, however, these large systems are great fun and are very useful. One of the best is The Source (1616 Anderson Road, McLean, VA 22102), a subsidiary of the Reader's Digest Association, started in June, 1979. The Source has a great deal to offer in the following categories:

News and Reference Resources: You can get the latest news, both local and national, from the United Press International service, and you can access information about government and politics, consumer information, science and technology reports, and even dining and travel information.

Catalog Shopping: The Comp-U-Star service gives you access to 30,000 brand name items. Through your computer, you can order these items at 40 percent less than retail price. You also can use Barter Worldwide Inc. to trade items with someone else on the network.

Mail and Communications: Electronic mail and the "chat" mode, much like the message library and "talk to SYSOP" features of BBSs, are available on The Source. You also can mail messages to any one of the thousands of individuals on the system, and you even can send electronic mail that will be printed on paper and delivered by the post office to the address you indicate. The chat option allows you to "talk" with dozens of people at the same time, making for some lively conversations.

Business and Financial Markets: With this service, you can get the latest stock quotes, commodity prices, and interest rates. The service also has a research and reference section along with a news and commentary section to assist investors in researching places to put their money.

Home and Leisure: Blackjack, Adventure, Tic-Tac-Toe, and dozens of other games are available on the network.

Education and Career: You can educate yourself with lessons in Greek, French, poetry, spelling, grammar, and other subjects. The service also provides information on education and careers to help you with college and job decisions.

Computer Languages: One advantage of being on-line with an enormous computer system like The Source is that you have access to many of its powerful languages and utilities. This section of the system lets you create programs using a variety of high-level languages. As powerful as the Amiga is, you still may want to experiment with other systems that have even greater capabilities.

Source Plus: Many business and educational journals are available electronically. A few of these are *Forbes, Harvard Business Review,* and *Venture* magazine.

For those who can afford the charges ($4.50 to $20 per hour), The Source is a powerful and interesting network.

Another system, with almost all the same features as The Source, is CompuServe (5000 Arlington Centre Blvd., P.O. Box 20212, Columbus, OH 43220). Although CompuServe doesn't have a start-up fee, its rates are $6 to $22.50 per hour depending on the time you call and the baud rate you use. The faster you transmit and receive data, the more expensive the service is.

In addition to Source-like features, CompuServe has some extras that might interest you:

The Multiple Choice (TMC): A giant trivia database will ask you questions on just about any subject you can imagine.

The CB radio: This is a sophisticated chatting system. Most people can get on a particular "station" (19, of course, is the most popular) and send messages to dozens of people simultaneously. When you type something into your computer, everyone on that channel sees what you type; and you and all the other users can see anything that anyone else types. Sentences that you type appear on the screen one at a time so they don't get too jumbled. People come up with all sorts of weird handles such as "I'm the Blue Knight." The CB is fun and can be addicting—and therefore expensive. If you want to have a conversation with one or more other individuals, and you don't want anyone else to "listen in," you can go to private scrambled channels.

Computer communications can be both entertaining and useful. Once you have purchased a modem and some software to support it, you are on your way to going on-line with the world. You can have access to information that is not readily available to noncomputer users. Also, you can expand the power of your Amiga by being in communication with different computers that have other features and languages.

Computer Crimes

Using modems with personal computers does have a "dark side." With all the power a modem can give to computer users, some misuse is inevitable. Modems provide the key to breaking into other computers, getting valuable telephone network information, and acquiring a large library of software for next to nothing in cost. Some people take advantage of technology by using phones illegally or duplicating copyrighted software. Two particular types of computer crimes, which have attracted publicity lately, are largely the result of individuals abusing telecommunications; these crimes are software piracy and phone phreaking.

Software piracy is the act of duplicating copyrighted software and giving away or selling the copies. Often people make copies for friends without realizing that they are stealing from both the software company and program author, who aren't earning the profits they deserve from sales of the product. The estimate is that for every program sold, five illegal copies are distributed.

Modems make the illegal exchange of software easy. Often this exchange is simply a matter of either downloading programs from a "pirate" bulletin board service or getting programs over the telephone from someone you are on-line with. You can send software to BBSs or other people just as easily, and these exchanges occur constantly over the telephone lines of the United States.

Tracking down software pirates who trade with friends, by mail, or with other individuals through a modem is practically impossible. However, the FBI has raided a number of bulletin board services that specialized in having copyrighted software available for downloading.

These bulletin boards also had information valuable to "phone phreaks." The phreaks are an advanced kind of computer pirate; they abuse the telephone system with stolen codes and secret telephone numbers. By using Sprint and MCI numbers that are not theirs, finding WATS line numbers, and stealing manuals and information from the telephone company, these people can make calls anywhere in the world for any length of time and not pay one cent. Some phreaks reach the point where they can shut off phone lines or break into bank computers to alter information or transfer money to their own accounts.

Fortunately, law enforcement agencies know considerably more about these crimes than they used to, and people who were "just having fun" are being fined and sent to jail more frequently for computer crimes. Remember that crimes with computers are illegal and are damaging to the businesses and the people affected by them. Getting involved with these activities can lead to much more trouble than the "fun" is worth.

Business Software for the Amiga

With the speed and memory of the Amiga, a business could be much easier to run with the help of this personal computer. The Amiga can work with the MS-DOS system, which is most commonly used with the IBM Personal Computer line. As a result, more than 11,000 programs have been developed to work with the Amiga when it is equipped with the IBM Emulator. A sampling of these programs follows.

1-2-3® and Symphony® from Lotus Development Corporation: These products are the most popular business software packages ever made for a personal computer. The Symphony package includes word processing, a database, a spreadsheet, telecommunications, and business graphics; and 1-2-3 has all but the last two of these features.

WordStar®: You can use this popular IBM PC word-processing program from MicroPro on your Amiga.

ThinkTank™: This program from Living Videotext helps you organize your thoughts and outline your plans so that you can perform a task better. You can use Thinktank for writing a report, outlining a book, or simply figuring out what you have to do in the next week.

These and the thousands of other programs made for the IBM PC are all on 5 1/4-inch disks, so you need to purchase the 5 1/4-inch disk drive from Commodore. You plug in the data cable, just as you do with a regular Amiga external disk drive, and load the Emulator program into memory. Although the Amiga is somewhat slower than the IBM PC at running these MS-DOS programs, the large amount of software available makes the compatibility an attractive option.

Several other sophisticated business programs have been introduced for making business or job responsibilities easier to handle. Descriptions of some of these programs follow.

Rags to Riches™ from Chang Labs (5300 Stevens Creek Blvd., San Jose, CA 95129-1088) will keep your ledger, receivables, payables, and sales in order by integrating the information from these four modules, which cost $99.95 each. The Ledger module keeps track of the income, expenditures, assets, and net worth of a company. With this module, you can determine where money is coming from and where it's going simply by entering the information requested into the various categories.

Receivables is an automated billing system that will show the status of a customer account at the press of a key. You can charge and credit an individual's account, and the module handles wholesale and retail pricing, volume discounts, and tax calculations. The Receivables module works with the Ledger to keep all your accounts current and in order.

The Rags to Riches Payables module monitors your expenses. Payables keeps track of vendor information, addresses, and terms so that you can make the best use of cash flow. You can identify expenses by purchase order numbers, project codes, or job numbers, and you can get a complete summary for any one vendor. Payables also works with the Ledger module.

Finally, the Sales module serves as an electronic cash register by recording the amount of each sale, computing the sales tax, printing the receipt, and performing all the other functions of a cash register. You can have 100 different categories for merchandise, and you can total the amount sold in any one group and determine the percentage of sales from any one group.

Maximillian is a $175 package from Tardis Software (2817 Sloat Road, Pebble Beach, CA 93953) that also uses four integrated modules. The MaxiCalc module is a spreadsheet program that gives you rows and columns of financial data that can be used in formulas to determine "bottom line" results in your business. When you alter any figures in your spreadsheet, the program automatically updates the other figures on the spreadsheet so that you can answer "what if" questions when you make a business decision.

MaxiWord module is a word-processing program for the Amiga with many of the same features as Textcraft. MaxiShare is a telecommunications program that can share information with other computers. MaxiGraph can draw line, bar, and pie graphs and print these graphs on a printer. With all four modules sharing the same information, you can do such tasks as download information with MaxiShare and later modify the data with MaxiWord, send spreadsheet information from MaxiCalc to another computer with MaxiShare, and have MaxiGraph put into picture form the numeric information from MaxiCalc.

Enable™ from The Software Group (Northway Ten Executive Park, Ballston Lake, NY 12019) has modules similar to Maximillian's as well as a database program. All five programs are integrated into one package, which costs $199. With the database program, you can store, format, and print large quantities of information. For instance, you can store and print labels from a long mailing list. This capability is excellent for both large organizations and small businesses.

Finally, VIP from VIP Technologies (132 Aero Camino, Santa Barbara, CA 93117) claims to have all the features of Lotus® 1-2-3® while maintaining the simplicity of the Amiga's operating system. Moreover, VIP costs only $199.95 compared to the much more expensive 1-2-3.

This book has only touched on a few of the business programs available for the Amiga. But by now, you should understand how the

Amiga can be a powerful business tool that can make running your own business or doing your job within a business much easier and more efficient.

Amiga Graphics Packages

The best graphics package for the Amiga is Graphicraft® (see color fig. 10.1 in center of book). The package, from Island Graphics of Sausalito, California, sells for $49.94 and is published by Commodore-Amiga. With Graphicraft, you can create pictures with up to 32 different colors. You can draw circles, rectangles, and freehand shapes; and you can alter the type of brush you are using. Graphicraft makes extensive use of the mouse as a drawing tool. You can "point and click" at different options and then move down to the drawing board to do the actual drawing.

At the top of the screen, the menu bar displays the options: Project, Edit, Special, Color, Shape, and Brush. Each option gives you a variety of other options and commands. For example, under the Color part of the menu bar appears a menu showing the 32 different colors and patterns available. You can alter the color and pattern of any of these and choose one for your drawing. You also can load and save your paintings for later reference.

The features of Graphicraft are amazing. To give you some idea of Graphicraft's power, here is a list of its capabilities:

Shapes available: You can select from freehand drawing, rectangles, lines, curves, circles, arcs, triangles, ellipses, parallelograms, and polygons. You also can fill entire areas with a certain color.

Text available: You can type words and numbers in the drawing area in Topaz, Diamond, Ruby, Garnet, and Sapphire fonts; and you can put any of these fonts into plain, italic, bold, or underlined mode.

Editing features: You can erase, move pictures around, cut and copy pieces of a picture, rotate a picture, flip it horizontally or vertically, or stretch it.

Colors and patterns: You can choose any of the 4,096 colors, and you can create any pattern you desire with the pattern editor. You also can change the brushes you draw with.

Special effects: You can draw repeating shapes, filled shapes, multiple shapes, and three-dimensional shapes. You also can "mirror" your drawing so that what you are drawing is duplicated according to which of the four drawing mirrors you select. Finally, you can get the colors of a picture to change in order to create the illusion of animation.

Graphicraft has many more capabilities than the Macintosh's MacPaint™. Commodore-Amiga's Graphicraft has unequaled features in developing pictures. Not only is the program fun to use, but you can draw pictures for use in business presentations, school reports, and financial planning. Moreover, you can print the pictures, and this feature is even exciting when you have a color printer. Island Graphics has done a commendable job of tapping the potential of Amiga's graphics.

Aegis Development (2210 Wilshire Blvd., Suite 277, Santa Monica, CA 90403) also offers a graphics package for the Amiga: Aegis Draw©. At $149, Aegis Draw is a fairly expensive program. The power of this package is that you can create the effect of animation by superimposing the picture frames you make. Although Aegis Draw has many of the same features as Graphicraft, the animation capability makes Aegis Draw even more fun to use.

Because the Amiga is such a great computer for graphics, a number of developers have undertaken the tremendous task of developing software that takes advantage of these graphics. As time goes on, more developers are likely to introduce even more astounding programs.

The Musical Amiga

Stereo sound and the capability to play four different tones ("voices") at once makes the Amiga an impressive musical instrument (see fig. 10.2). Commodore-Amiga and Cherrylane Technologies (P.O. Box 430, Port Chester, NY 10573), along with many other companies, are introducing musical keyboards that connect to the Amiga so that you can use it as a music machine.

With the Amiga's MIDI interface, you also can hook up full-blown synthesizers to create a seemingly infinite variety of sound effects, tones, and musical pieces. MIDI is the music industry's standard interface between music synthesizers and computer equipment. The Music Construction Set from Electronic Arts works with a MIDI interface and a synthesizer to create stereo music (see fig. 10.2).

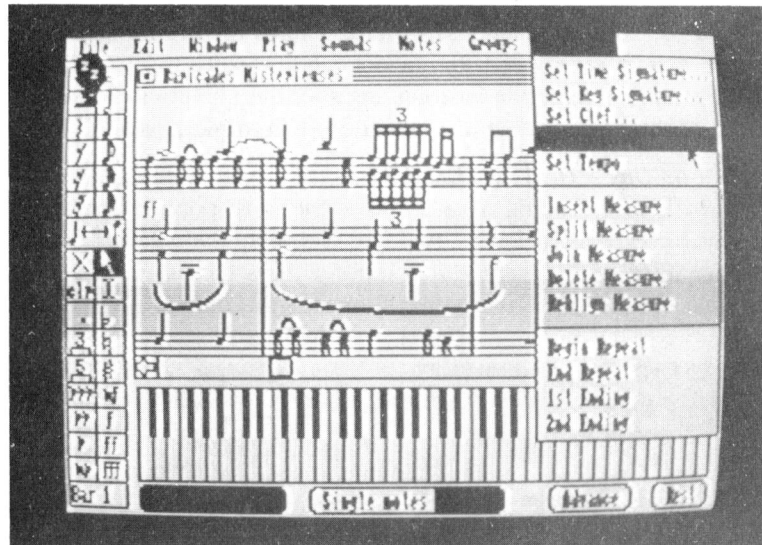

Fig. 10.2. Music Construction Set from Electronic Arts.

Cherrylane Technologies is the most active in developing musical applications for the Amiga. Harmony, one of the first software packages they introduced, uses the four voices of the Amiga with the MIDI interface not only to play music but also to teach you to play music. On your Amiga, you can play along with one of the songs that comes with Harmony or with your own creation. Harmony will keep pace with you if you fall behind or go too fast. In this way, you can use the Amiga as your backup band.

Harmony features incredible graphics, which show the sheet music being played; an extensive library of prerecorded arrangements; and the capability to record the musical notes you are playing on the piano keyboard. Harmony, which costs $79, can open up a whole new world of music for you.

The Entertaining Amiga

Because the Amiga has such incredible sounds and graphics, a fast microprocessor, and large memory capacity, many people regard the Amiga as the most sophisticated game computer ever introduced. Of course, Amiga users know that their computers can be used for many other things besides games, but the fact remains that the Amiga is a great game machine. Many software publishers have developed programs for the Amiga that are entertaining and often educational as well.

Electronic Arts (2755 Campus Drive, San Mateo, CA 94403) was
one of the first companies to develop games for the Amiga. Electronic Arts is recognized for its outstanding software, which has
sophisticated graphics and astounding sound capabilities. These are
some of the games being introduced by Electronic Arts:

One-on-One™: Dr. J and Larry Bird play a one-on-one game
of basketball (see fig. 10.3). This is the most popular sports
game ever written for a computer. You play the role of
Larry Bird or Dr. J, and the computer plays the other man
while the Boston Garden crowd cheers you on.

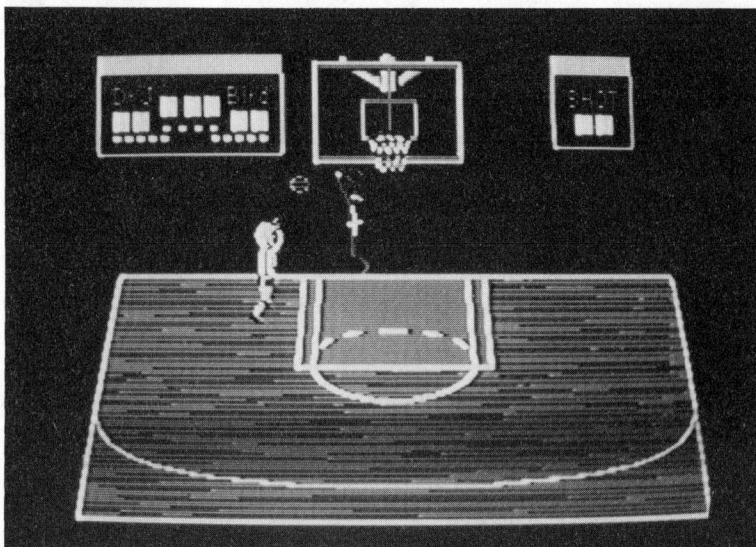

*Fig. 10.3. One-on-One with Dr. J
and Larry Bird.*

Skyfox™: This program gives you the pilot's "eye view" from
a sophisticated jet complete with radar. Your mission is to
attack enemy jets and tanks.

Seven Cities of Gold™: You learn history and geography as
you play the role of Christopher Columbus seeking new
lands.

Archon™: This sophisticated board game is a mix of chess
and Dungeons and Dragons.

Deluxe Video Construction Set™: Computer graphics,
animated scenes, sound effects, and titles are easy to create
with this program. You even can record the routines on a
videocassette so that you can watch them on a VCR.

Arcticfox™: You are in command of a futuristic tank—the Arcticfox—and your mission is to defend the landscape. This game features amazing three-dimensional scenes and realistic sounds.

Return to Atlantis™: In this three-dimensional simulation, you are an oceanic hero, Indiana Cousteau.

Other Electronic Arts programs are Marble Madness™ (see color fig. 10.4), which has the same amazing three-dimensional graphics as the pinball version, and Bill Budge's Pinball Construction Set® (see fig. 10.5), with which you can create your own computerized pinball games.

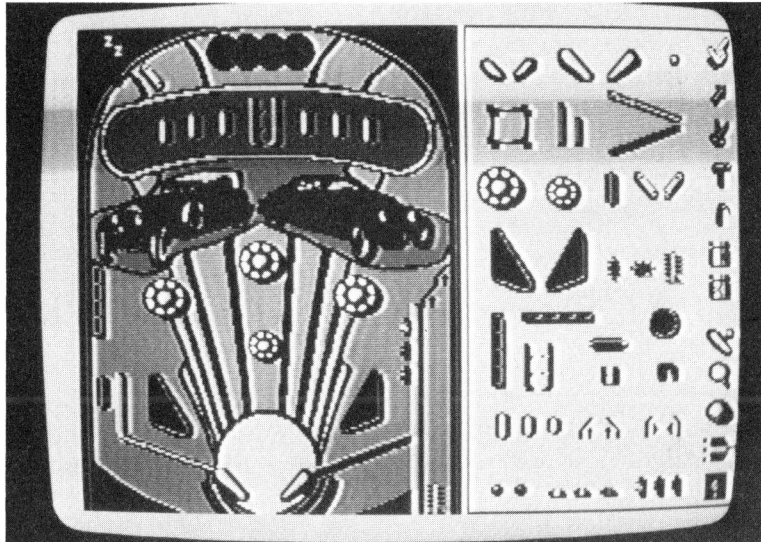

Fig. 10.5. Bill Budge's Pinball Construction Set: software that lets you create your own games.

A number of other companies have introduced video games for the Amiga. For example, Synapse Software (Richmond, California) has come out with Mutant, Wyndwalker, Essex, and Brimstone, all of which are sold by Commodore. Although the video game craze of the early 1980s is long gone, the Amiga is still an outstanding way to while away the hours (hopefully not too many of them) in a fast-paced, entertaining way.

Besides video games, some of the most popular entertainment programs for personal computers are those from Infocom (125 Cambridge Park Drive, Cambridge, MA 02140). Founded by eight MIT computer scientists in 1979, InfoCom publishes a host of "interactive fiction" games in which you solve murders, explore dungeons, and voyage into space. However, these games are not the simple "shoot-em-up" games known to most personal computer users. Infocom games are text-only interactive programs that are incredibly sophisticated and challenging. No matter what problem you face in one of these games, you can rest assured that you will be hooked to the computer screen for hours (or days) trying to be a Sherlock Holmes, a Buck Rogers, or a noble knight.

The most interesting aspect of Infocom's software is that you can enter full sentences, and the Amiga usually will understand what you are telling it. In other adventure-type games, only two- or three-word commands, such as GO NORTH or GET LAMP, are accepted. In Infocom's software, however, sentences like HEAD NORTH AND GET THE LAMP THEN GO THROUGH THE DOOR will be understood by the computer, as long as you can head north and a lamp and a door do exist in the game. The *parser* in the games is the interpreter for the computer. Because English is such a complicated language, the parser will weed out the words that are not in the game's vocabulary or that are not used in one of the 300 sentence forms that the game can understand.

The 16 programs are broken into the 4 genres of Infocom software: fantasy, mystery, tales of adventure, and science fiction. The games range in price from $39.95 to $49.95. Some of the games available are the following:

Zork I®, Zork II®, and Zork III®: In this trilogy of games, you are a freebooter questing through the Great Underground Empire—a labyrinth dungeon with treasures, traps, and trolls. Your mission is to stay alive and collect as many treasures as possible before reaching the end of the game.

Wishbringer™: This game makes you a postal clerk with a temperamental boss, Postmaster Crisp, who gives you a mysterious envelope to deliver to the Old Magick Shoppe on the other side of town. At the Shoppe, you learn that the owner's cat has been catnapped by "the Evil One." When you leave, you discover that the whole town has changed and has become sinister and threatening. You have been told by the owner of the Shoppe, however, that a hidden stone named Wishbringer will grant you seven wishes to help destroy the Evil One and restore the town to its former self. Of course, the Shoppe owner did not tell you where the stone is because the Evil One will read your mind and get it for himself. The game even includes a glow-in-the-dark "wishbringer stone."

Enchanter®: You are an apprentice sorcerer doing battle with the Evil Warlock. While finding your way through the enemy's stronghold, you have to figure out magic spells that you hope will come in handy later.

Planetfall®: As an ensign 7th class aboard the damaged spaceship Feinstein, you escape the exploding vessel and land on a decaying planet with a lost high-tech civilization. Your mission is to save the planet with the help of a little robot named Floyd.

Suspect™: You are a journalist who has received an invitation to the annual Halloween party thrown by Veronica Ashcroft at her Maryland estate. During the party, as you mingle and talk with other guests (your Amiga, actually), someone is murdered; and you are the prime suspect. You have to find clues to prove the identity of the real murderer while the other guests sometimes try to foil the investigation.

A Mind Forever Voyaging™: For a real twist, this game puts you in the role of a computer. After decades of work, scientists have finally taught a computer to think like a child, slowly developing its intelligence and self-awareness. When you (the computer) reach age 20, you are told of your true form and of the next phase you are about to enter. Your mission is to guide the United States into the year 2031 in the best way possible. This "interactive fiction plus" game has a 1,700-word vocabulary and is a huge step forward in computer entertainment.

Other games from Infocom are Starcross®, Cutthroats™, Hitchhiker's Guide to the Galaxy™, Infidel®, Seastalker®, The Witness®, and Suspended®. All Infocom games are excellent, and if you would like a change of pace from the fast-action graphics and sounds games most often associated with Commodore computers, these products are an excellent choice.

Other Languages

To expand your knowledge of computer programming, you might want to try other programming languages available for the Amiga. This experience will not only increase your knowledge of computing but also will help you become a better programmer, because you will see the advantages and tricks used in other programming languages.

You already have explored Logo and the C programming language, both of which are worthwhile to purchase and use. Here are some other languages available for the Amiga:

Pascal: This highly structured language from Metacomco (201 Hoffman Avenue, Monterey, CA 93940) is often recommended as the best way to start programming. Learning Pascal is actually pretty difficult for the person who has never worked with computers before, but after you have had experience with C, you probably will be well prepared for Pascal.

LISP: The Learning Company's Logo has some of the characteristics of LISP, but this is a full-featured version from Metacomco. LISP is recognized as the most popular language in the United States for developing artificial intelligence programs.

Assembler: Also from Metacomco comes Amiga Assembler. Computers use three different types of languages: high-level, which include Amiga BASIC, Pascal, and LISP (sophisticated languages that pack a lot of power into single commands); mid-level, which include the C programming language; and low-level, which is the category for assembly language. When you work with assembly language, you have to deal directly with the registers, memory locations, and other fundamentals. Although the Assembler requires many program lines to accomplish what a single Amiga BASIC statement does, the advantage is much faster results. The program you produce will be as fast as possible (assuming you have done a good job with it), and you can take advantage of all the features of the Amiga directly because you are working with the machine on a level very close to its own 1s and 0s.

Turbo Pascal®: Borland International (4585 Scotts Valley Drive, Scotts Valley, CA 95066) has introduced its version of Pascal for the Amiga: Turbo Pascal. Turbo Pascal is already used on other computers by more than a million people. The Amiga version's extensive use of graphics procedures and its helpful Turbo Tutor® (which will help beginners) make it an outstanding way to learn Pascal and write fast high-quality programs.

You will discover that as you learn more computer languages, learning still other languages will become easier. Of course, you can get confused sometimes because different languages use different forms of syntax and entirely different command sets; but once you become a multilingual programmer, you usually won't have trouble shifting from one language to another.

Enhancements and Expansions

With an 800-kilobyte floppy disk drive, unequaled graphics and sounds, 512K of memory (with the capability to expand memory even farther), and other great features, the Amiga may seem to "have it all." However, you will soon find that what you once thought was an incredibly powerful computer could still use a little help. The computer may not be quite fast enough in processing or large enough in memory to serve your needs. These problems are solved easily, however, because the market provides an abundance of hardware (electronic devices) and software (programs on a diskette) to make your Amiga an even more powerful and versatile machine.

If you find that your floppy disk drives don't provide enough storage space and speed (for example, if you use your Amiga for business applications), you may decide that a hard disk would be a worthwhile purchase. A hard disk is different from a floppy disk because (1) the hard disk is much faster, (2) the hard disk can hold 25 times as much information as a single floppy disk, and (3) the hard disk cannot be removed from its drive. The hard disk, which is extremely sensitive to outside elements, is permanently encased in its drive; but because you probably can store all your files on this single drive, this shouldn't be a problem.

The hard disk for the Amiga is Tecmar's T-disk,™ which sells for $995. (Tecmar also produces the T-modem, discussed earlier.) This small hard disk drive sits on top of the Amiga and can hold more than 20,000,000 bytes of information (20 megabytes). Even though this hard disk is an excellent product, you still should back up the information on this disk. Because backing up 25 disks could be very time-consuming, Tecmar also manufacturers the T-tape™. This $595 tape system can back up the contents of the hard disk in a relatively short time. Because you can back up 20 megabytes in just a few minutes, using the T-tape is an easy way of ensuring that your information won't be destroyed accidentally by a power surge or computer failure.

One other Tecmar product that is a good way to expand your Amiga is the $799 multifunction expansion module, the T-card™. This card will expand the memory of your computer to a full megabyte (in other words, you will have twice as much memory to work with). The T-card also will give you a full-time clock-calendar, a standby battery in case the power goes dead, a serial and a parallel port for extra add-ons, and a hard disk interface. You will need this card if you plan to get the T-disk hard disk drive.

One of the most exciting features about the Amiga is that it can run software made for the IBM PC. The Trumpcard®, an add-on from Commodore-Amiga, costs $299, and the 5 1/4-inch disk drive (which most IBM PC diskettes work with) costs $325. With these extras, the Amiga can run most IBM PC software just as fast (and sometimes faster) than a PC. The advantage of this capability is the great amount of powerful software made for the IBM PC. An Amiga owner needing a particular piece of software can have that need satisfied simply by going to an IBM software dealer. Although the compatibility of the Amiga with the IBM PC probably will not put a dent in PC sales, the fact that you have a wealth of software already available makes the Amiga an even more worthwhile machine.

Commodore-Amiga has other add-ons that enhance the graphics and sound capabilities of the Amiga. The Genlock Interface®, for example, will merge your computer with a videocassette recorder. You can superimpose images from your computer on video signals on the videocassette tape so that when the tape is played back, both the television signal and the computer graphics are on the screen. The Digitizer® has the reverse function: you can take a video image (from a video camera, the television, or a videocassette recorder) and have the Amiga "digitize" the picture into computer graphics (see fig. 10.6). Once you have the graphics on the screen, you can alter the graphics to create whatever effect you want.

As far as sound is concerned, the MIDI interface in your Amiga can be hooked up to sophisticated synthesizers to produce sounds you have never heard before. Although the Amiga probably won't be in any big rock bands any time soon, you can create your own

Fig. 10.6. A digitized picture of programmers at Electronic Arts.

sophisticated songs and sounds with the help of the Amiga and Commodore-Amiga's musical keyboard. You even can connect more sophisticated synthesizers (such as those from Roland or Sequential Circuits) to the Amiga and store sounds and songs on the disk for later use.

As powerful as the Amiga is, you always can find room for improvement. You now know several ways to give the Amiga more memory, more speed, more disk storage, and more potential; but a tidal wave of other products is sure to be introduced for this machine. One way to keep up with all the changes is by subscribing to a magazine devoted to the Amiga. At present, the only one published is *Amiga-World* (80 Pine Street, Peterborough, NH 03458). This is an excellent publication with plenty of color photos and informative articles. Besides this, you should consider joining a Commodore or—better yet—an Amiga users group in order to keep up with all the exciting changes and improvements in the Amiga system.

Your Future with Amiga

The Amiga personal computer was introduced at a time when many people were giving up hope for home computers. Indeed, maybe not everybody needs a computer on the kitchen table because not all people need to use spreadsheets, word processors, and telecommunications to keep their lives in order.

However, you will soon discover that a personal computer gives you a decided advantage in your work and life. A computer makes tasks easier and less time-consuming, and in many cases you will find that what used to be work is now fun. More important, by using your Amiga regularly, you will be prepared for all the exciting events of the near future; you will have a head start by understanding what a computer can do for you and having a machine do repetitive, boring work that you shouldn't have to do.

You now have the knowledge to use and program your system successfully and to build on your computer later. The Logo, Amiga BASIC, and C languages will give you a firm foundation for writing programs now and for moving on to other languages. In addition, your knowledge of the available hardware and software tools will let you customize your Amiga to suit your needs. Remember that your Amiga is a tool that can help you improve yourself, enjoy your work and free time more, and teach yourself about exciting new worlds in high technology.

Index

More Computer Knowledge

LOTUS SOFTWARE TITLES

1-2-3 Business Formula Handbook	19.95
1-2-3 for Business	18.95
1-2-3 Financial Macros	19.95
1-2-3 Macro Library	19.95
1-2-3 Tips, Tricks, and Traps	19.95
Using 1-2-3, 2nd Edition	19.95
Using 1-2-3 Workbook and Disk	29.95
Using Symphony	23.95
Symphony: Advanced Topics	19.95
Symphony Macros and the Command Language	22.95
Symphony Tips, Tricks, and Traps	21.95

IBM TITLES

IBM PC Expansion & Software Guide	29.95
IBM's Personal Computer, 2nd Edition	17.95
Networking IBM PCs: A Practical Guide	18.95
Using PC DOS	21.95
PC DOS Workbook	14.95

APPLICATIONS SOFTWARE TITLES

dBASE III Plus Application	19.95
dBASE III Advanced Programming	22.95
dBASE III Handbook	19.95
Multiplan Models for Business	15.95
R:base 5000 User's Guide	19.95
Using AppleWorks	16.95
Using Dollars and Sense	14.95
Using Enable	17.95
Using Excel	19.95
Excel Macro Library	19.95
Using Javelin	19.95
Using Paradox	19.95
Using Reflex	19.95
Using Smart	22.95

Que Order Line: **1-800-428-5331**
All prices subject to change without notice.

Books from Que

Que Order Line: **1-800-428-5331**
All prices subject to change without notice.

MORE COMPUTER KNOWLEDGE FROM QUE

C Programming Guide, 2nd Edition
by Jack Purdum, Ph.D.

To accommodate current revisions of the
C language, Que has published a second edition
of the *C Programming Guide.* This tutorial book
expands and updates the reader's knowledge of the
applications introduced in the first edition. The
second edition of the *C Programming Guide* gives
numerous examples and illustrations to help you
learn how to program in C. You won't want to
miss the second edition of one of the best-selling
C programming tutorials on the market.

Using 1-2-3, 2nd Edition
by Douglas Cobb and Geoffrey LeBlond

Nationally acclaimed, *Using 1-2-3* is "the book" for
every 1-2-3 user. Whether you are using Release 1A
or 2, you will find *Using 1-2-3,* 2nd Edition, your
most valuable source of information. Spreadsheet,
database, graphics, and macro capabilities common
to both Release 1A and 2 or new to Release 2 are all
covered in depth. Notations in the text and a
tear-out command chart help you locate quickly the
differences between Release 1A and 2. Like
thousands of other 1-2-3 users, you will consider
this book indispensable. "A valuable text. Should be
part of every PC library."—*PC BookSource*

C Self-Study Guide
by Jack Purdum, Ph.D.

Using a unique question-and-answer format, Jack
Purdum takes you through the basics and into
advanced areas of the C programming language.
Purdum's answers to the questions he raises include
many complete programs for testing new functions
and for illustrating tips, traps, techniques, and
shortcuts. This self-directed study guide can be
used with any C book. Whether you're a perplexed
beginner asking for help or an experienced
C programmer looking for a challenge, this book
has the answers.

Using WordPerfect, Revised Edition
by Walton Beacham and Deborah Beacham

Revised and updated, this popular book explains in
detail the expanded capabilities of Version 4.0 and
discusses those features common to all versions of
WordPerfect. A clear and informative user's guide.
Using WordPerfect covers the basics of this popular
program and provides many practical applications.
Special attention is given to WordPerfect's file
management features and report generation
capability. If you rely on the power of WordPerfect,
this book is an excellent resource.

Mail to: Que Corporation • P. O. Box 50507 • Indianapolis, IN 46250

Item	Title	Price	Quantity	Extension
188	C Programming Guide, 2nd Edition	$19.95		
176	C Self-Study Guide	$16.95		
130	Using 1-2-3, 2nd Edition	$19.95		
11	Using WordPerfect, Revised Edition	$18.95		

Book Subtotal

Shipping & Handling ($1.75 per item)

Indiana Residents Add 5% Sales Tax

GRAND TOTAL

Method of Payment:

☐ Check   ☐ VISA   ☐ MasterCard   ☐ American Express

Card Number _____ Exp. Date _____

Cardholder's Name _____

Ship to _____

Address _____

City _____ State _____ ZIP _____

If you can't wait, call **1-800-428-5331** and order TODAY.

All prices subject to change without notice.

Place
Stamp
Here

Que Corporation
P. O. Box 50507
Indianapolis, IN 46250

FOLD HERE

Place
Stamp
Here

Que Publishing, Inc.
P. O. Box 50507
Indianapolis, IN 46250